OUR CHILDREN

For Elaine and Patricia

Our Children and Other Animals

The Cultural Construction of Human–Animal Relations in Childhood

MATTHEW COLE
Open University, UK

KATE STEWART
University of Nottingham, UK

Routledge
Taylor & Francis Group

LONDON AND NEW YORK

First published 2014 by Ashgate Publishing

Published 2016 by Routledge
2 Park Square, Milton Park, Abingdon, Oxfordshire OX14 4RN
711 Third Avenue, New York, NY 10017, USA

First issued in paperback 2016

Routledge is an imprint of the Taylor & Francis Group, an informa business

British Library Cataloguing in Publication Data
A catalogue record for this book is available from the British Library

The Library of Congress has cataloged the printed edition as follows:
Cole, Matthew (Matthew Daniel), date.
  Our children and other animals : the cultural construction of human-animal relations in childhood / by Matthew Cole and Kate Stewart.
    pages cm
  Includes bibliographical references and index.
  ISBN 978-1-4094-6460-0 (hardback) 1. Children and animals. 2. Human-animal relationships. 3. Animal welfare--Moral and ethical aspects. I. Title.
  BF723.A45C65 2015
  179'.3--dc23

                                                                            2014023418

ISBN 13: 978-1-138-21571-9 (pbk)
ISBN 13: 978-1-4094-6460-0 (hbk)

Contents

List of Figures

Acknowledgements

We are very grateful to vegan illustrator *extraordinaire* Hayley Wells for the front cover and the images that grace the figures in this volume. To learn more about Hayley's work, please visit:

theillustratedvegan.blogspot.co.uk
hayleywellsillustration.blogspot.co.uk

We are obliged to the *Journal for Critical Animal Studies* for the kind permission to reproduce, with some modifications, our review of *Puss in Boots* in Chapter 6, which first appeared as: Cole, M. and Stewart, K. 2012. Puss in Boots. *Journal for Critical Animal Studies*, 10(1), 200–210.

We are indebted to the support of many colleagues in innumerable discussions and especially through the opportunity to present portions of this volume at various conferences and other events over the last few years. In particular we would like to thank Marcel Sebastian and Julia Gutjahr for the invitations to speak in Hamburg and Bochum and to the Childhood Research Group at Cardiff University, who gave us our first chance to present the ideas that ended up in this book, way back in 2008. Thank you also to Karen Morgan and Claire Molloy for your advice and encouragement with the completion of the book, and to Neil Jordan at Ashgate for your interest and faith in the project. Coping with the stresses and strains of completing this volume was made much easier by being able to draw on the inspirational writings and work of the pioneers of the early Vegan Society in the 1940s and beyond, especially Donald Watson, Leslie J. Cross, G. Allen Henderson and Faye K. Henderson. Thanks are due to Joshua and Dylan, who have on occasion felt as if their own joyful childhood memories have been under scrutiny, and also to our animal companion Barney who shared that life and ours since as a much loved part of our family. Finally, it is customary to acknowledge the bottomless, fortifying and inspiring love and support of one's partner. Clearly, we couldn't have written this book without each other, but our co-authorship is only a fraction of the reason why.

PART I
Conceptualizing Western Human–Nonhuman Animal Relations

Chapter 1

Introduction

"Chicken Run is an innovative, witty movie that will appeal to Burger King customers of all ages" said Richard Taylor, vice president of marketing for Burger King ... *Chicken Run* follows a group of chickens imprisoned at Tweedy's Egg Farm, where any chicken who doesn't put breakfast on the table can wind up as dinner. But Ginger and her fellow flock are determined to break out before they meet a "fowl" fate. Time is running out as the greedy owner of the farm, Mrs Tweedy, finds a new way to feather her nest – by turning chickens into chicken pies. (Extract from the Burger King press release about its *Chicken Run* tie-in (PRNews 2000))

In 2000, Aardman Animations released their first feature length movie in collaboration with Dreamworks. *Chicken Run* (2000) involves a plot in which hens seek to escape from their confinement in a 'chicken farm', stylized as a World War II prison camp, before they are killed, butchered and served up as 'chicken pies'. The film, rated suitable for all viewers by its U certification in the UK and G certification in the USA, invites children to identify with the nonhuman characters in their struggle to avoid ending up as food. At first glance then, *Chicken Run* subverts food norms by destabilizing the taken-for-granted exploitation of chickens; 69 million chickens ('broilers') were slaughtered in the UK for human consumption in the last month for which statistics were available at the time of writing (DEFRA 2014). This represents an average of 26 chickens being killed per second; an even faster pace of killing than in the equivalent month in the year that *Chicken Run* was released: an average of 22 per second (DEFRA 2011). If *Chicken Run* was subversion, it apparently failed to have any lasting impact on the scale of the exploitation of chickens. The fast food chain Burger King offered promotional tie-ins at the time of the film's release, allowing children to take home a toy representation of the characters with which they had been invited to identify, while simultaneously consuming actual animals who had been subjected to the very fate the film's heroes had fought against, which the audience had been encouraged to support. So confident that this dissonant practice would not be received problematically by the audience, Burger King even managed to promote the products with quips revolving around this contradiction in their press release.

The Juxtaposition of Death and Delight: A Sociological Conundrum

Our interest in children's relations with other animals was sparked by this specific contemporary cultural artefact: the promotional tie-in meal offered by fast food chains that juxtapose nonhuman animal 'characters' as images and toys alongside the mangled body parts of other animals. Movies aimed at children featuring nonhuman animals formed one topic in a series of screenings at a Human Animal film group with which we were involved in the late 2000s, at Cardiff University. Our conversations prompted by this event came to focus on the conceptual crucible represented by these children's fast food tie-ins. How could it be that presenting children with a figure of a loved animal character alongside dead pieces of other animals is not only tolerated but enjoyed by children? What happens in the walk across the multiplex car park, from screen to restaurant, which transforms the strong affective feelings towards nonhumans represented and encouraged in themes common in children's films to an acceptance of the utility of nonhumans as toys or food? How do we teach young humans so swiftly and so robustly that these contradictory relationships are 'normal' and unproblematic? In exploring these issues in the specific context of fast food–film tie-ins (for a full discussion, see Stewart and Cole 2009), it swiftly became clear to us that the processes we identified there are also identifiable across the full range of social processes and cultural artefacts that collectively shape humans' early experiences with other animals in the UK; at home, at school, at leisure or in the virtual worlds of digital media. Additionally, as our study of these processes proceeded, an equally clear question emerged: why is the ubiquitous presence of nonhuman animals in children's lives largely unaddressed by scholars of the cultural and social domains in which we identified them?

We do not claim to be able to fully address all of these issues across all of the relevant disciplines and subdisciplines in this one volume. Our aim for this book is to offer an invitation to enquire, by uncovering the interconnectedness of studies of childhood, culture and human–nonhuman animal relations. Through doing so, we aim to establish the importance of human–nonhuman animal relations in sociology, by describing the sociological importance of other animals in children's lives, and of children in other animals' lives and deaths.

Context: The Destructive Legacy of Majority Human–Nonhuman Animal Relations

Throughout the unfolding of modernity there has been an acceleration in the rates of exploitation of other animals as or for 'food', as 'tools' in vivisection laboratories, as 'entertainment' or 'educational' spectacles in the media, sport, 'zoos', schools and so on. Throughout this process (and before it), opponents of exploitation who we might now characterize as ethical vegans, as activists for other animals, have offered visions of alternative ways of living, foregoing the exploitation of vulnerable others, dismantling specious justifications for that exploitation and establishing the moral indefensibility of continuing to inflict confinement, pain and death upon hundreds of billions of our fellow earthlings (Cole 2014, Davis 2012, Walters and Portmess 2001, 1999, Leneman 1999). An under-life of non-exploitative discourse and practice therefore runs beneath the mainstream 'progress' that has succeeded in shedding ever more blood in modernity. But that bloody process has also been paralleled by a proliferation of bloodless cultural representations of animals directed towards children. The coincidence of these developments merits sociological investigation in two key respects. Firstly, as scholars who are opposed to the exploitation of other animals, we present a critical sociological examination of the reproduction of dominant human–nonhuman animal relations in childhood. This task remains perpetually urgent given the consequences of those dominant human–nonhuman animal relations: an almost incomprehensible scale and intensity of suffering and death being inflicted at every moment on other animals (Masson 2009, Mann 2007, Eisnitz 2007, Marcus 2005, Coats 1989, Vegan Society no date); a pattern of global environmental destruction being wrought as a consequence of 'animal farming' (Twine 2010, Baroni et al. 2007, Steinfeld et al. 2006, Horrigan et al. 2002, Fox 2000, White 2000); an ongoing history of massive human suffering interlinked with the oppression of other animals. The latter encompasses the intersection of patriarchal, colonialist, classist and other forms of intra-human oppression with inter-species oppression (DeMello 2012, Adams 2004b, Patterson 2002, Spiegel 1996); the relationship between the displacement of indigenous peoples, the immiserated experience of working in the slaughter industry and the capitalist commodification of other animals (Nibert 2013, 2002, Eisnitz 2007, Torres 2007, Mason 2005, Schlosser 2002); the diversion of plant foods to the 'livestock' industry in the context of global human hunger (Horrigan et al. 2002, Marcus 2001); and the chronic and zoonotic disease implications for human populations of dependence on dietary 'animal products' (Tonstad et al. 2013, Aston et al. 2012, Pan et al. 2012, Tantamango-Bartley et al. 2012, Aune et al. 2009, Greger 2006).

These developments, and the relationships between them, are suggestive of a field of inquiry that can aid our understanding of how that destructive pattern of exploitation is sustained, and therefore our understanding of how it might be challenged and one day, ended. Secondly, these processes suggest that a specifically *sociological* analysis is necessary to explore the relationship between how and what children learn about other animals, and what happens to other animals through their, often violent and fatal, interactions with humans. We therefore aim to provide a sociological contribution to the emerging interdisciplinary field of human–animal studies, especially Critical

Animal Studies (CAS), in which sociology has played a less prominent part than other disciplines so far, not least due to its humanist–speciesist legacy (Peggs 2012, Nibert 2003). Thirdly, and related to Kay Peggs's wider critique of the inattention to other animals in the sociological tradition, the particular importance of other animals in children's lives raises questions about why that importance has been substantially ignored in the sociology of childhood, not simply in terms of the importance of the relationship for human children, but also in terms of the implications for nonhuman animals. Taking these last two points together, our aim is to evidence Erika Cudworth's argument that, 'the discipline of sociology has much to offer those who seek to understand our relationship with Other animals' (2011: 54).

While the exploitation of other animals and the legitimation of that exploitation is increasingly well-documented and critiqued (for instance see Taylor and Twine 2014, McCance 2013, Nibert 2013, 2003, Cudworth 2011, Kheel 2008, Kalof and Fitzgerald 2007, Adams 2004a, 2004b, Baker 2001), the intersection of childhood and nonhuman animal exploitation has been largely neglected. This volume focuses on the *socialization* of the human use of other animals, especially as 'resources' for food, clothing, play, entertainment, education and so on. This is pursued through a consideration of the interlinked roles of *practices* and *representations* in this socialization process. Dominant practices involving other animals in childhood, include the feeding of 'animal products' and the selective exposure of children to particular 'types' of animals, for example 'pets' or 'zoo animals'. Children encounter dominant representations of other animals through, for instance, engagement with the mass media and social media; through playing with toys and games based on other animals; and in the formal education system. The primary focus of our empirical research is the UK, although much of the content of the book will be relevant to wider Western society and beyond, especially given the globalizing reach of many cultural representations of other animals. Whilst we do not claim generalizability for the substantive content of our analyses, we do assert that the processes we identify in the examples we present are relatable to a wider range of cultural contexts.

We therefore identify five key themes addressed by this work, which can be summarized as follows:

1. A critical examination of the early socialization of the human use of other animals in UK society;
2. The interconnection of dominant practices and representations in this socialization process;
3. The sociological importance of nonhuman animals in human children's lives;

4. The consequences of these early socialization practices for other animals' lives and deaths;
5. The ways in which these dominant practices and representations are and can be challenged.

We pursue these themes by approaching the topic in three parts: the historical and conceptual basis of children's relations with other animals; the analysis of substantive contemporary examples; and the emergent and potential counter-discourses to the processes we have identified. Part I of the book therefore explores the theoretical and historical basis of the argument, and situates the work within both the sociology of childhood and in (critical) human–animal studies. In Part II, we present contemporary empirical examples of childhood practices and representations of other animals in a broadly biographical-chronological order, that is, as they become part of children's experience as they grow up. Finally, Part III examines emergent counter-discourses that aim to destabilize the socialization of dominant human–animal relations. It thereby addresses the extent of 'our' responsibility, as critically engaged sociologists, and as Western citizens, to contribute to those counter-discourses and to challenge the socialization of dominant human–animal relations. Throughout this volume, cognizant of the role of language in shaping our relations with other animals (see Cole 2011, Nibert 2003, Dunayer 2002), we have chosen to add denaturalizing quotation marks around words and phrases which euphemize and thereby normalize exploitative, violent or derogatory practices or discourses towards other animals, such as 'meat'.

Part I: Conceptualizing Western Human–Nonhuman Animal Relations

The empirical analyses we present in the book as a whole draw on a conceptual model of dominant human–nonhuman animal relations in the contemporary UK, and Western societies more broadly. In essence, this approach illustrates how nonhuman animals are primarily defined according to their form of relation with human beings, which broadly depends on the perceived utility of those animals to humans. In other words, other animals tend to be socially constructed in ways which legitimate human uses of them. Its focus on the inter-relation between representations and practices is informed by a Foucauldian analysis of the relationship between discourse and power relations (Foucault 2002) interwoven with an interpretation of Weber's typology of social action (Weber 2004). The theoretical grounding of this model, its emerging historical salience as a conceptualization of human–other animals relations, and the problematic ignoring of its salience in the sociology of childhood, form the basis of the first part of the book.

In Chapter 3 we consider how this schematic emerged as a salient model for human–nonhuman animal relations by exploring the re-shaping of material and discursive relations between children and other animals between the eighteenth and twentieth centuries in the UK. This period witnessed a series of developments that combined to construct these dominant relationships from the perspective of children, by reducing sensibility to exploitative *practices* at the same time as cultivating and channelling empathy, through relationships with animal companions or 'pets', and through imagined relationships with *representations* of other animals, such as toys or sympathetic characters in children's literature.

In Chapter 4 we critically examine the inattention to the importance of real and represented other animals in childhood socialization within much of the sociology of childhood literature, and argue for a fresh focus on children's relations with other animals within this and related social science disciplines. In doing so we identify key parallels between the analyses of the theoretical and social construction of human childhood, and the processes underpinning our conceptual model introduced in Chapter 2. We acknowledge a profound irony in the creation of the special status of childhood that we establish in Part I of the book. The great majority of exploited animals are infants or at most young adults themselves at the moment they are killed for human food, a fact which is assiduously removed from childhood experience and cognizance, as exploitative practices are removed from everyday life more generally. In light of this, the second part of the book aims to develop a sociology of childhood that is focused on the importance of practices and representations that socialize children into norms of human–nonhuman animal interaction, and which also exploit the children of other species.

Part II: The Contemporary Socialization of Human–Nonhuman Relations in Childhood

The second part of *Our Children and Other Animals*, applies the conceptual model from Part II in four empirical contexts in the UK: the family, mass media aimed at children, the formal education system, and digital media. These are conceived as four spaces in which children are socialized into dominant practices (such as eating other animals' flesh) and in which they encounter dominant representations of other animals. These representations tend to legitimate or conceal those dominant practices, as well as cultivating and channelling children's empathy in ways which tend to insulate dominant practices from critical questioning. Children thereby tacitly learn to internalize and reproduce the conceptual model and the skills of 'correctly' positioning other animals, and therefore their 'correct' relationships with them (to eat them, love them, spectate them and so on). However, we are not conceiving of children as passive dupes of this socialization process; the processes we describe are precarious, and each socialization space can be, and often is, a site of contestation over the 'correct' forms of relationship with other animals. Children can and do exercise their ethical agency to resist this socialization process. The four spaces are organized to roughly correspond to the biographical order in which children first enter into them, and are separated for analytical purposes; we acknowledge that the sites are intermingled in practice, and we highlight this in the course of the analysis.

Chapter 5 focuses on the family, considering how family interactions and practices shape and divert children's empathy for other animals in ways that reproduce the conceptual model introduced in Chapter 2. This includes consideration of how children are taught to consume the body parts (flesh) and reproductive products (milk and eggs) of other animals while simultaneously diverting their attention from the origins of these products. Key to this process is the nexus of public health policy and education which encourages parents to teach non-vegan ways of eating to children; the targeting of animal-based foods to children from the food industry, for instance in supermarkets or in fast food restaurants; and the ways in which animal foods are invested with symbolic status in the structuring of meals (see also Fiddes 1991, Twigg 1979, 1983). Taken together, this nexus automatically excludes vegan food practices as a viable, mainstream alternative. The chapter highlights the intersecting role of gender in shaping girls' and boys' relations to other animals, and how reciprocally these relations contribute to the construction of girlhood and boyhood; and we also address the fostering of empathic relationships with 'types' of animals (notably 'pets' and various representations, such as animal-based toys) that do not trouble the dominant practices of consuming other animals.

In Chapter 6, we build on the role of toys in socialization, by focusing on contemporary popular representations of other animals, and human–nonhuman animal relations, that direct children's empathy towards animal 'characters' and away from animals exploited for human use. Here, we focus on an exemplary filmic representation of other animals, *Puss in Boots* (2011), and a genre of children's animal-themed magazines, including titles such as *Animal Cuties*, *Animal Friends* and *All About Animals*. These are strongly gendered, explicitly targeting girls as their intended readers. These magazines emphasize the 'cuteness' of baby animals, abstracted from their material contexts and re-presented in posters, games or magazine features. The dominant theme of the magazines is the celebration of affective feelings towards 'cute' (which generally means infant) animals. So, caring about 'animal cuties' is a gendered practice in these magazines. This intersects with the same gender pattern examined in the context of family socialization discussed in Chapter 5. Furthermore, the forms of relationship which are encouraged and valorized in the magazines do not trouble dominant practices of exploitation, and in some instances reproduce them. For example, some magazines give away sweets containing gelatine (derived from the carcasses of slaughtered animals) or include cake recipes containing hens' eggs.

In Chapter 7, we focus on formal education in schools. By the time children enter this arena, they have already been immersed in the practico-discursive spaces of family and mass media socialization outlined in the previous chapters. In Chapter 7 we consider how the education system builds on that prior learning by a combination of tacitly and explicitly teaching the normality of human dominance over other animals. The tacit reproduction of human dominance includes formal and informal education about food practices in schools, which reproduces the normality of consuming other animals and compounds the marginalization of non-exploitative, vegan food practices. This is further entrenched by the practices and discourses associated with meals taken while at schools, in the forms of lunchboxes, school meals and snacks. More explicitly, children are formally educated about 'animal welfare' in ways which build on the empathy cultivated in the family and mass media, but which do not question the morality of using other animals, and which mask the most violent practices involved in exploiting other animals.

Chapter 8 presents the final empirical context examined in Part II, and focuses on new digital media, specifically handheld console games and 'free' social media games that interactively facilitate children's 'positioning' of other animals in our conceptual model. Social media and gaming allows children to actively practice the positionings that they have learned about in the family, mass media and formal education system, by manipulating other animals as entertainment spectacles, as instrumental in the acquiring of in-game rewards or as opportunities to express virtual 'caring' relationships. Following the pattern established in the socialization sites examined so far, those caring relationships are restricted to 'types' of animals that reproduce dominant human–nonhuman animal relationships and do not disturb exploitative practices. To illustrate by contrast, counter-scenarios in which children act out rescuing and caring for exploited animals from 'farms' or vivisection laboratories do not feature in these games.

Part III: Reconstructing Children's Relations with Other Animals: Vegan Practices and Representations

The dominant model of human–nonhuman animal relations that we present is not uncontested, and in the final part of the book we examine some of these contestations. Fundamental to reconstructing children's relations with other animals is recognition of the contingent and unstable character of our conceptual model. On the one hand, it is built on constructed human 'needs', for other animals' flesh, milk, eggs, skin, hair, companionship, spectacle, etc. On the other hand, our model illustrates how the risk of collapse is always embedded into the architecture of human–nonhuman animal relations as a whole, because it cultivates empathy for other animals as such, but then attempts to limit its effects by constructing 'appropriate' outlets which, roughly speaking, only exist in certain contexts. So, while particular constructions of other animals do predominate, they are continuously vulnerable in a number of ways: vegan practices destabilize the 'needs' of humans for exploitative relations with other animals; vegan discourse also undermines constructions of the 'nature' of nonhuman animals as exploitable resources; and finally some types of animals are ambivalently positioned in our model, increasing its instability when that ambivalence becomes available for critical reflection.

The penultimate chapter of the book therefore considers examples of vegan-themed children's literature that deliberately dismantles the architecture of our conceptual model, by directing children's empathy towards other animals who could most benefit from it, exposing and critiquing exploitative practices and providing a model of alternative, non-exploitative forms of relation with other animals. In doing so, this literature simultaneously reconstructs human ontology as peaceable and humble in contradistinction to a critique of human arrogance and violence, albeit obfuscated and euphemized, in dominant human–nonhuman animal relations. In the final chapter of the book, we conclude by addressing the implications of failure to embrace these and other vegan interventions, and the globalizing reach of our conceptual model as dominant Western patterns of human–nonhuman animal relations and media representations proliferate. It thereby addresses the extent of 'our' responsibility, as critically engaged sociologists, and as Western citizens, to contribute to those counter-practices and discourses and to challenge the socialization of dominant human–animal relations. In so doing, we can work towards ending the moral tragedy of children being systematically deceived about the violence of human practices with other animals, through immersion in an affective representational milieu populated by animals who they are encouraged to identify with. Furthermore, that process is implicated in the self-identification of children, and by extension humans as such, as benevolent protectors of other animals, rather than their vicarious gaolers and killers.

Chapter 2
The Use of Names: Socially Constructing Animals as 'Others'

"Of course they answer to their names?" the Gnat remarked carelessly.

"I never knew them to do it."

"What's the use of their having names", the Gnat said, "if they won't answer to them?"

"No use to THEM", said Alice; "but it's useful to the people who name them, I suppose. If not, why do things have names at all?"

"I can't say", the Gnat replied. (Carroll 1993: 185–6)

Discourses and Practices about Animals: Knowledge, Power and Social Construction

This exchange between Alice and the Gnat encapsulates the key concern of this chapter: that the naming of other animals is *useful* for human beings, while it is *dangerous*, and frequently lethal, for other animals. This is because the words we use to name other animals are saturated with common sense knowledge claims about those animals, which legitimate their habitual use for humans. Here then, we take a broadly social constructionist approach to the problem of human–animal relations, attending to how *we* humans 'think about and interact with *them*' (Arluke and Sanders 1996: 9, emphasis added). However, this is not to imply, as Keith Tester argues, that other animals are only 'a blank paper which [*sic*] can be inscribed with any message, and symbolic meaning, that the social wishes' (1991: 46). For example, other animals' resistance to those inscriptions, to their naming as 'types' and bearers of categorical fates, has been documented by Hribal (2010). In *Fear of the Animal Planet*, Hribal bears witness to animals fighting back against their human captors, refusing their work as providers of consumer spectacle, escaping from violent constraints. Hribal's work is especially disturbing because the acts of resistance he documents are historically exceptionalized; most of the time, social constructions are 'successful' in reducing other animals to physical or discursive matter for redeployment in human practices and representations. Hribal's account therefore jars the assumption that other animals are non-agential (see Kowalczyk 2014). As Alice implies, the naming of types of animals, that is, their categorization, is the key to their thingification; their reduction to non-agential manipulable resources for discourse and practice. Alice's epiphany, we argue, cuts to the heart of Foucault's approach to the inter-relationship between knowledge and power, or between discourse and practice, which we use in this chapter to examine the construction of hegemonic human–nonhuman interactions in contemporary Western societies. That is, we describe the inter-relation of:

1. How discourses conceptualize other animals as particular kinds of entities (relations of knowledge);
2. How other animals are physically positioned in different spaces and subjected to specific practices (relations of power).

To elaborate points 1 and 2: Foucault's understanding of discourse, according to Colin Gordon, can be understood as, 'identifiable collections of utterances governed by rules of construction and evaluation which determine within some thematic area what may be said, by whom, in what context, and with what effects' (2002: xvi). Discourses about animals which legitimate and reproduce their oppression are dispersed across the social (Johnson 2012), but our focus in this book is in their presence within the social worlds of children's culture and practice, traceable in the indissociable interaction between childhood representations of animals and the ways that children are enjoined to act in relation to other animals, including the practice of incorporating parts of other animals' bodies into their own. A central preoccupation of Foucault's work was the 'knowable individual', who 'has been the individual caught in relations of power, as that creature who is to be trained, corrected, supervised, controlled' (2002: xvi). Although Foucault's concern was with human animals, these concerns are apposite to the situation of nonhuman 'knowable animals'. Therefore, the inter-relation between points 1 and 2 above, can be thought of as a mutually reinforcing cycle: specific spaces facilitate specific practices, which both enact and reproduce discursive conceptualizations; the practice of placing an animal in a 'farm' is an enactment of the concept 'farm animal' which also reproduces the meaning of that concept, through the juxtaposition of the animal with the location and their subjection to 'farming' practices. Furthermore, these discursive utterances are diffused through cultural representations of animals, including children's culture of stories, films, magazines, food packaging, toys, digital media, educational materials and so on (see chapters 5–8 of this book).

Discourses about other animals have very specific, often lethal, effects in the practices of 'farms', laboratories, sporting arenas, and other contexts of human–nonhuman animal relations. At the same time, practices of supervision, control, correction, training and dismemberment constitute the 'knowable animal' within those contexts. By inculcating ways of conceptualizing and locating other animals in human beings, these discourses and practices also help to shape what it means to be and behave as 'human' ('the people who name'), in contemporary Western societies, in contradistinction to 'animal'. The empirical focus of the book is on how children are socialized into reproducing these discourses and practices, and thereby on how they come to shape our experience of ourselves as 'human', as we grow up in the contemporary West. Our emphasis in this chapter is also on *problematizing* majority human discourses and practices about other animals. This is primarily because they have injurious and often fatal results for those animals from slaughterhouses to vivisection laboratories. But also because they have injurious and sometimes fatal results for humans too, as contributors to heart disease, cancer or type-2 diabetes in the form of 'animal products' (Stewart and Cole 2013, and see Chapter 1 for a fuller discussion of the intersection of human and nonhuman animal exploitation), as well as the moral injury resulting from the deformation of children's relationships with other animals. None of this is to deny the existence of alternative discourses and practices, of alternative ways of naming the other, an issue we return to in detail in Chapter 9; the task of documenting the social construction of other animals has important consequences for nonhuman *and* human ontology (Cole 2014). So, while the spirit of this book is critical but ultimately optimistic, we first need to describe and understand where we are, in order to inform how we might move beyond our present circumstances.

Structure of the Chapter

The remainder of this chapter is organized into two major sections. The first sketches out those majority discourses and practices that largely govern the interface between human and nonhuman animals in contemporary Western societies. It is our own looking glass panorama of the culture that we inhabit; an effort to estrange habitual ways of thinking about human–nonhuman animal relations and thereby make them available for critical reflection. This section therefore traces the development of a conceptual model, or map (see Figure 2.1 below) that summarizes the key shared features of Western culture's discourses and practices about other animals, and which provides us with a tool for analysing their manifestation in specific sites: family, education, mass and social media, in chapters 5–8 respectively. The second section then elaborates a sociological key to reading this map, based on Michel Foucault's writings on power-knowledge (Faubion 2002, Rabinow 2000) and Max Weber's typology of social action (2004). This is placed in the context of an overview of previous sociological literature that has schematized human–nonhuman animal relations. Here we argue that our conceptual model is especially well-suited to describing and understanding the complexities of the relationship between discourses and practices, in shaping human–nonhuman animal interaction in childhood (and beyond). Taken together then, this chapter provides the theoretical and conceptual grounding for our analyses of both majority and alternative practices and discourses pertaining to human–nonhuman animal relations. It also provides a preliminary answer, and a way of answering, to the problem outlined in Chapter 1: the normalization of the massive scale and intensity of 'legitimate' violence meted out against other animals.

Defining and Locating Animals: Sketching a Practico-Discursive Map

It isn't etiquette to cut anyone you've been introduced to. (Carroll 1993: 268)

Nonhuman animals are primarily defined and categorized according to their form of relation with human beings. Broadly speaking, these forms of relation depend on knowledge claims about the utility or disutility of those animals to humans. In everyday life, to 'know' other animals in our cultural context is to be familiar with the enactment of those claims about utility and disutility. We 'know' that chickens are 'useful' *because they are used*, as 'food'. We 'know' that rats are 'not useful' *because they are killed*, as 'vermin'; that is, discourse and practice mutually recall, reinforce and legitimate each other. There are variations and ambiguities in judgments of utility and disutility within Western culture (discussed further below, and see Cole and Stewart 2010, Stewart and Cole 2009), but a common feature across all such variations is that utility/disutility forms the basis of 'common sense' typologies of other animals, which are taken for granted by most human members of Western societies, in most circumstances. These typologies are the means by which particular species, and members of those species, are grouped together, both figuratively and spatially. This can be illustrated by considering how nouns are placed in front of the word 'animals' to pin down their meaning, purpose and appropriate physical location: 'farm animals' are located on 'farms' for the purpose of 'food production'; 'zoo animals' are located in 'zoos' for the purposes of 'entertainment', 'education', or 'conservation'; 'laboratory animals' are located in 'laboratories' for the purpose of 'research'; 'companion animals' are located in 'domestic space' for the purpose of 'companionship'; 'endangered animals' are located in 'reservations', for the purpose of 'preservation', etc. However, utility is precarious. 'Unproductive' diseased or injured 'farmed' animals may be left to die or purposely killed, being re-conceptualized as 'waste' or 'costs' (see Marcus 2005), while rats are, 'vermin in the pipework under the lab but a useful piece of equipment in the lab' (Birke 2003: 220).

In some cases, a noun serves on its own to group together a collective of animals and also to imply their meaning and location: 'pests' are *wrongly located* in competition with human resources, while 'vermin' are *wrongly located* as threats to human health or well-being. The meaning of both is determined by the assertion of their disutility. However, in both cases, the commercialized slaughter of animals thus conceptualized demonstrates a murderous alchemy, by which the 'useless' animal is transmuted into profit. This is exemplified in the company name Rentokil, which euphemistically promotes itself as, 'the UK's leading provider of pest control' (Rentokil 2013a). Part of Rentokil's framing of its own expertise inheres in its ability to appropriately locate animals in space, according to common sense knowledge, as in this example: 'Immediate steps for rat control [...] Use tamper resistant bait boxes – designed specifically to encourage rodents to enter and consume rodenticide bait, but not allowing inquisitive children, pets or non-target wildlife to gain access' (Rentokil 2013b). In this configuration, the only appropriate location for rats is a killing space (though even here, killing is euphemized as control), which other *types* of animals are excluded from; the shared inquisitiveness of human children and rats is suppressed, because only one 'must' die and must therefore be discursively differentiated from 'non-targets'. Fixing the meaning and 'appropriate' location of animals in these ways, shapes what the 'appropriate' human dispositions and behaviours towards them are. That is, the meaning of the locations and therefore the particular animals who occupy them, is dependent on human discourses and practices of categorization, of naming. The name of 'pest' *is* the discursive target that legitimates killing, and its absence is the guarantee of protection from this particular lethal practice. This common sense knowledge therefore systematically denies or attenuates the capacity, or at least the legitimacy, of other animals' determining of *their own* 'meaning', purpose, or movement through space. The fact that other animals do not answer to the human names of 'vermin', 'tool', or 'food' are irrelevant, let alone that they may violently resist those categorizations (Hribal 2010); these are purely matters for human discourse and practice within hegemonic human–animal relations.

A Continuum of Human–Animal Relations: Friend or Food?

The way that humans conceive of and behave towards other animals, as suggested by the discussion so far, rest on common sense judgments of (dis)utility. This means that other animals tend to be placed on an instrumental continuum. The intensity of instrumentalization though, varies according to the addition of affectivity or moral concern, which may in turn sediment into habitual, or 'traditional' ways of relating to other animals. This tempering of instrumentality may be exemplified in the 'friend or food?' distinction between 'pets' on the one hand and 'food animals' on the other (see Cole and Stewart 2010, Stewart and Cole 2009). So, discourses about 'pets' tend to construct them as deserving of affection and care (Franklin 1999), therefore shaping the appropriate disposition towards an animal defined as 'pet'. This disposition is culturally habituated to the extent that its disturbance can produce cultural shock effects, as in recent UK parliamentary (BBC 2013d) and media (BBC 2013b) responses to the 'horsemeat' scandal in the UK and elsewhere in Europe, where 'conventional' animal products were found to have been 'contaminated' with DNA from horses (BBC 2013a). Affective dispositions are generally more benign than instrumental ones, in terms of their results for individual nonhumans, although it should be noted that affectivity may also be manifested in the form of violence against nonhuman animals. But, even relatively benign forms of affectivity are also precarious, exemplified by the scandalous commodification of horses' flesh, the abandonment and killing of 'unwanted pets' (Ward 2012) or the status of ambiguously conceptualized animals such as urban foxes, squirrels, or pigeons (Cole and Stewart 2011a, Cole and Stewart 2011b, Jerolmack 2008). In these kinds of examples, 'positive' affect can quickly switch to 'negative' affect (fear and loathing) with frequently lethal consequences, and the instrumental continuum can be seen to exert a constant pull towards calculating the (dis)utility of other animals. The affective polarity of love or companionship on the one hand and hatred and revulsion on the other, contrasts with the dispassionate assessments of human–animal relations on the instrumental continuum. For instance, the appropriate disposition and behaviour towards an animal defined as 'food' (and therefore utterly thingified) is instrumental and calculative. In 'farmed animal' welfare discourses and practices, concern for the physical, mental, or emotional well-being of those animals may be instrumentalized as economic and gustatory benefits: increasing profits for 'farmers' and taste sensations for 'consumers' (see Cole 2011). In the case of 'food' animals, even those subjected to 'welfare-friendly' regimes, instrumental dispositions are therefore, at root, exploitative and calculated to maximize perceived human benefits. Although there are undeniable diminutions of harm that may result from animal welfare measures, the practice of harm-reduction itself can therefore be instrumentalized; such as a 'feel-good factor' deriving from consuming signs of 'care' for other animals in the purchase of 'welfare-friendly' labelled food (Cole 2011, Cole and Morgan 2011). In other cases, instrumental dispositions take annihilatory, rather than exploitative, forms: either nonhuman animals are 'useful', in which case they are segregated, confined and frequently killed (exploitative); or they are 'useless' and interfere with human interests, or contribute nothing to them, in which case they are exterminated, exiled, or excluded from human milieus (annihilatory).

Humans, taken as a privileged group constructed as distinct from other animals, are therefore free to construct, enter and leave physical and discursive spaces more or less at will, and engage with a range of relations and conduct a range of practices with other animals in those spaces, on the basis of this instrumental continuum. However, a crucial exception is the exclusion from those spaces of humans who seek to disrupt, protest or prevent hegemonic relations, for instance by facilitating animals' escapes from various sites of captivity; this is exemplary of the exclusionary effects of discourse about other animals and the normalization of exploitation as the bottom line, despite the self-conscious cultivation of affect and moral concern in welfarist discourses (see Cudworth 2011: 74). By contrast, other animals are generally reduced to non-agential entities, blank or near-blank slates awaiting the inscription of human meanings and practices that will define their purpose and mortal fate. Here we do not deny the capacity for nonhuman agency, but point to the general *inefficacy* of nonhuman agency in the face of the great lengths that humans have gone to in order to subordinate other animals. In other words, the majority of human–animal relationships are characterized by the more or less successful attempt to channel, minimize, or stifle nonhuman agency. At the same time, the agency of humans, 'the people who name', is constructed on the basis of that capacity to channel, minimize or stifle the agency of the nonhuman other. This can be illustrated in the context of specific human occupations that are implicitly defined by the management of nonhuman agency, such as 'farmer', 'animal experimenter', 'zoo keeper', 'gamekeeper', and so on. More widely, humans as such exercise this management of nonhuman agency by proxy, through the division of human labour that sustains them. In summary then, the location of other animals in discourse and space can be understood as a process of objectification, with varying levels of intensity. The most intense forms of objectification are meted out to the greatest number of animals who regularly encounter human practices: the confinement, execution and dismemberment of 'farmed' animals. Some animals are afforded a level of protection from the extremes of objectification, through the attenuating force of positive affect, and are therefore treated as at least quasi-subjects. This is sometimes manifested in recognition of the legitimacy of their having some agency, some influence on the circumstances of their lives, such as responding to an animal companion's invitation to play or request for food. However, even these cases tend to diminish the subjectivity of other animals relative to humans, in ways that echo the attenuated subjectivity of human infants – in both cases the adult human remains in ultimate control of the dispensation of material and affective goods. The inter-relationship between the infantilization of animal companions and the petification of children is explored further in Chapter 4.

So far, the discussion has highlighted the ways that animals are positioned in one dimension: along a continuum of instrumentalization, or objectification, with countervailing tendencies of positive affect and moral valorization. The discourses and practices that effect that positioning however, also instantiate an intersecting dimension relating to the *sensibility* or *non-sensibility* of other animals. Western culture is dominated by the visual, not least in respect of the representation of other animals (Baker 2001). One consequence of this is to draw attention away from the difficulty in fully sensing and experiencing other animals. That is, hearing, smelling, touching as well as seeing other animals, through the morass of visual representations. We therefore generally refer to the sensibility or non-sensibility of other animals in this book, rather than their visibility or invisibility, in order to deprivilege the visual and acknowledge the impoverishment of the depth with which humans generally attend to other animals (Cole and Morgan 2013, Kheel 2009). There is also a punning second meaning to this choice of language, as it draws attention to how it is conventionally 'sensible' to accept dominant meanings and practices relating to other animals, but non-sensible, or even non-sensical, in the sense of being contrary to human privilege, to resist those dominant meanings and practices. Attending to the agential interventions of other animals, minimally depends on interactional co-presence or representational verisimilitude, that is, on humans being sensible of the corporeal existence and actions of other animals. Broadly speaking, co-presence becomes more likely for a greater number of humans the less an animal is objectified in discourse and practice. To illustrate by extremes: few of us do, or can, visit slaughterhouses or laboratories to see, hear, smell or touch animals as they are taken to their deaths (Smith 2002, Vialles 1994), but most of us do encounter 'pets' or 'wild' animals (such as urban foxes and so on) in everyday life, even if we do not personally choose to live with other animals. The same general principle holds for the cultural representation of animals in these different situations, with some exceptions, such as activists' use of undercover images or footage of slaughterhouses or vivisection laboratories. Simultaneously, Western culture is inundated with the products of objectification, in the form of processed and packaged body parts ('meat'), reproductive products (milk, cheese, butter, etc.), skin and hair (from 'leather' sofas to woollen clothes) as well as the less overt commodification of animals' bodies as ingredients in medicines, toiletries, or cosmetics. The ubiquity of the products of objectification is compounded by their representation in cultural forms: in advertising, in cookery books, magazines and television programmes, on restaurant menus and as 'props' in fiction across all forms of media, from Fonzie's 'leather' jacket in the *Happy Days* sitcom, to J. Wellington Wimpy's consumption of hamburgers in the *Popeye* cartoon. So, the pleasurable consumption of other animals, as objects and representations, is a cultural norm, but the connection between the animals and the object/representation is severed by the relative non-sensibility of the *processes* of objectification. The massive cultural sensibility of the results of objectification (hamburgers, leather jackets and all) serve to legitimate the continued (hidden) objectification of animals, and continued insensibility to them, through manifesting their 'usefulness'. This has a profound consequence of making opposition to the instrumentalization of other animals appear self-evidently irrational, because contrary to human self-interests. This in turn creates a background assumption that non-exploitative practices such as veganism, are ascetic, in a narrow pejorative sense of pleasure-denying (see Cole 2008). This is an assumption which we critique in Chapter 9, in the context of vegan children's literature.

An important aspect of cultural insensibility to the processes of objectification, is the saturation of culture with representations of living animals who function as repositories of affect and sentiment, alongside products (real or representational) of (hidden) exploitation, many of which are also loaded with affective meanings ('comfort food', etc.). Examples abound in children's cartoons, comics, books, toys or games. For instance, the Ladybird *First Picture Dictionary* (Berry no date), aimed at toddlers, uses humorous illustrations of animals (among other images) as examples for 24 of the 26 letters of the alphabet. None of the images shows animals in captive situations, with the partial exception of a 'zoo' depicted without enclosures and with a snake, big cat, elephant and giraffe amiably hanging out with a 'zoo keeper'. It also includes images of animal products, such as 'egg' represented by a drawing of a fried chicken's egg. Most incongruously, it juxtaposes an illustration of a salami sausage being sliced (to illustrate 'knife') with drawings of a koala and a kangaroo. The fact that what are being sliced are the body parts of other animals is of course hidden from the toddler reader. So, the overall effect is to make idealized representations of other animals sensible, but also to make animal products sensible, while the situations and experiences of the real animals exploited to 'manufacture' those products are absent. What is especially significant is that there is no attempt to account for the incongruity of this kind of juxtaposition. For the young reader, the incongruity doesn't exist; *habituation* to cultural and personal denial of exploitation proceeds smoothly. The cultural sensibility of affective representations, alongside the results ('products' like the flesh components of 'happy meals') of some of the most intense forms of objectification, is a social fact dependent on the non-sensibility of the practices of objectification themselves. This is illustrated in Figure 2.1.

Figure 2.1 maps some of the *uses of naming* that Alice intuited in her conversation with the Gnat. From her dream vantage point through the looking glass, Alice is estranged from the banality of real human–nonhuman animal relations, and can therefore make them fleetingly evident for readers. Back on this side of the looking glass however, children enter into an adult culture habituated to that banal conceptualization of other animals according to their (dis)utilities.

A dramatic way to illustrate this, appropriately enough in the context of the Alice novels, is to consider the example of rabbits (Stewart and Cole 2009). Rabbits are positioned across almost the entire geography of Figure 2.1. They are 'farmed' for their flesh, their fur and as experimental 'tools', out of cultural sensibility. The products of these most intense forms of objectification, contrastingly, are highly visible in food and fashion culture. Meanwhile, rabbits

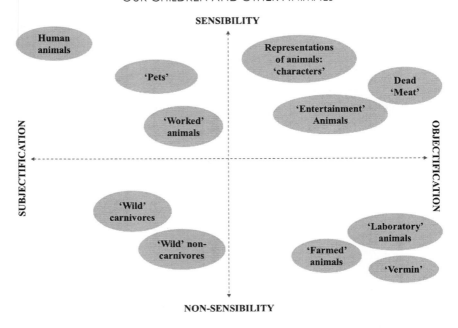

Figure 2.1   A conceptual map of the social construction of 'other' animals

'entertain' as they emerge from magicians' hats or facilitate human 'care' as hutched 'pets', but are also exterminated as 'vermin' when they impinge on human interests. They symbolize the promiscuity of 'nature' as 'wild' animals while they also symbolize the limpness of 'lettuce eating' in anti-vegan stereotypes. Either way, biologically determinist discourses reduce rabbits to helpless dupes, of their fecundity or of their herbivorousness respectively. All the while, they feature most prominently of all as anthropomorphized representations, which, despite their cultural valorization, often remain infused with these same kinds of derogatory stereotypes, from Jessica Rabbit to Bugs Bunny. These different constructions of 'rabbit' entail very different fates for particular rabbits, according to the corresponding spatial locations in which these discourses are enacted. None of them are much good for the rabbits; and no rabbit ever chose to answer to any of these category names. This illustration therefore shows that the fates of individual rabbits are largely dependent on the ways in which they are defined by humans: the ways in which the meaning of 'rabbit' is enacted in different practices of confinement, exclusion and, often, killing. In each case, there is an evident relationship between the intensity of suffering experienced by individual rabbits and the extent to which we treat them as objects or subjects, and the extent to which the experiences of those rabbits are culturally sensible.

The ambivalence of the social construction of rabbits, also noted by Fiddes (1991: 132) and echoed in other species with multiple 'uses', such as squirrels, foxes or horses, highlights the peculiar skill acquired through socialization: to successfully (that is, unresistingly) inhabit a cultural milieu that mixes up affect, objectification and denial, often in respect of the *same* species of animal. This balancing act depends on material and discursive practices of separation, of instrumentalization, of literally and metaphorically removing from human sensibility. It is crucial to note that children are first habituated to the more 'innocent' constructions of rabbits (for instance), anywhere on Figure 2.1 but the south-eastern killing zone (see Chapter 5). Children's attention is focused resolutely above the equator, on 'cute' rabbit representations, or on idealizations of the south-western 'wild' rabbit in nature. It is much less likely that children will encounter constructions of rabbits that legitimate human violence towards them because, for instance, the history of intensive animal (including rabbit) farming has led to a progressive removal of the most exploited other animals from public life, though relocating farms, increasing security measures and the use of the laws of trespass to inhibit the exposure of violence and exploitation (Best 2004). This historical event is considered in more detail in Chapter 3, but to help us think through its result in contemporary Western culture, Carol Adams's concept of the 'absent referent' is useful:

> Behind every meal of meat is an absence: the death of the animal whose place the meat takes. The "absent referent" is that which separates the meat eater from the animal and the animal from the end product. The function of the absent referent is to keep "our" meat separated from any idea that she or he was once an animal, to keep the "moo" or "cluck" or "baa" away from the meat, to keep something from being seen as having been someone. (Adams 2004b: 14)

In other words, the absent referent prevents us recognizing objects (such as 'meat', but also hair/'fur', skin/'leather', etc.) as being the fragmented bodies of subjects (animals). Adams (2004b: 51–2) argues that animals become absent referents in three ways. First, they are literally absent through having been killed. Second, they are definitionally absent through being misnamed, not as killed animals, or the body parts thereof, but as euphemisms like 'pork', 'hamburger' and so on. Third, they are metaphorically absent when meat is invoked as an expression of human suffering, as when victims of sexual violence report, or are described as, being treated like pieces of meat. In the latter case, Adams stresses that the real fates of *killed* nonhuman animals are absent from the use of the metaphor to describe *lived* human experiences. In these ways, the mediated *presence* of exploited animals in everyday discourse is part of what enforces their unmediated *absence* in everyday discourse; that is, they circulate among human-controlled milieus as objects and representations, but not as living, breathing individuals. A salient example for children's experience of other animals is promotional fast food tie-ins with Hollywood animal characters, in which 'meat' is highly visible, but materially and discursively disconnected from its source. Killed animals are literally and definitionally absent from a 'happy meal' box (which, for example, packages a 'burger' and not 'cow's muscles, fat, skin, connective tissue', etc.), but that definitional absence is facilitated by the intervention of an anthropomorphized animal character, who alone invites (which is not to say determines) the focus of affective sentiments towards 'animals' for young consumers. In this way, the capacity to distinguish some animals (characters) as appropriate repositories for affect from others (killed) as misrecognized objects is encouraged. In both cases, this is a social process that is disarticulated from the 'nature' of either the killed animals or the real animals anthropomorphized as 'characters'. Habituation to use and channelled affect in childhood instantiates a powerful motivation for denial for the rest of our personal lives, and for the reproduction of collective denial through the massive cultural labour that sustains attention, especially children's attention, above the equator of Figure 2.1.

The next section of this chapter pursues the theme of the inter-relation between discourse and practice, representation and materiality, by reviewing extant sociological literature on the categorization of other animals. In that light, we go on to argue that Foucault's insights on the nexus of power-knowledge and Weber's fourfold typology of social action, can help make our sociological understanding more sensitive to the nuanced complexity of those categorization processes. We therefore conclude the chapter by returning to Figure 2.1 and considering it as a representation of an interlocking, but unstable, network of territories for social action, the boundaries of which are constantly policed by the circulation of discourse.

Critical Sociologies of Human–Nonhuman Animal Relations

[…] a horse never knows who may buy him, or who may drive him; it is all a chance for us. (Sewell 1994: 14)

The argument that humans relate to other animals according to the uses that we do or do not make of them, has been central to sociological analyses of human–nonhuman animal relations over the last two decades. These use-based relations have been analysed to generate typologies (Peggs 2012, Cudworth 2008, Hirschman and Sanders 1997, Arluke and Sanders 1996, Benton 1993), membership of which circumscribes the probable fate of nonhuman animals when they enter into contact with humans. In some senses, hindered by humanist conceptual baggage, sociology has been slow to catch up with, or to attend to, popular nineteenth-century critiques of human–animal relations as exemplified in the quotation from *Black Beauty* above (critical analyses of anthropocentrist bias within sociology have been made by Peggs (2012), Cudworth (2011) and Nibert (2003)). While the discourse of the Alice novels, *Black Beauty* or other children's novels featuring animals is complex and uneven (discussed in more detail in Chapter 3), and certainly not straightforwardly critical, the extracts quoted in this chapter arguably go further towards a critical analysis of human–nonhuman animal relations than was evident within the discipline of sociology, before a more recent challenge to its humanist preoccupations. However, critical elements of nineteenth-century children's fiction can give us a useful way into understanding the importance of social constructionism in sociological critiques of human–nonhuman animal relations. As Anna Sewell highlighted, from the perspective of other animals, 'all is chance' in their encounters with human discourse and practice; despite his narration of his autobiography, Black Beauty's destiny is largely dependent on the meanings constructed for him by his human 'masters', with the intensity of his instrumentalization tempered according to how far he is led northward and westward through Figure 2.1, in the course of the novel. While Sewell exposes and denounces the capriciousness of the uses that humans make of horses in *Black Beauty*, recent critical sociological approaches interrogate the wider socially constructed and contingent character of judgments of utility and associated category allocation. Arluke and Sanders argue that: '"Being" an animal in modern societies may be less a matter of biology than it is an issue of human culture and consciousness' (1996: 9). The contingency of that culture and consciousness is most clearly demonstrated by the variability across time and place in the species and individual animals assigned to different categories, being arbitrarily (from other animals' perspectives) switched between 'friend' or 'food' (Arluke and Sanders 1996: 10–18, and see Cole and Stewart 2010). As Kay Peggs argues, the practice of constructing other animals is the key to their subordination (2012: 40). In this section we therefore begin by briefly reviewing this broadly constructionist sociological work.

Hirschman and Sanders have the most obvious salience to our own focus on socialization, as they identify three categories of animals in children's fiction: 'utility animals', who are portrayed as objects not individuals, and whom Hirschman and Sanders refer to as farmed or working animals; 'wild animals', beyond human control and representative of forces of nature; and 'pets', who are the most analogous to humans in fictional narratives. This tripartite distinction is a useful starting point, and corresponds with Figure 2.1: 'utility animals' tend to be located towards the south-east region (although we would argue that 'working animals', such as Black Beauty, may sometimes be constructed as quasi-subjects rather than purely as objects); 'wild animals' tend to be located in the south-west region – with relatively greater autonomy and therefore relatively less visibility (the construction of autonomy as an especially human characteristic must be defended, by obscuring the autonomy of others when it cannot be directly controlled); 'pets' tend to be located in the north-west region, closest to humans. However, as we argued above, all nonhuman animals (representational *or* real) tend to be constructed according to their relative (dis) utility to humans, that is, along the equatorial continuum of Figure 2.1. 'Wild' animals in this schema still serve human *uses* as symbols, for instance, while the use of 'pets' includes the affective functions they can fulfil in a human-dominated household. So, even though they come much closer than Hirschman and Sanders' utility or wild animals to being treated as autonomous subjects, they only exist as such because of the quasi-subjectivity conferred on them by their human 'owners'. And, for real animals, even this quasi-subjectivity is precarious – all 'pets' are not universally recognized by all humans as individual subjects – it is a consequence of a particular relationship with a particular set of humans (the 'owners'). The subjectivity of 'pets' is therefore always precarious and contingent, including the risk that the human 'owners' will get bored with and abandon or kill the 'pet', or that the 'pet' will transgress its proper role, for instance in the case of dog attacks on humans (a similar point is actually made by Sanders elsewhere (Arluke and Sanders 1996: 11)).

Drawing on Ted Benton's analysis of the categorization of other animals (1993), Cudworth provides a more detailed typology than Hirschman and Sanders, as follows: 'wild' animals (in conditions of limited incorporation with humans), the use of animals as a labour force, as entertainment (e.g. 'recreational fishing') and edification (e.g. 'wildlife' documentaries), as household companions, as symbols (often representing certain human qualities) and as food (Cudworth 2008). Cudworth's approach more fully captures the view that all nonhuman animals are usually defined according to the form of utility/disutility relationship they have with humans (even 'wild' animals can have edificatory as well as symbolic uses). However, some important forms of relationship between human and nonhuman animals remain missing from Cudworth's model. For instance, animals categorized as 'vermin' or 'pests' do not find a place in this schema, although Benton's original ninefold typology may reaccommodate the latter, as one of his categories of human–nonhuman animal relations is as 'sources of profit' (1993: 64), recalling the Rentokil example discussed earlier. Benton's final category, 'wild' animals who evade human discourse and practice in relation to their constructed (dis)utility, escape Figure 2.1. It therefore offers a utopian outline in its assertion of the thinkability of post-oppressive human–animal relations, which we return to below and in Chapter 9.

A focus on oppression itself has come to the fore, in sociological analyses of the intersection between the social construction of human–animal relations and intra-human difference and inequality. This is especially, but not only, in respect of gender, sexuality, class, 'race' and colonialism (Nibert 2013, 2002, Cole et al. 2012, Peggs 2012, Cudworth 2011, Torres 2007, Arluke and Sanders 1996). Cudworth argues that any 'critical sociology of species […] cannot only theorize notions of human domination and difference from Other animals. Rather, it needs to take account of the ways in which oppressions are multiple and intersecting' (2011: 15). The category of 'humans' in the north-west corner of Figure 2.1 may be fragmented in many complex ways, not least through the 'downgrading' of certain humans by association with nonhuman animals (see Cole and Morgan 2011 for an application of an earlier version of Figure 2.1 to 'raced' and gendered oppression). At its worst, this process facilitates gross acts of violence against humans, as in the equation of Jews to 'vermin' in the Holocaust (Arluke and Sanders 1996), or of Tutsis to cockroaches in the Rwandan genocide (Adams 2006). Arluke and Sanders conceptualize the discursive equation of different categories of humans with more or less abominated categories of nonhumans in their metaphor of a sociozoologic 'ladder of worth' (1996: 168), which recalls the equatorial continuum in Figure 2.1; objectification being inversely related to worth. Peggs (2012) draws on Arluke and Sanders's sociozoologic scale, and also on Nibert's framing of speciesism as an ideology that legitimates oppression, to focus on the importance of 'othering' in the human oppression of other animals. Oppression, for Nibert, inheres in the enmeshment of economic exploitation, inequalities in power and the ideological devaluation of 'others' (Nibert 2002, and see Peggs 2012: 37, Cudworth 2011: 46–50); a nexus that captures subordinated humans just as it does subordinated nonhumans. Cudworth's own approach to intersecting oppression is the development of a theory of anthroparchy: 'a social system, a complex and relatively stable set of hierarchical relationships in which "nature" is dominated through formations of social organization which privilege the human' (2011: 67). Cudworth argues that anthroparchy captures the interplay of the material and discursive constitution of domination, which resonates with our own consideration of the indissociability of discourse and practice. Cudworth's elaboration of anthroparchy also suggests that nonhuman resistance to human oppression is possible, as are co-constitutive relations across species that contest anthroparchy. But Cudworth also implies that human beings (including sociologists), are the beneficiaries of anthroparchal relations, and therefore have a responsibility to oppose them (2012: 78).

So, there is much in common between these previous sociological examinations of the social construction of human–nonhuman animal relations and our own. All draw attention to the uses made of other animals and therefore to the primacy of human interests (excepting Benton's somewhat subversive ninth category, of which more below). Although there is no space here to do justice to the nuanced development of Cudworth's theory of anthroparchy, the term is a useful way of concisely conveying the systemic appearance of oppressive or exploitative human–animal relations in Western society. Although our argument is that different positions in Figure 2.1 are contingent and inherently unstable (see below), they are anthroparchal in their specific effects; that is, they each advance human primacy, albeit in different ways depending on the specific discursive and material context. Anthroparchy also avoids the sociologically problematic reduction of 'speciesism' to an individualized focus on attitudes or beliefs in many applications of the term (Nibert's analysis of speciesism notwithstanding), and therefore we refer to 'anthroparchal relations' in our empirical analyses later in the book. Kay Peggs points out the complicity of sociology itself in reproducing human primacy:

> Sociology has typically opposed biological classifications that have been used to explain inequalities among humans (e.g. related to gender and "race") but has done relatively little to challenge biological explanations for inequalities between other animals and humans. Indeed, sociological analysis has often served to entrench such inequalities by either ignoring them or by explaining them away as natural. (2012: 36)

In common with Peggs, we seek to challenge that legacy and assert the value of sociology *for* other animals, which we pursue in detail in Chapter 4, in an examination of the lacuna about other animals in the sociology of childhood. We also address a hitherto under-explored aspect of intersecting oppressions: the tripartite intersection of oppression in relation to species, gender and age, especially in the trivializing feminization/infantilization of affective relations with other animals in childhood. Our approach eschews the addition of further categories of relationships in order to compile a more comprehensive catalogue. This is reflected in the organization of our empirical chapters on the basis of socialization sites, rather than on constructed categories of animals. In assembling Figure 2.1, we are therefore attempting to facilitate analysis of the specific relationships between different positions/categories, within an unstable network (for instance the contingent mutual interests served by 'happy meal' style film tie-ins), as well as the key dimensions of both discourses and practices that attempt to fix other animals within them (the subjectivity–objectivity equator and the sensibility–non-sensibility meridian of the map). The map can accommodate new forms of discourse and practice that are organized on the basis of (non-)sensibility and degrees of objectification, without modifying its essential geography. Likewise, it would be possible to map the positions of individual humans and human collectives differentially, according to discourses and practices associated with oppressions on the basis of age, 'race', class, gender, sexuality, and so on; capturing the fact that any given individual might suffer from one form of oppression, while benefiting (even if unwillingly/unconsciously) from another (see Peggs 2012: 44–5).

There are three, mutually supportive, advantages to this approach. Firstly, it enables us to present an at-a-glance snapshot of the entirety of hegemonic human–nonhuman animal relations in contemporary Western cultures, both in terms of representations and in terms of practices, while not necessarily claiming that they constitute an imperviously totalizing system. It thereby portrays complex interacting discourses and practices across which the apparent incongruities of 'friend or food', or cuddling a teddy bear while eating a hamburger, remain sensible (in both senses), in that the network as a whole serves multiple human 'needs' simultaneously. But, while the interaction of these discourses and practices is complex, we hope that our representation of them is simple; simple enough, for instance, to have practical pedagogical applications in helping children and adults to critically trace their own socialization routes towards the privileged position in the north-west corner of the map (discussed further in Chapter 10). Secondly, by definition, any forms of human–nonhuman animal relations that cannot be captured by Figure 2.1 are ones which do not manipulate the agency of, and sensibility towards, other animals for human ends, and which do not construct 'human' on the basis of subordinating the animal other. The map can therefore also serve as a tool for critically evaluating human–nonhuman animal relations. Ted Benton's ninth category cannot be mapped in Figure 2.1, because it involves humans leaving other animals alone (although the extent to which that is really possible at this juncture is moot, given the far reaching ecological impacts of human activity on the planet). Thirdly, Figure 2.1 allows us to recognize the contingency of animals' fates in their perilous relationships with humans, to attend to the experiences of individual animals as well as to groups of animals, and to conceptualize the way that the positioning of animals on the map is frequently ambivalent and can and does shift according to practico-discursive modification or contestation. These features of Figure 2.1 are integral to our empirical analyses throughout this book. But the point about positioning leads us to an important question: *what are we humans doing* when we distribute animals across Figure 2.1? To provide a sociological answer to this question, we borrow from Weber's typology of social action, and Foucault's work on power-knowledge.

Othering Animals as Social Action

While the range of Max Weber's sociological concerns is breath-taking in scope, arguably his central preoccupation, or at least legacy, was with understanding the role of rationalization in providing the globalizing force of modern Western culture (Craib 1997, Weber 1992, Schluchter 1985). Western rationalization, for Weber, inhered in the 'disenchantment' of the world: the retreat of mystery and the decline in the significance of emotion or tradition in informing human action. In their place, human action comes increasingly to be shaped by a calculative attitude in more and more areas of life. There is no space to recapitulate Weber's arguments in detail here, but a salient element of his analysis of rationalization, was his construction of four 'ideal types' of meaningful social action: instrumental-rational, value-rational, affective and traditional (2004: 329). The imaginative construction of ideal types was a key innovation of Weber's approach to sociology (Craib 1997). They are idealized models of a topic of study (not 'ideal' in the normatively desirable sense), which provide a point of comparison against which to measure empirical evidence and which also facilitate the imaginative reconstruction of how actors may behave in different contexts. The ideal type method has proved highly influential within sociology, and might also be related to the construction of Figure 2.1. So, we do not claim that Figure 2.1 represents a rigid code for relating to other animals that is internalized and reproduced through a monolithic socialization process. Instead, it is an idealization of the paradoxical hegemony of human–nonhuman animal relations in contemporary Western society, which socialization processes tend to be orientated towards, but which is not necessarily ever fully achieved for any individual. But, the specific elements of Figure 2.1, the categories of 'food animal' and so on, also tell us something about human 'meaningful social action', as well as about the fates of other animals. To understand this, we need to examine Weber's typology further.

Weber argued that for human action to be genuinely social and meaningful, it had to take account of the behaviour of others. So, action that was habitual to the extent of automaticity was not properly meaningful, or social, for Weber. Meaningful social action therefore had to have a specific motivation in a specific social context for the actor. So, Weber argued that it was possible for sociologists to interpret 'the subjectively intended meaning of a social actor's behaviour' (2004: 303) through empathetic understanding of the motivation of actors, in light of empirical evidence of their action. In the empirical analyses in chapters 5–8, we make use of this insight to frame our reading of socialization sites, as contexts for children's social actions, or meaningful practices, with other animals or representations of other animals. That is, we adapt the Weberian framework to facilitate our understanding of what it means for children to relate to other animals as living quasi-subjects (e.g. 'pets'), as characterful representations (e.g. cartoons), as utterly objectified matter (e.g. 'meat'), etc. in a discursive context framed by Figure 2.1. The empirical evidence of action includes the practices enjoined within socialization sites (eating, spectating, cuddling, etc.) and the 'appropriate' motivations that are discursively embedded within them. The meaningfulness of children's practices with other animals therefore inheres in the extent to which children are enjoined to be mindful of the constructed subjectivity of other animals (including the 'subjectivity' of representations) and the performativity of practices vis-à-vis other humans, especially socializing agents and peers. That is, 'normal' socialization in anthroparchal contexts requires evidence of 'appropriate' practices towards, and understandings of other animals on the part of children. Weber's contention was that instrumental-rational action had become the most dominant type in modernity and that it therefore shaped the modern individual. Instrumental-rational action disenchants and objectifies the world, rendering it predictable and manipulable. Although not part of Weber's own analysis, crucially, this objectification of the world has included nonhuman animal life. This was an insight intuited by a non-sociological contemporary of Weber, vegetarian pioneer John Howard Moore: 'Others [animals] live, not as ends, but as means and conveniences' (1895: 33). So, the calculative attitude is central to the manipulation of nonhuman animals in factory 'farms' and more generally across the south-eastern region of Figure 2.1. Close confinement, mutilations, unnatural diets, etc. are efficient means to the ends of maximizing weight gain and therefore profitability for agribusiness. In chapters 5–8, we explore some of the ways in which children are socialized into reproducing instrumental-rational relations with other animals, primarily as consumers of 'animal products', but the inherent violence of this process necessitates a more subtle inculcation of discourses and practices towards other animals, that simultaneously facilitate the denial of that violence and the development of children as caring and compassionate beings.

Weber's second type, value-rational action, is that which is meaningful in relation to specified ultimate ends (such as 'honour' or 'dignity') which are valuable in themselves. In our present context, we might consider caring for animals removed from factory 'farms' in a sanctuary or adoptive home as value-rational action. However, as argued above, contemporary 'animal welfare' discourses instrumentalize caring for other animals. That is, they relegate it to a means for augmenting human self-interests, in minimizing costs, maximizing gustatory pleasures, or augmenting a vicarious 'caring' identity for humans. Welfarist 'care' cannot be interpreted as an end in itself, because 'welfare-friendly' regimes still confine, segregate, control and ultimately kill other animals to satisfy human desires, notwithstanding differences in the intensity of suffering which various systems of 'farming' inflict. Welfarist discourse therefore exemplifies Weber's concern that there had been a slippage from value-rational to instrumental-rational action in modernity. A similar point was made by Weber's contemporary, Georg Simmel, whose concept of 'axiological trivialisation' (1984) captures the relegation of ultimate ends to mere means in modern culture. However, while we contest the meaning of welfarism, that contested meaning is embedded in the socialization process as a reframing of instrumental-rational relations, which we explore in the context of our empirical analyses, and especially education about other animals, in Chapter 7.

While the first two types of social action are both rational in Weber's formulation, the remaining two are described by Weber as irrational: affective action is motivated by emotion or feeling, while traditional action is motivated by habituation to custom. Irrational social actions are, for Weber, less meaningful than rational social actions, as they are inherently less cognizant of others. In the case of affect, this may be disputed in so far as empathetic affect is arguably an invaluable social resource for contesting the exploitation of other animals (Kheel 2008, Donovan and Adams 2007). Indeed, from an ecofeminist perspective, Weber's typology may itself be critiqued for constructing a patriarchal hierarchy of social action, which privileges rationality while it undermines the value of affect; patriarchy and anthroparchy are articulated at this point. Nevertheless, what Weber alerts us to is that the trivialization of affective action (typically as sentimentality) is a social fact in modernity. An important outcome of the socialization process is to associate affective action towards other animals with human infancy. As children age, affectivity is progressively, albeit unevenly, downplayed and gives way to a gendered inculcation of instrumental-rational action; 'livestock transporters' usurp plush animals as appropriate toys (see Chapter 5 for an extended discussion of animal-related toys and gender). Therefore, affect may itself be instrumentalized. Figure 2.1 illustrates the cultural sensibility of commodified representations that act as lightning rods for children's affectivity. The denial of exploitation that is facilitated by these representations is also extremely profitable for the culture industries, and for their fast food industry partners (Stewart and Cole 2009). This is not to deny that the experience of affective relations towards other animals (including representations of other animals) is profoundly meaningful for children, but to point out how that affectivity may be diverted, and denied its full expression in resistance to anthroparchal relations. This is a theme which we return to in Chapter 9, where we consider anti-anthroparchal alternatives to mainstream children's culture.

In the case of traditional action, meaningfulness begins to be elided entirely as actions shade into unthinking habit. A critical question therefore concerns under what social conditions do certain kinds of social actions become sedimented as habit? Once again, traditional action is itself commodifiable, sucked into the vortex of instrumental-rational action. This is evidenced through the evocation of timeless rural idylls of animal 'husbandry' in children's culture (see Chapter 8 for a discussion of the reproduction of the rural idyll in children's digital media). Through playing with 'farmyard' toys children are encouraged to (profitably) reproduce a fabricated 'tradition' of human–nonhuman animal relations that obfuscates the extant practices of industrial 'farming' and slaughter. So, in light of Weber's typology, a reading of Figure 2.1 is that it depicts the triumph of instrumental-rational action, but often disguised as value-rational action ('caring' for the welfare of commodified others), affective action ('loving' representations) or traditional action (rehearsing the rural idyll). Recalling that these are analytical ideal types, it is no surprise that Figure 2.1 represents an arena for the complex comingling of different types of social action, or different practices with other animals. Figure 2.1 is also evocative of Weber's wistful declaration at the climax of *The Protestant Ethic and the Spirit of Capitalism* that 'the idea of duty prowls around our lives like the ghost of dead religious beliefs' (1992: 182). Weber's point here was the fading of the religious motivation for the work ethic and its replacement with the instrumentalized work ethic as an end in itself (Weber's famous 'iron cage'). Non-instrumental social action (value-rational, affective, or traditional) similarly prowls around the edges of our instrumentalized relations with other animals, but is tamed as soon as it enters. Figure 2.1 therefore illustrates the *apparent* re-enchantment of human–nonhuman animal relations in Western culture; the representation of fundamentally instrumental relations as otherwise, especially beneficently otherwise. But it also makes sense as an interpretation of human action in respect of other animals, in that it illustrates how we may experience our discourses and practices towards other animals being based on normatively sanctioned ultimate values, or feel-good affectivity, or the good old way that things have always been done, in spite of their instrumental-rational underpinnings. Using Weber's typology as part of the key to reading Figure 2.1 therefore enables us to interpret the meaning of discourses about and practices with, other animals and to make sense of the bewildering incongruities of extreme violence juxtaposed with sentimental affection in our culture.

This provides a point of intersection with Foucault's theory of power-knowledge, to complete our key to Figure 2.1. Foucault (1980: 230–31) rejected the notion of rationalization itself as an ideal type, against which specific rational practices might be measured, and therefore at this point disidentified as a 'Weberian'. Instead, he attended to 'how forms of rationality inscribe themselves in practices or systems of practices' in specific empirical contexts (such as prisons, hospitals or asylums). Foucault famously insisted that there, 'is no knowledge without power, no power without knowledge' (2000: 17). As we argued in the first section of this chapter, the positioning of other animals depends on discourses, or knowledge claims about them, and those various claims to knowledge legitimate specific uses of other animals. Therefore, our approach follows Foucault's concern with the diverse rationalities of specific socialization contexts or spaces, rather than analysing different uses of other animals in terms of their proximity to a rational ideal. In this light, it should not be surprising that Figure 2.1 depicts what might be interpreted as regressive, in terms of an historical narrative of advancing rationalization as such. The diverse positions that it maps vary according to the contingencies of specific discourses, whereas a map informed by a narrative of overarching rationalization would depict a progressive eastward drift of *all* of the positions, or meanings, of other animals. Such an historical drift *is* apposite for the specific case of 'factory-farmed' animals (see Novek 2005, Coppin 2003), but not necessarily for other positions on the map.

Different uses of animals are enacted through specific practices which enmesh humans and other animals in relations of power. Objectifying knowledge (as opposed to empathetic understanding perhaps), for Foucault, involves a 'radical malice', in that it depends on a distancing gaze which separates the knower from the known (1973: 12). Notwithstanding Foucault's distancing from a particular reading of Weber as author of a grand narrative of rationalization, there is an affinity here with Weber's argument that rationalization tends to reduce the constituents of the world to manipulable matter, including, we argue, other animals in some contexts of human–animal relations, especially those in the south-eastern region of Figure 2.1. Those manipulations are authorized by rational knowledge of the manipulated object. To illustrate by example, the maximizing of efficient weight gain of animals incarcerated on factory 'farms', in terms of financial cost and time, demonstrates that those animals *are* manipulable 'matter', but it does so because of the 'radical malice' of knowledge: the separation of human from nonhuman animal life as distinct ontological categories, which terminates in the physical destruction of animals as known objects. Figure 2.1 illustrates this separation through the maximum distance between humans in the north-west corner and the most thoroughly objectified of nonhuman animals in the south-east corner respectively. Objectification, and 'legitimate' violence, increases the more thoroughly other animals are 'known' to be manipulable. Perhaps the starkest illustration is the industrial 'manufacture' of animals as tools for vivisection laboratories. As Foucault argues, knowledge is generated in specific contexts, especially disciplinary contexts such as prisons, barracks, schools and so on (1991). Such knowledge is intrinsic to the practices of 'correction' and normalization of the prisoner, recruit or pupil, individualizing at the same time as it homogenizes categories of knowable others (Foucault 1973, 1991). An analogous argument is made in Novek's Foucauldian analysis of the regime of the factory farm (2005, see also Cole 2011, Coppin 2003). Material practices of confinement, surveillance, feeding, weighing, etc. generate knowledge that in turn facilitates refined relations of power. This exemplifies Foucault's argument that, 'space is fundamental in any exercise of power' (Foucault 1982a: 361), an insight that is germane to the capturing of animals within places of confinement, but also to the locating of children within spaces of socialization, whether institutional (such as the home, or the school) or cultural (for instance the cinema, or the virtual spaces of digital media). However, an important caveat is that Foucault's understanding of power always keeps open the possibility of resistance

(Foucault 1984); without that possibility, animals (human or nonhuman) are more properly described as being in a helpless state of domination (Foucault 1998). In their applications of Foucauldian power relations to the discipline of the 'factory farm', Coppin (2003) and Novek (2005) respond to this point by drawing attention to the imperfection of factory farm discipline. This is evidenced through the biological resistance of animals to the imperatives of maximally efficient growth and reproduction, attempts to destroy or escape from constraints, or through the necessity of animal welfare science interventions to combat 'inefficient' behaviours such as stereotypies. Meanwhile, Hribal's documentation of nonhuman animal resistance clearly contests a monolithic reading of human–animal relations as pure domination, and Kowalczyk (2014) argues for the possibility of collective human–nonhuman animal agency in resistance to the subordinating effects of capitalism. Indeed, a core contention of this book is that childhood socialization of dominant discourses and practices about other animals is, and has to be, extremely thorough, due to the very contingency and precariousness of those discourses and practices. Mapping the messy incoherence of contemporary Western hegemonic human–animal relations gives us a starting point for our empirical analyses, but beyond this, 'We need to know the historical conditions that motivate our conceptualizations. We need a historical awareness of our present circumstance' (Foucault 1982b: 328). In short, we need to understand how we ended up in this mess. To that end, the next chapter considers the historical emergence of Figure 2.1, with special reference to changes in the relationship between children and other animals through the emergence of modernity in Britain.

Chapter 3
The Historical Separation of Children from Other Animals

For those countries touched by the first wave of the industrial revolution, the period from the mid-eighteenth to the end of the nineteenth centuries saw rapid and significant changes across many domains of human and nonhuman life. These changes, as they affected human children and nonhuman animals, were the context for the emergence of the specific rationalities that continue to echo through contemporary relationships between these two groups, and between these groups and wider society. Between the sixteenth and nineteenth centuries there had been major but gradual change in humans' relationships with nonhuman animals, but urbanization and industrialization heralded a much more rapid pace of change (Franklin 1999). The UK was the first country to experience urbanization and industrialization, from the mid-eighteenth century onwards. Elsewhere in Europe and the USA, the process started later but moved forward faster. The nineteenth century in particular saw unprecedented urban growth in the UK: at the start of the century less than 20 per cent of the human population lived in towns or cities with populations exceeding 10,000, and no provincial town or city (outside London) had a population exceeding 100,000; by the end of the century around three quarters of the human population lived in towns or cities exceeding 10,000 and 17 provincial towns or cities had populations over 100,000. During the century, the human population of the capital alone grew from 1.1 million to 7 million. This rapid change did not unfold in a planned or orderly fashion, but was chaotic and disorganized, and associated with a proliferation of public health hazards (Giddens and Sutton 2013, Szreter 2001). This transformation of public health since the eighteenth century was especially marked for infants and children. It was associated with a decrease in deaths from infectious diseases, which was observed across the human population, but this had particular significance for this group (McKeown 1977). Prior to the expansion of urban living, the majority of humans lived in rural locations in close proximity to nonhuman animals, and shared accommodation with them, especially during the winter months (Franklin 1999).

The events and developments associated with industrialization and urbanization have been well documented previously (see for example Allen 2009, Griffin 2010), but for the purposes of our analysis, we present a particular emphasis which has not been explicitly addressed: the significant changes of this period will be revisited and examined from the perspective of the relationship between human children and nonhuman animals, in order to facilitate an understanding of the emergence of the discourses and practices that provided the topography of Figure 2.1. While the intensities of objectification and (non-)sensibility of different forms of human–nonhuman animal relations have waxed and waned in the intervening period (notably with the advent of 'factory farming' in the early twentieth century), the twenty-first-century relationships discussed in Part II of this book were substantially shaped through the industrialization and urbanization process. The confluent identities, functions, roles and experiences of human children and nonhuman animals have been, we hope to demonstrate, key factors in the historical developments we outline in this chapter. Yet hitherto, they have remained hidden in plain sight in the academic literature that provides historical accounts of the period. The relationships between nonhuman animals and human children have been key factors in areas such as public health developments of the period and the withdrawal of children from the workforce and the associated enforced relocation to educational establishments, as we will explore below, and in chapters 4 and 5.

New Ways of Living and New Concerns

Industrialization and urbanization saw changes in the uses of nonhuman animals for human purposes, and inevitably children's participation in those practices. A key feature in the changes witnessed over this century and a half is the shift in the sensibility (that is, what we might interpret as affect and value-rationality) towards nonhuman animals in these changing roles and functions, and an increasingly prominent viewpoint that the sensibility of certain forms of relationship and practices involving nonhuman animals were morally harmful, especially to children. Discourse and practice then, can be seen to be articulated, in that a motive force for the exile of violent practices towards the south-eastern region of Figure 2.1 is provided by emerging discourses of childhood, especially the notion of 'innocence' (discussed further in Chapter 4). In comparison to rural living, urban-dwelling humans lived at greater distance from the nonhuman animals they used and consumed. Initially, rural animals and the associated practices of 'keeping' them were brought by the mass human population into urban areas, which had previously been the preserve of the aristocracy and upper classes. Significantly, the latter viewed cities as centres of civilization (Franklin 1999), an elitist conceit destabilized by the arrival of more chaotic, less governable, human and nonhuman migrants.

During the eighteenth century, concerns were increasingly voiced about issues relating to density and proximity in growing urban environments, revolving especially around public health issues such as the cleanliness of the water supply, sewerage and ventilation (Mason 2012). The appropriateness of certain kinds of animals (and the uses to which they were put) in new urban spaces became challenging with the simultaneous rise of public health issues and the continued popularity of hunting and fishing among the urban gentry, and the increasing popularity of animals as 'pets' within urban households (Franklin 1999). While these concerns were articulated across a number of domains (e.g. religious, artistic and literary) in the eighteenth century (discussed below), significant progress that impacted on the circumstances and uses of nonhuman animals associated with these concerns was not wholly evident until the nineteenth century when cultural and legislative changes (also discussed below) that physically and discursively repositioned them came to pass.

Over the latter part of the eighteenth century, the artistic representations that formed the basis of some of the work of the childhood theorists discussed in the following chapter, formed part of a wider cultural discourse about the appropriate uses and places of nonhuman animals. Representations of nonhuman animals in eighteenth-century art were peculiar to British art at this time, but did not feature significantly in wider European art. They served to convey messages about the status of humans (for example though portraits of nonhuman animals, such as in Stubbs's portfolio of equine portraiture), as well as more philosophical and moral themes. Hogarth's 1742 painting *The Graham Children*, depicting a family 'pet' cat in a room with the eponymous children and a caged bird, overseen by a statue of Father Time, may be interpreted as a representation of the threat to childhood innocence of the implied violence between the cat and bird, but acted out within the safe sphere of the home, between nonhumans under the care and control of the human household, overseen by a male adult figure. Nonhuman animals therefore serve symbolic and morally edificatory purposes in the painting, in addition to their overt positioning as 'pets', somewhat protected from the extremes of objectification, but nonetheless instrumentalized through their edificatory representations. They also serve to demonstrate a patriarchal nexus of control-as-protection, intersecting with the anthroparchal message of the composition. Joseph Wright's 1768 *An Experiment on a Bird in the Air Pump* shows a scene from a domestic parlour where a family 'pet' bird is being used for a scientific experiment. The painting features two apparently distressed female children witnessing the experiment – one averting her eyes and being comforted, and the other looking on anxiously. Of the assembled group, the children are the only ones showing sentiment or concern for the animal; affective action is trivialized through its association with infancy. The only other female depicted is distracted by the attention of a young man by her side, leaving only the adult males present who are attending, unemotionally, to the scientific demonstration. While affective concern for the bird is therefore acknowledged to have a place in the picture, it is depicted as something to be set aside and associated with immaturity (Kean 1998). In contrast, maturity is associated with the control of emotion/affect, with masculinity, and with the objectifying gaze of 'science'; Foucault's concern with a 'radical malice' of knowledge, discussed in Chapter 2, is demonstrated not only through these gendered and aged constructions of appropriate forms of inter-species (non-)relationship, but also through the physical confinement of the bird: practice and discourse once more reinforce and reproduce each other.

There was also around this time a growing body of philosophical and religious writings engaging with the discomforts that accompanied changes in use and sensibility of other animals. The Reverend Humphrey Primatt's 1776 work *The Duty of Mercy and the Sin of Cruelty to Brute Animals* asserted that if abuse based on appearance was wrong, then that should extend to other animals on the basis that they also feel pain. Jeremy Bentham's work, such as *An Introduction to the Principles of Morals and Legislation*, first published the following decade, while focussed on legal and prison reform, nonetheless also made comparisons between the treatment of oppressed and abused groups of humans and the treatment of nonhuman animals (Bentham 1781). Bentham's work famously provided an inspiration for Peter Singer's *Animal Liberation* (1975), drawing on the philosophical tradition of utilitarianism as the basis for its arguments against some of the most objectifying uses of other animals, such as vivisection and 'meat'-eating. John Wesley, the founder of Methodism, held that animals too had an afterlife, and ruled that travelling preachers should not mistreat their horse nor feed and rest themselves until their horses had first been attended to: 'Everyone ought – 1. Never to ride hard. 2. To see with his own eyes his horse rubbed, fed, and bedded' (Wesley 1993: 17). Writers such as Joseph Ritson and John Oswald extended moral concerns for the care of animals to the practice of 'meat'-eating, associating the practice with harm to the character of those humans who ate the flesh of other animals, in addition to the obvious harms to the animals being killed for 'meat'. By the end of the eighteenth century then, concern with the treatment of animals had become a focus of interest across religious, philosophical and cultural fields and had come to be associated with the moral character of the humans engaging with a range of practices involving nonhuman animals. Then as now, human ontology was bound up with our relationships with other animals: a central theme of contemporary anti-anthroparchal discourse, which we discuss in Chapter 9. Treatment of nonhuman animals was coming to be a signifier of moral worth in Britain, whether as a totem of middle-class status, or a symbol of respectability among the working classes (Kean 1998). Concern for animals therefore, was clearly emerging as an issue for education, especially in the form of moral edification, and education increasingly was being defined as an important part of childhood to which all children should have access, a process discussed further in Chapter 4.

The end of the eighteenth century also saw a burgeoning of children's literature, which incorporated this emergent morally educative approach to human–nonhuman relations. Mary Wollstonecraft's *Original Stories from Real Life; With Conversations Calculated to Regulate the Affections, and Form the Mind to Truth and Goodness* was first published in 1788 and followed by a second edition illustrated by William Blake three years later, with its purpose for the moral instruction and improvement of middle class girls evident in its title, and executed through stories featuring nonhuman animals. It provided the reader with advice on the treatment of nonhuman animals, acknowledged to be inferior to humans, but to whom a duty of care was owed, not intrinsically for the good of the animal, but for the moral improvement of the (female) human.

> I, who never wantonly trod on an insect, or disregarded the plaint of the speechless beast, can now give bread to the hungry, physic to the sick, comfort to the afflicted, and, above all, am preparing you, who are to live for ever, to be fit for the society of angels, and good men made perfect. This world, I told you, was a road to a better – a preparation for it; if we suffer, we grow humbler and wiser: but animals have not this advantage, and man should not prevent their enjoying all the happiness of which they are capable. (Wollstonecraft 1906: 9)

Wollstonecraft then, by targeting her socializing narratives towards girls, ironically exacerbated the gendered difference in affect versus instrumentalism depicted by Joseph Wright. Whereas earlier key texts featuring stories about nonhuman animals, such as Aesop's (1998) fables (first translated into English in the fifteenth century), had presented other animals in essentially human roles and as characters offering moral instruction in the treatment of other humans, books such as Wollstonecraft's were now using stories to instruct children in the treatment of the animals who were represented in the books. This shift is consistent with Cosslett's (2006) contention that there were two strands to children's literature about animals through the late eighteenth and nineteenth centuries: moral instruction and 'pure' entertainment without edificatory intentions. This dual function, as we will discuss later in this chapter also became evident in other cultural sites aimed (at least partially) at children, such as 'zoos' which were positioned as places of both delight and instruction. The specific rationalities of cultural artefacts and sites thereby also position the contents of those artefacts and sites: nonhuman animals as educational tool or entertainment spectacle for children.

As the eighteenth century drew to a close, discourse about the treatment of nonhuman animals by humans extended beyond the philosophical, intellectual and artistic concerns where they had previously been more apparent and entered political debate, and along with it emerged the special status of the relationship between human children and nonhuman animals that these fields had established. Together with the continued growth of urbanization and industrialization, as the nineteenth century began, treatment of nonhuman animals and the nature of their relationship with (and treatment at the hands of) humans featured heavily across artistic, political, philosophical, and commercial discourses. While in each of these spheres differing sensibilities and rationalities were pulling in different directions to different ends, value-rational and/or affective concern for nonhuman animals was becoming increasingly fashionable in cultured circles, as a counterpoint to the instrumental rationality of some forms of human–nonhuman animal relations. The character of this recoil from the eastward movement across Figures 2.1 is discussed in the next section.

Value and Danger: The Sensibility of Nonhuman Animals in the Nineteenth Century

Around the start of the nineteenth century, there was an increase in the conspicuousness of a growing variety of nonhuman animals in urban space, by way of touring menageries, bull baiting, dog fighting, markets and slaughter of 'livestock' for food, as means of transport, in public vivisections and as 'pets' (Kean 1998). The history of 'animal welfare' at the start of the nineteenth century has the issue of sensibility and cruelty at its centre, with change driven often by how and by whom the treatment of other animals was witnessed, rather than (in the main) a critique of the principles of instrumentalizing animals at all (Burt 2001).

There were, at this time, attempts to legislate for the end of certain violent and publicly conspicuous practices, but these were characterized by motivations relating to the humans engaging in these abuses of nonhumans, rather than through direct concern for the nonhuman animals themselves. For example, William Pulteney's 1800 Bill to ban bull-baiting was as much linked to attempts to regulate working hours by depriving the working classes of a popular pastime which was seen to contribute to absenteeism, as it was to the condemnation of perceived brutality (Kean 1998). In this instance, the anthroparchal privilege of being entertained by violence and injury to nonhuman animals was subordinated to classist hierarchy in the form of the disciplinary rationality of industrial production. The speciesist linkage of violence with 'brute' behaviour (misrecognizing the violence as distinctively *human*) also illustrated the instrumental imperative to 'uplift' working class men in particular, from their association with imprudent animalism, in contradistinction to the sober industriousness demanded of the wage labourer. However, a more radical ethic of the consideration of other animals for their own sake, that did not merely focus on particular (ab)uses of particular animals was also present, if perhaps only fleetingly, in the birth of the modern vegetarian movement. This marked the emergence of distinctively value-rational action, orientated to the intrinsic worth of nonhuman animal life, rather than apparently value-rational action disguising the instrumental rationalities of work, sobriety, etc.

Joseph Ritson's 1802 publication 'Essay on Abstinence from Animal Food as Moral Duty' combined the health and moral dimensions of consuming animal foods, articulating the importance of, and challenging, children's socialization into morally harmful practices: 'Our children are bred up, and one of the first pleasures we allow them, is the licence of inflicting pain upon poor animals' (Ritson 1802: 97). Ritson advocated the adoption of the 'vegetable regimen' in the education system, and suggested that the high rates of infant mortality in London and its suburbs at the start of the nineteenth century were as a result of the 'untimely and unnatural use of animal food' (Ritson 1802: 147).

The work of Dr William Lambe, a Fellow of the Royal College of Physicians and a pioneer of what we would now call vegan nutrition (although the word vegan was not coined until 1944), remained influential for many decades following his first publications in 1809. While Lambe's defence of the vegan diet was on health grounds, he strongly influenced the work of one of his patients, John Frank Newton, who developed Lambe's advice to include ethical issues relating to the use and treatment of nonhuman animals. Newton in turn influenced other prominent figures including the poet Percy Bysshe Shelley, whose debut published poem, *Queen Mab* in 1813, was prefaced with his essay 'A Vindication of Natural Diet', which linked both the health and moral well-being of humans to Lambe's 'vegetable diet' (which also included fruit, grains and legumes, but was named thus by Lambe and his advocates). Shelley was briefly part of the vegan commune at the London home of Harriet de Boinville, Newton's sister-in-law, which advocated (and practiced) the health and ethical dimensions of living without using nonhuman animals (Davis 2012). This encompassed not only the forgoing of 'animal products', but also avoiding exploiting the labour of animals, which remained a significant form of publicly visible animal use prior to its gradual usurpation by mechanical labour in agriculture, transport and industrial processes such as mining. This early challenge to the nascent anthroparchal network of Figure 2.1 was somewhat derailed by the drift of the vegetarian movement towards a more contemporary understanding of vegetarianism as being a plant-based diet plus some 'animal products', especially 'dairy' and birds' eggs. It was this drift that eventually fomented the emergence of the contemporary vegan movement in the mid-twentieth century (see Cole 2014, Davis 2012), which in turn infuses the anti-anthroparchal interventions into children's culture described in Chapter 9.

In 1809, Thomas Erskine introduced a Bill into the House of Commons which sought to establish that nonhuman animals had rights and should not be treated as property. Erskine recognized that harms to nonhuman animals were only acknowledged as harms inasmuch as they were harms against the property of humans (and human males, specifically), but as nonhumans shared the same senses as humans, they should also have rights to reflect this and not be regarded as property.

> Almost every sense bestowed upon man is equally bestowed upon them; seeing, hearing, feeling, thinking; the sense of pain and pleasure; the passions of love and anger; sensibility to kindness, and pangs from unkindness and neglect, are inseparable characteristics of their natures as much as of our own … I say their rights, subservient as they are, ought to be as sacred as our own. (Hansard 15 May 1809: col. 555–6)

Although 'subservience' is perhaps incongruous alongside a call for equal sacredness, this remains a radical call over 200 years later, demonstrating the depth with which anthroparchal relations have inveigled the culture as a whole in the intervening period. In the same speech at the second reading of the Bill in the House of Lords, Erskine made a connection between the treatment of nonhuman animals, his proposal to grant them rights, and the moral education and well-being of children. This in turn, he argued, through the legislation he proposed, would be progressively socially transformative and furthermore on a global scale (Hansard 15 May 1809: col. 571). The Bill got no further than this second reading in the House of Lords before being defeated in the House of Commons, due to opposition from those who saw that it threatened pastimes such as fox-hunting (Kean 1998); Weber's iron cage thesis evidenced by the triumph of instrumentalism over value-rationality. The radical nature of Erskine's proposal is also underlined by the fact that at this time and for some decades yet in both the UK and the US, women were still regarded in law as the property of their husbands, as illustrated by William Blackstone's often quoted description of women's traditional legal status in Britain: 'the very being or legal existence of the woman is suspended during the marriage' (Blackstone 1765: 430).

Erskine's Bill is important, despite its defeat, in that it not only made an explicit connection between the status of animals, the moral education of children and the moral worth of society, but also in that, consistent with the ideas of writers such as Primatt (1776), it attempted a cohesive approach to the status of all nonhuman animals, irrespective of their uses by humans, that is, it (implicitly at least) traversed most of the terrain of Figure 2.1. Subsequent legislative attempts, both successful and unsuccessful, took a far more fractional approach, focussing on particular uses of particular nonhuman animals, connected to particular concerns about the impacts of these uses on humans from moral, health or economic standpoints; the specific rationalities of the diversity of discourses and practices militate against a holistic refusal of anthroparchal relations. 'Protecting' children from engagement with some of these aspects of use came to be a core theme in the pursuit of managing and regulating these concerns.

This fractional approach to subsequent regulation and legislation is crucially dependent upon the variable perceptibility, or sensibility, of different animal uses. The first successful piece of legislation in the UK – *The Cruel Treatment of Cattle Act* in 1822, also popularly known as Martin's Act – was introduced by Richard Martin MP, and outlawed the cruel treatment of a category of animal whose use (for the purposes of a reliable food supply for the growing urban population) was increasingly visible in the rapidly expanding centres of population. The concern here however is arguably not really with the use of animals but with the corrupting effects on the human populace of the visibility of their use in an urban milieu.

The following year saw the establishment of the Regent's Park Zoological Gardens, which provided the opportunity to directly observe and admire (certain) nonhuman animals. The Gardens' aim was explicitly educative (but also covertly entertaining) with a clear moral intent to foster respect and proper treatment, but again confined to only certain 'exotic' species of animals. The latter had previously only been 'knowable' through representations in books, but the advent of 'zoos' made them available for human encounters, which although mediated through the practice of confinement and the discursive constructions of exotica, did involve living nonhuman animals (Kean 1998).

In 1824 the Society for the Prevention of Cruelty to Animals (SPCA, later the RSPCA after being granted Royal status in 1840), was established by a group of campaigners including Richard Martin MP, in order to support the implementation of the 1822 Act. Several other similar organizations were established shortly thereafter for the same purpose. Nonhuman animals were to be watched over, either in zoological gardens for educative purposes, or by protectors of new laws and morals that regulated 'proper' treatment of those nonhumans destined to be consumed as food. The principle of surveillance of other animals as a 'proper' form of human–nonhuman animal relation was therefore inculcated in children as 'zoo' visitors at the same time as 'animal welfare' began to be regulated through the surveillance of instrumental practices. In both cases, instrumental uses were subsumed by value-rational veneers; the putative intrinsic worth of the education of children or the 'welfare' of 'farmed animals', through the mechanism of an objectifying gaze. In terms of Figure 2.1, these forms of relations illustrate the related processes of increasing the sensibility of some anthroparchal practices and discourses at the same time as the most instrumental practices sink towards the south-east of the conceptual map. This is not to deny that ameliorations of some of the most egregious harms of other animals did not result from the actions of the RSPCA et al., but to argue that the thrust of welfarism was to regulate instrumental use insofar as to render it legitimate, morally untroubling, and therefore discursively non-sensible even (especially) while under the gaze of welfarists.

In 1828, parliament was petitioned to debate the conditions at Smithfield market, and the issue was investigated by a parliamentary committee. Smithfield was the oldest and largest of London's cattle markets, dominating London's bovine 'livestock' trade, occupying over 4 acres and surrounded by inns and butcheries. It had been open since 1660 and trebled its business between 1732 and 1846, roughly in line with human demographic growth. In 1828, the year of the parliamentary enquiry, there were 161,600 sales of cattle and 1,438,790 sales of sheep at Smithfield. The market's strength owed much to its central position, with direct access from north, east and west of the city. This also fostered some of its unpopularity, causing congestion (and associated noise and dirt) in routes into central London as live animals were driven to the market. At Smithfield, trading began as early as midnight, which caused unpopular disruption locally. Concerns also revolved around the perceived monopoly some saw Smithfield to hold, with rival markets struggling to be established or compete, even though 'livestock' traders supported the benefits they saw in having a central, sizeable facility (Smith 1999). Once again, disquiet about the use of nonhuman animals was focussed on a highly visible, audible, specific context, in which emerging pseudo-value-rational sensibilities were being challenged. Yet despite these growing concerns that would be sustained for many years after the 1828 enquiry, but before the market eventually ceased to sell live animals, Smithfield market and Newgate shambles continued to grow in proportion with the growth of the urban populations – undergoing building work to expand in the 1830s, and increasing the numbers of live animal sales (Smith 1999).

There was as yet no cohesive movement to connect and oppose these issues; different contexts were dealt with separately for separate purposes. A more connected approach, that might be more recognizable to contemporary animal rights or vegan activists, was perhaps not entirely absent though – for example, Lewis Gompertz, an early secretary of the SPCA held what we would now recognize as a vegan position of opposing all animal use, but by the 1830s he had been side-lined and ousted from the SPCA, ostensibly for 'anti-Christian views' (Davis 2012). The SPCA had a much more conservative approach to change, and relied on the law to change behaviours, with a particular focus on nonhuman animal use in the public sphere: they opposed legislation to protect animals kept at home as 'pets' as inappropriately intrusive (Kean 1998), in an eerie analogy to the discourse of 'privacy' that has historically masked and facilitated multiple forms of violence within domestic space, not least physical and sexual violence towards children. Other groups, including the Animal Friends' Society established by Gompertz in 1832 after his departure from the SPCA, looked to change behaviours without seeking changes to the law. They were part of a movement to use education as a vehicle for behaviour change, through museums, galleries, public gardens and ironically, 'zoos'; to manifest their ethical concerns about relations with nonhuman animals, through increasing direct encounters with them and thereby the sensibility of nonhumans, rather than by campaigning to remove the *results* of exploitative practices, especially 'animal products', from public space.

The emerging concerns for certain types of treatment of certain types of nonhuman animals in the 1820s and 1830s coincided with other social movements challenging the prevailing social order. Increasingly from this time and throughout the century, women in particular were becoming politicized across a range of social movements including but by no means limited to animal rights and welfare movements. In 1825 Britain's first anti-slavery society was founded by Lucy Townsend (Midgley 1992) and in the wake of the publication of Wollstonecraft's *A Vindication of the Rights of Woman* in 1792, female philanthropy and an organized feminist movement grew in prominence (Midgley 2007, see also Adams 2004). Around this time also, performed concern for nonhuman animals became a distinctive feature of those seeking to identify as 'respectable', manifesting in the types and contexts of animal use that were successfully regulated or outlawed; dogfighting, associated with lower-class groups was outlawed in 1835 (Kean 1998). This period also saw the growth in popularity of an organized vegetarian movement in the UK. Alcott House, in South West London, opened in 1838, and is closely associated with the Victorian vegetarian movement. It was a progressive school and community which was what we would now call vegan from its inception – as noted above, early on in this period the term 'vegetarian' still referred to practices which we now classify as vegan, not just limited to the exclusion of meat from the diet but the exclusion of all animal products as well as the rejection of other instrumental relations with other animals (Davis 2012). The vegetarian movement of the mid-nineteenth century was aligned with some pioneering socialist idealistic thinkers, such as the pioneering socialist, feminist and co-operator William Thompson, but the movement was also popular in response to issues of poor food quality (thereby kicking back against another manifestation of instrumental rationality: the hiking of profits through food adulteration). The Vegetarian Society, which held its founding conference in 1847, described animal food disparagingly as 'second hand food' (Kean 1998: 54). The vegetarian movement drew together disparate concerns of health and morality regarding the use of nonhuman animals, but these concerns arguably co-existed within the movement without there being a united ethic connecting them, or in other words, without a coherent opposition to anthroparchal discourses and practices that could comprehensively redraw the map of Figure 2.1.

Victorian Public Health Reform

The concern with the quality of food was also an important part of ongoing public health concerns regarding the use of nonhuman animals in growing urban settings. During the middle of the century these concerns began to manifest in steps towards formal regulation and control. As discussed above, disquiet had long been voiced about large 'livestock' markets such as Smithfield and Newgate, but now there was a collective momentum of anxiety about the moral harm of the sensibility of slaughter practices, especially to impressionable children, together with public health concerns about the spread of disease through contaminated food, unclean water and insufficient sewerage and street cleansing. Implicitly and explicitly, these public health debates about the spread of disease had children as a fundamental concern: childhood mortality from infectious diseases being employed as a barometer of the health status of the populace more widely is a familiar theme of the history of Victorian public health (McKeown 1977). Victorian public health discourses were very much concerned with separating children (as a group particularly susceptible to infectious diseases) from the health risks that contact with nonhuman animals brought. Alongside these, there was also more and more palpable concern that these practices posed moral as well as mortal dangers to the impressionable. The 1847 *Town and Police Clauses Act* classifies the slaughtering and 'dressing' of cattle as an obstruction that threatened public order (Mason 2012); a measure to remove these practices from view rather than to end them, suggesting that while the instrumental practice (of animal use) was still acceptable, its means was problematic: 'If cruelty was to take place, it was to be behind closed doors and under license' (Burt 2001: 208). So, while an intensification of instrumental relations with other animals is evidenced by the burgeoning trade of Smithfield, the removal from public view of those relations also effected their discursive transportation to the distant, hidden lands of the south-east of Figure 2.1.

The RSPCA was by now targeting educational establishments, attempting to introduce issues of animal welfare into school curricula. In the mid-1850s they were preparing a school textbook, and forging links with the government school inspectorate to the extent that they had a voice in the inspectors' work, who in turn co-operated in the distribution of RSPCA literature to schools (Harrison 1973). Education therefore emerges as a site for the socialization of anthroparchal relations, with 'welfare' giving a value-rational gloss to the inculcation of instrumental norms, an issue we return to in the context of current education about human–animal relations in Chapter 7.

Throughout the nineteenth century, the regulation of children in the workplace had been subject to a series of 'Factory Acts', limiting hours worked according to age. These moved forward a shift in acceptance of the appropriateness of work environments as spaces for children, and were long couched as measures to protect both moral and physical well-being among them. Historical accounts constructing the moral progress underpinning the origins of the British Welfare State have focused on the role of nineteenth-century legislative changes relating to public health, factory working and education, but those relating to nonhuman animal treatment have been overlooked, despite their shared legitimation of social well-being and physical health (Harrison 1973). A more rounded account of this history should recognize these changing roles of and attitudes towards nonhuman animals, and their spatial and conceptual reorganization considered alongside those also affecting children (see Chapter 4).

Formal regulation of spaces with regard to children and animals is also evident among these measures, such as attempts to prohibit children under 14 from being present in slaughterhouses to witness slaughter (Burt 2001). Describing the presence of 'livestock' markets and the visible practice of slaughter in central London, Charles Dickens offers a description of the corrupting influence on children:

> ... you shall see the little children, inured to sights of brutality from their birth, trotting along the alleys, mingled with troops of horribly busy pigs, up to their ankles in blood but it makes the young rascals hardy. Into the imperfect sewers of this overgrown city, you shall have the immense mass of corruption, engendered by these practices, lazily thrown out of sight, to rise, in poisonous gases, into your house at night, when your sleeping children will most readily absorb them. (First published in *Household Words* 8 March 1851, reprinted in Pascoe 1997: 429)

The role of nonhuman animals in mid-nineteenth-century Victorian public health discourses is interlaced in the timeline of these moral concerns, but has also been somewhat lost in history's retelling. Famously, in 1854 Dr John Snow turned medical wisdom on its head by demonstrating the role of water supplies contaminated by human and nonhuman animal waste in the spread of cholera in London. What is less well remembered about Snow is his longstanding advocacy of the works of Lambe and Newton, the pioneering early nineteenth-century nutritional scientists who advocated the adoption of what we would now call a vegan diet for health reasons, and Snow's own commitment to the wisdom of following such a diet himself for his own health (Davis 2012). Lambe's work had continued to be influential and in 1850 his second book (published in 1815 in Britain) was republished in the USA, where it also became popular. The Gamgee brothers, a vet and a doctor, writing in the 1850s and 1860s, asserted that around a fifth of 'meat' eaten in the UK came from diseased animals, and that these diseases were transmittable to humans (Kean 1998). These accounts establish that the connection between animal foods, the conditions in which animals were kept, and human health and morality were integral to prominent medical discourses at this time. However, it is the issues of the cleanliness of human living conditions and the spread of disease among humans that have tended to endure in historical accounts of the period. While concerns about zoonotic disease in the new urban context accelerated the *physical* separation of humans from other animals in the nineteenth century, their *conceptual* separation is subsequently compounded by the near erasure of this development of human–nonhuman animal relations from historical accounts; it is almost as though (particular types) of other animals were never there at all, that is, human responsibility for their location in marginal spaces of confinement is also effaced.

Remove, Reconfigure and Refresh

The mid-nineteenth-century expurgation of nonhuman animals from urban spaces applied only to certain kinds of nonhuman animals. That is, those who were used for the most nakedly instrumental purposes (such as to be killed and eaten) and objectified the most intensely, steadily discursively shifting these groups of nonhumans into the south-eastern region of Figure 2.1. As with the earlier introduction of zoological gardens, such as the Regents Park Zoological Gardens, or the Bristol Zoological Gardens in 1836, certain types of rare or exotic animal were simultaneously being introduced to cities for use as educative spectacle rather than as food; the spectacle of exotica accompanied and arguably exacerbated the banalization of 'domestic' animals, compounding their cultural non-sensibility. The other groups of animals being encouraged in urban spaces in the middle of the century were those with roles as companions ('pets') directly within households, as well as some labouring animals, especially horses (of whom more below). During this period, animal companions were allowed, or encouraged, to remain in the human home, but subjected to physical and behavioural normalization to remove their perceived 'animality', also evidenced by the introduction of dog licences to tackle the perceived threat of unsupervised dogs (Mason 2012). From the 1850s onwards, books on 'pets' and 'pet care' became increasingly popular, shifting towards discourses of improvement in behaviour achieved through kindness rather than punishment (Kean 1998), perhaps imitating the contemporaneous drift from sovereign to disciplinary power in the human carceral archipelago of prisons, barracks, schools and so on (Foucault 1991). Other animals, whose presence and role in the urban landscape was already well established, found themselves subject to neither the expulsion of 'livestock' nor the remoulding of 'pets'. Despite the rise of the railways, horses were still (and for some time yet), crucial to the transport needs of the city, and so while numbers of cattle, sheep and pigs in city centres fell, numbers of urban horses rose (Kean 1998). For them, a more munificent response was evident, with echoes of Wesley's edicts that a preacher take care of 'his' horse's comfort before his own at the end of the day. In 1859 the Metropolitan Drinking Fountain and Cattle Trough Association was founded, to provide free water for human and nonhuman animal travellers in major British cities, recognizing the integral role that some kinds of animals had in urban workers' daily lives, and the duty of care owed by humans to them. While horses were increasingly cared for in their urban roles (albeit under an instrumental rubric that continued to demand their labour as exchange for that care), the growth of the railways did facilitate the removal of 'livestock' from the cities, who previously by necessity had been raised close to the human populations who consumed them. Now, they were being moved further out of sight of the life of the city and transported post-mortem by the new, speedier rail links. In 1855 a new cattle market in Islington opened, facilitated by the new rail line (Kean 1998), diminishing the importance of the convenient centrality and easy road access of Smithfield market, which had shored up its continued success despite the moral and health concerns that had long been voiced. Sites which had previously served as areas where 'livestock' were rested before their final journey into central London were now able to host sites for 'livestock' markets and slaughterhouses, tucked away from sight (Smith 1999). Across major cities in Europe, slaughterhouses were being removed to the outskirts, and given more anonymous architectural appearances (Burt 2001), sinking into non-sensibility at the same time as the processes of objectification were industrialized and scaled up. Vialles (1994) describes how French abattoirs were being 'banished' beyond city walls as a result not only of town planners' public health concerns, but also a powerful shift in sensibilities about death, suffering, violence, waste, and 'miasmas'. These shifting sensibilities also saw nonhuman animals increasingly viewed as lesser beings. Technological advances meant slaughter could become almost entirely non-sensible – the process removed from the sight, smell and hearing of the masses who continued to consume its end products (Vialles 1994). Smithfield market finally ceased as a 'livestock' market in 1868, and was replaced by a dead animal market, with Newgate shambles also shutting at this time. Three years later, a large live cattle market for the foreign cattle trade was opened in Deptford in South London (Kean 1998), with spatial necessity and moral qualms respectively facilitated and soothed by improved transport links – the consumption of animals was not significantly challenged, but at least the city, and the morally vulnerable eyes therein, were no longer directly confronted by the violent practices that they involved.

This period also saw the emergence of a prominent anti-vivisection movement in the UK. It had by now been long accepted that nonhuman animals felt pain and emotion, meaning that their treatment and use for experimental spectacle had become a moral issue. During the seventeenth century vivisection had been conducted in public; the public were able to spectate rather than participate, with the activities of experimentation conducted by appropriate 'experts'. Guerrini (1989) argues that this contributed to the creation of the laboratory as a 'disciplined space'. As attitudes to nonhuman animals changed, although the practices continued, from the eighteenth century they continued chiefly in private spaces, spatially and conceptually demarcated as the domain of the expert (Guerrini 1989). In the 1870s however, the practice of vivisection did become a public issue and subject of heated debate. This was not solely driven by the issue of the proper treatment of nonhuman animals; Frances Power Cobbe, a leading spokesperson for the anti-vivisection movement, argued that the practice would lower the morals of the population (Harris 2002). The anti-vivisection movement in England at this time included multiple groups and societies, often opposing each other's tactics as much as the practice of vivisection itself. For example, the British Union for the Abolition of Vivisection sought single legislation to abolish vivisection while the National Anti-Vivisection Society favoured a gradualist approach. This variance had parallels in other social movements of the period, for example Millicent Fawcett sought women's suffrage through successive reforms, while the Pankhursts sought a single legislative act. The anti-vivisection movement as a whole also faced barriers from those who might ostensibly appear allies, for example some of the RSPCA's council were vivisectors themselves (Lansbury 2007). These anxieties about the use of nonhuman animals for the pursuit of science were reflected in contemporary culture in these closing decades of the nineteenth century, such as in H.G. Wells's *The Island of Doctor Moreau*, in which the eponymous protagonist is a vivisector. In the novel, Moreau's devotion to scientific research is set against his attitude to the pain he inflicts on other animals, reflecting the contemporary tensions between the pursuit of scientific knowledge and changing attitudes to nonhumans (Harris 2002). In terms of our analysis of the use of nonhuman animals addressed in this book, a key issue in the management of concerns regarding vivisection is that of how sensible the practice was at the time. Writing in 1865, the French physiologist and vivisector Dr Claude Bernard wrote how a scientist 'no longer hears the cry of animals, he no longer sees the blood that flows, he sees only his idea' (Bernard 1865: 103, quoted by Harris 2002: 103). The anxieties about this practice, like so many others we have discussed, cut not to whether they are done, but whether we see them to be done.

New Positions, Consolidated by Instruction

This separation and compartmentalization of different groups of animals in new urbanized societies now spawned an increased focus on instructing the population, and children in particular, in the proper use of this newly reorganized nonhuman life. 'Pets' living in family homes was not a new phenomenon, having been a feature of British life since late medieval society, but the practice of 'pet-keeping' became more 'refined', subject to stricter social rules and etiquette (Franklin 1999), and their endurance following the reorganization and removal of other nonhuman animals previously present in domestic spaces required a re-education, and a rewriting of their 'proper' place and function, which now, transformatively, included love as a central feature. Publications such as *Beeton's Book of Home Pets*, published in the 1860s, instructed children in 'proper' standards of care and familiarity among one group of nonhuman animals, still permitted space and function within urban and domestic spaces (Kean 1998). The instructive function of animal companions instrumentalized and undercut the affective gloss discursively constructed by Beeton and others; while children might well feel genuine love for their nonhuman companions, the latter were incorporated into domestic space as a tool in a socialization process that morally aggrandized humans, all the while that they remained complicit in the newly non-sensible most violent forms of anthroparchal relations. Beeton's particular book (first published as a series of weekly pamphlets) was part of a range of works carrying the 'Beeton' brand, either edited, compiled or authored by Samuel Beeton, the publisher husband of Isabella Beeton, more familiarly referred to simply as Mrs Beeton. Her famous *Book of Household Management* was first published in 1861, so as her husband instructed in the proper care of some kinds of animals granted domestic sanctuary, so she wrote authoritatively and popularly on the cooking of those other animals now largely removed from urban sight. Even in death, those animals used as food were subjected to further effacement, with the carving of recognizable body parts at the dining table becoming less acceptable, and progressively a task given to the head of the table alone, or the removal of carving to side tables or 'specialist enclaves' being seen as ever more appropriate in civilized circles (Elias 1978).

In the latter part of the nineteenth century, behaviour modification in 'pet' dogs focussed on techniques couched as compassion and firmness rather than punishment; dogs were argued to have a conscience of sorts, an ability to discern right from wrong, which lent them a quasi-subjectivity and therefore made them suitable for membership of a family unit and who would be obedient, playful and tolerant of children's (uncivilized) behaviours. Periodicals such as *The Strand Magazine* were also publishing articles on cats and cat care to reinforce and regulate their suitability as domestic animal companions (Mason 2012).

By the end of the nineteenth century, zoological gardens were hugely popular, with Regent's Park Zoological Gardens now attracting over half a million visitors a year. Although ostensibly established for education not entertainment, they were now a regular part of social as well as educational life for the Victorians. Their entertainment value was now recognized and accepted as legitimate (Kean 1998), and 'zoos' were opening in large cities across the world: for example Stuttgart (1850), Philadelphia (1859), Copenhagen (1859), the Jardin d'Acclimation in Paris (1860, following an earlier Parisian Zoological Gardens in 1795), Central Park in New York (1864), Sofia (1888), Helsinki (1889) and Barcelona (1892). 'Zoos' faced (and still do) a tension between serving the recreational motivations of visitors from the general public and pursuing loftier goals that are often constructed as value-rational, notably through conservation discourses. This tension continues today in practices in educational and recreational spheres which make cross-claims to the other, as we discuss in Part II of the book. Although this period at the end of the nineteenth century saw many 'zoos' open, they struggled financially because of the unmanageability of this tension, and for some the scientific goals fell away in favour of the more successful role as an attraction popular with children (Osborne 1996); another triumph for instrumental rationality.

Representations of the New Orders

Entertainment and recreation provided other means by which children began to be taught appropriate relationships with other animals. At the end of the nineteenth and start of the twentieth century, toys and books representing nonhuman animals (but not those abominated in the south-east of Figure 2.1) became increasingly popular, acting as lightning rods for childhood empathy. Anderson and Henderson (2005) argue that there is a dissolution of the distinction between humans and other animals in children's stories. The portrayal of nonhuman animal characters with what we assume to be uniquely human qualities is commonplace in children's fiction, with an emphasis on domesticated animals and 'pets', which communicates 'pet-keeping' as the only emotionally important relationship with other animals. Narrative traditions common in children's stories include the message that there is a duty of care owed to those nonhuman animals positioned towards the north-west of Figure 2.1, and that loss of sympathy or empathy with nonhuman animals is an inevitable part of the process of growing up (Stewart and Cole 2009). The former is perhaps most famously illustrated by the impact of the publication of *Black Beauty* in 1877, which is thought to have contributed to the ending of the use of the bearing rein – a painful harness used to keep the head high, which caused damage and pain to horses' necks (Anderson and Henderson 2005). The latter theme is well illustrated by the narrative of Kipling's *Jungle Book*, published in 1894, which tells a story of a boy raised by a motley assemblage of nonhumans, the end of whose childhood is signalled by his vanquishing of his nonhuman foe (Shere Khan the tiger) and his return to the human village, where he also struggles to fit in. Essentially rejected by both human and nonhuman social worlds in the story, we are told that the boy eventually becomes 'a man' and marries – a tale of a childhood characterized by association with nonhumans, an adolescent phase as an outsider struggling to shake off their childhood symbols, and eventual return to a 'human' life. Anthropomorphized nonhuman characters continued to be popular in children's fiction, deftly combining invited sympathy for the stories' protagonists while reinforcing the normative order of nonhuman animal use by humans (Coslett 2006). This adroit device is exemplified in Beatrix Potter's extremely successful series of animal stories, the first of which was published in 1902. In the period before World War I, she published 19 story books, but then only two more stories and two nursery rhyme collections before she stopped writing in 1930. The majority of the chief protagonists in her stories (excluding the title characters in the nursery rhyme collections) were small mammals with identities as both domesticated and free living creatures (cats in five of the stories, rabbits in four and mice in four), and the characters were usually presented in quasi-human homes, wearing clothes, carrying out human practices, such as shopping and so forth. While some story plots involved the rescue of the nonhuman characters from humans and nonhumans who would eat them, the stories also routinely included practices of the human use of nonhumans: while in the *Tale of Peter Rabbit* (1902) the eponymous hero is seeking to escape the clutches of the human who wishes to put him in a pie, his siblings' good behaviour is rewarded with milk; in the *Tale of Two Bad Mice* (1904), two mice attempt to eat the ham, fish and lobster dishes laid out on the dining table of a dolls' house, only to be angered when they find the items to be made of plaster. Saved from a mouse trap laid by the nurse of the girl who owned the dolls' house, they atone by clearing up the house; in the *Tale of Jemima Puddle Duck* (1908), Jemima (but not her eggs) is saved from being eaten by the fox hounds who are summoned by the local butcher's dog. In Potter's writing then, the seismic convulsions in anthroparchal relations since the eighteenth century can be seen to have more or less settled into the familiar geography of Figure 2.1, discursively reproducing the physical categorization and dispersal of other animals, according to their differential positioning along the intersecting continua of objectification and sensibility.

Conclusion

The intensification of the reordering of relationships between humans and nonhuman animals that had been in progress before and without industrialization and urbanization, required corresponding intensification of efforts to educate, re-educate and reinforce these changed orders, and children were at the heart of both the re-ordering and the strategies to consolidate this new order through the socialization mechanisms of edification and entertainment. The fractional nature of the reordering, dealing piecemeal with different uses of different animals according to their contingent rationalities left the modern era without a unifying logic underpinning the relationship between humans and other animals. This required and still requires an ongoing process of legitimation of this precarious ordering as 'proper', and the channels through which this process continues are addressed in Part II of this book.

Chapter 4
The Construction and Study of Children and Childhood

Children's ties to animals seem to have slipped below the radar screens of almost all scholars of child development. (Melson 2005: 12)

As Melson (2005) observes, a critical analysis of children's relationships with nonhuman animals has been neglected in the study of children and childhood, which we argue is untenable given the ubiquity of children's interactions with other animals as well as the ubiquity of cultural representations of other animals in children's culture. In order to facilitate the analyses of those interactions and representations that we present in Part II of this book, this chapter introduces some of the ways in which scholars have addressed the early years of human life. To this end, we begin the chapter with a discussion of how childhood has been recognized as a cultural construct, beyond simply a physiological pre-adult stage of development. Secondly, we discuss social science research on children and childhood that highlights the emergence of socialization sites relevant to our empirical analyses in Part II of this book. We conclude by asserting the indissociability of children and other animals for a full sociological account of the construction of each, in the context of the emergence and trajectory of modern Western societies.

Constructing Childhood

The importance of childhood as a conceptual category, and discrete social position has shifted over time, although quite how is subject to some considerable academic dispute. It is important to acknowledge these themes as historical perspectives on childhood promise to elucidate and inform contemporary perspectives in potent ways (Kehily 2009). Our analysis of the construction of childhood therefore intersects with that of the construction of other animals, or rather, building on Chapter 3, we are interested in the ways in which children and other animals have been *mutually constructed* through discourse and practice, in ways which have entrenched exploitative, anthroparchal relations. However it is questionable whether a meaningful history of the concept of childhood is possible. It is considered unstudiable by some, as the limited, partial, sources used in many accounts are so problematic; while widespread in the study of childhood, the use of personal documents has drawn criticism for its tendency to be used for selective, illustrative purposes rather than for systematic and rigorous analysis (Pollock 1983). Certainly all attempts to construct such a narrative must always accept that they can only ever be regarded through the contemporary lens of the viewer, so whether the issue is of the selectiveness of the questions we ask, or the context in which we understand the answers we identify, we cannot remove our understanding of the present from the picture of the past that we draw. As this book seeks to also challenge the norms of our present(s), this challenge of determining a history appears to become more problematic still. However, we are concerned with the versions of the history of childhood which have become influential, precisely because they reveal much about the mutual constitution of childhood and 'animalness'. That is, key markers of childhood that are taken for granted as common-sense in the present, such as 'innocence' or 'sentimental' affectivity in relation to other animals, gain cultural purchase partly through their reification in academic discourse as 'true' outcomes of an historical process.

Despite these issues with studying childhood then, and the particular criticisms levelled at the selectivity of sources in his work, Philippe Ariès's *Centuries of Childhood* (1962) continues to be influential with scholars in this field. Ariès's argument held that childhood was not considered to be worthy of cultural representation until the seventeenth century in Europe, but that it was through these representations that childhood was first afforded a privileged status. The nature of this status, argues Ariès, has changed over time, (as outlined in 'The "Grand Stages" of Childhood' below), a process which is traceable through changing portrayals of children in cultural representations. The continued prominence of Ariès's work is particularly due to his acknowledgement of childhood as a social construction that requires serious consideration: that 'children' existed was of course a matter of straightforward physiological fact, but the notion of 'childhood' being a particular, socially constructed category and therefore 'children' having a distinct ontological status was not, he argued. Furthermore, Ariès is also still valuable as he is credited with instigating a focus on the history of childhood in academia (Postman 1994). Otherwise, much of the substantive claims within his work have become untenable, in no small part because the bulk of his analysis related to a relatively narrow range of sources such as specific types of medieval writings, and the portrayal of children and childhood in medieval art (Corsaro 2012, Clarke 2004). Yet it is important to recognize that meaningful interpretations of social mores can be interpreted through media analysis, as illustrated also by the depictions of children and animals in the paintings of Hogarth and Wright discussed in Chapter 3, and indeed as we engage with contemporary representations of both human children and nonhuman animals in Part II of this book. By considering the intertextuality of representations in different socialization fields, and their enmeshment with dominant practices (such as eating other animals), we can also infer the potency and social currency of these representations.

The 'Grand Stages' of Childhood

Ariès is referred to as one of the 'Grand Stage Theorists' of childhood, who also included deMause (1974) among others (Corsaro 2011). Grand Stage Theories supported the view that childhood developed in distinct historical stages, and asserted that childhood both developed as a concept and 'improved' as a lived experience in historically identifiable stages. Broadly speaking, the stages proposed by Ariès charted the representation of children shifting from being not humans, to an angelic motif, to coddled amusements, to adults in training. Ariès's thesis held that childhood had not been recognized, or constructed, as distinct from adulthood in the medieval period, with children becoming recognized as fully human, or entering the 'adult world', at around the age of 7 years. Children were not deemed to merit representation before this age, roughly identified as the age they could be without the care of mother or nurse (Corsaro 2012, Pollock 1983). Ariès was by no means alone among scholars of childhood in asserting that there was 'no childhood', with children 'held in such low esteem that they were not even regarded as human' (Shorter 1976: 169, cited by Pollock 1983: 3). This theme of identifying children as nonhuman, or pre-human, is evident in many of these academic accounts of how childhood was conceptualized prior to the twentieth century, and these historical resonances between how human children and nonhumans were viewed and treated are evident elsewhere in the chapters in Part I. A key motif here is the hierarchization of the human and the nonhuman, with children needing to be discursively 'uplifted' from a pre-human or nonhuman ontological status in order to accede to adulthood. One way to conceive of this process is the 'rescue' of children from the southern regions of Figure 2.1 (i.e. as either 'wild' or, perhaps more well-meaningly, exploited) through their elevation to the security of the north and west of the conceptual map. In this process, children, through their ascension, leave other animals behind. An approximate equivalence of certain key features associated with human childhood and nonhuman animals remains in contemporary social discourses of both groups, including this process of distancing. This is explored further in Part II of this book. Thus we see that the processes described in Chapter 2, whereby individuals are granted varying levels of subjectivity and sensibility through dominant human worldviews and power relationships do not simply apply to relationships with nonhumans, but also to how other humans (in this case children) are and always have been granted (or denied) status, subjecthood and cultural sensibility. The relationship between human children and nonhuman animals, when considered in this light, within hierarchical social structures, assumes a new layer of interest – beyond the relationships that are observed, fostered, constructed or denied *between* members of these groups, to also invite a consideration of the shared otherness of those within these groups.

The picture of a social world without childhood that Ariès and others described gradually changed from the thirteenth century onwards when depictions of children as angels in contemporary art (such as the ornamental, angelic motifs in the work of painters such as Titian) suggested the start of the 'special status' associated with childhood (Corsaro 2012): still not quite human, but not negatively defined or 'ignored' either, starting to now enjoy the status of an object to be enjoyed or admired. Although qualitatively different from celebratory or eulogistic representations of other animals, there is a resonance with the latter's positioning in the north-east of Figure 2.1: highly culturally sensible, but also highly objectified and arguably instrumentalized in relation to the pleasurable consumption of images of childhood or of other animals, by adult humans. If we accept that these depictions of children as angels give access to at least a partial understanding of the nature of relationships between adults and children between the thirteenth and fifteenth centuries, this therefore suggests a relationship with characteristics of observer and observed between adults and children. In terms of attempting to position children in this era in the terms of the typology we propose in Figure 2.1, children are being afforded greater sensibility than previous analyses of childhood suggested, but at a price, with the ideology of these idealized representations limiting still fuller subjectivity. This theme of the distancing, objectifying gaze was explored in Chapter 2, in the context of Foucault's concerns with the mortifying potential of knowledge practices, and recurs in our empirical analyses in Part II; even 'celebratory' representations are problematic in the context of wider sets of discourses and practices which they obscure or legitimate.

An iconography of childhood as a period of innocence and sweetness, in which children were a source of amusement or escape for adults, particularly women, emerged in the sixteenth century (Corsaro 2012). Children were, according to this thesis, special types of humans, with a function of amusing or distracting adult humans. This function of distraction or amusement, and its inevitable association with increased interaction between children and adults (as opposed to observation of children by adults) perhaps starts to shift children a little further to the north and west in terms of Figure 2.1, impacting on not only sensibility but also subjectivity. Implicitly, children are being moved further away from the nonhuman others with whom they were discursively more closely associated in earlier eras, echoing the physical and spatial reorganisations and relocations discussed in Chapter 3.

In turn, this emergence of a 'cherished' aspect to views of children was seen to then move into a reactionary 'moralistic' period between the sixteenth and eighteenth centuries, rejecting this earlier 'coddling' in childhood but retaining the view of the child as a special kind of human, with scholars and moralists viewing childhood as a period of immaturity, for the training and disciplining of children (Corsaro 2012). The theme of 'uplifting' children persists, but the representations and practices which facilitate that uplift have a disciplinary rather than idealizing character. High levels of infant mortality meant that emotional attachments to children were interpreted as being tempered by self-preservation; prior to the nineteenth century the inevitability of not being survived by most of one's children was accepted, and arguably accommodated (Postman 1994). However unknowable the 'reality' of childhood was in earlier centuries, our knowledge of wider social conditions reminds us that they cannot be understood without the contexts within which they were set, and some of those contexts (such as high levels of infant mortality), can be more surely evidenced, and therefore accepted, than others.

According to this 'Grand Stage' history of childhood then, in the broadest terms 'children' as a conceptual category can be regarded to have been repositioned from 'nonhumans' to 'angels' to 'pets' to 'adults inchoate' (which, we note, are comparable to some of the key positions identified in Figure 2.1, such as 'vermin', 'characters', and 'pets'), and arguably our modern conceptualizations of children and childhood retain elements of all of these. To return to our map then, the contemporary view of children and childhood accepts (or expects) an ideal in which *practices* involving children often vacillate around the central point of our map, while our *aspirations* for them pull inexorably towards the upper left, or north-west, corner, where full adult human status can be afforded. This aspirational pull does not, of course, capture all human children and the exploitation characteristic of a south easterly position on Figure 2.1 also persists.

Critics of the Grand Stage Theorists, most notably exemplified by Linda Pollock's (1983) detailed refutation of the work of Ariès and others, highlight that the nature of the historical materials used to support these ideas inherently mobilize a social bias, among other flaws such as the partial drawing of medieval life and the argued misinterpretation of certain aspects of the materials studied. The details of Pollock's critique are without the scope of our analysis, but one of the most important consequences of this, in terms of how comprehensively childhood was or was not drawn through analysis of these sources, is that the perceptions and experiences of children in poorer communities were largely overlooked. Despite this robust challenge to generalizability, childhood thus conceptualized is easy to grasp and to accept. Its plausibility to the contemporary mind benefits from the clear parallels between this view of children as innocent amusements and the modern concept of the animal companion or 'pet', who occupies a similarly comparatively privileged north westerly position, while still falling short of the furthest corner of optimum sensibility and subjectivity. These parallels between human children and animal companions are articulated in many of the practices and cultural artefacts which we discuss in Part II of this book, and we argue that these parallels are not only analytically interesting commonalities but serve as mutually reinforcing of the status of both children and nonhuman animals. This also suggests that while the robustness of the approach of Grand Stage Theorists as a historically accurate analysis may be in doubt, its outward credibility perhaps tells us more about how we currently conceptualize children and childhood. Critiques of Grand Stage Theories of childhood have successfully challenged the thesis that 'childhood' progressed through these stages in chronological steps, but they nonetheless provide us with a valuable analytical insight into the functions and features of childhood as it has been conceptualized, and as it continues to be conceptualized; they provide plausible and useful categories for the analysis of childhood, and for the understanding of relationships between human children, human adults and nonhumans.

Studying Children and Childhood

The study of children was established long before the emergence of the discipline we now recognize as Childhood Studies. It may come as a surprise to those unfamiliar with that field to learn how relatively young this discipline still is. Children were for a long time, as Jenks (2005) puts it, paradoxically absent but present in studies of social life; implicitly children were addressed in studies of family life, socialization and education, but as a 'natural' unit rather than a contextual social construction. For readers more familiar with the even newer field of Critical Animal Studies, a parallel will be instantly apparent here: how immediately curious and obvious these two omissions from social science are, how much they offer to our understanding of all aspects of the social, and how necessary in our study of social worlds their inclusion is. Furthermore, with the notable exception of works such as Gail Melson's (2005) *Why the Wild Things Are*, few childhood studies scholars have specifically explored what is often but only lightly acknowledged passim as the special and significant relationship between children and nonhuman animals: relationships which do not endure into adulthood without all facets thereof being either cast off, or modified, or preserved as a semi-detached precious past token of a past innocence; all variations on the theme of distancing that we have already explored in the earlier chapters of this book. That is, affective child–other animal relations tend to be usurped by more instrumental relations, albeit ones that are frequently enchanted with an aura of affectivity, or even value-rationality. Where nonhumans have been present in the academic study of children and childhood, they have appeared in respect of their function in the development of the child, such as the role of nonhuman animals in children's exposure to death and bereavement, or in learning and practicing power, domination and kindness (Melson 2005). Inevitably therefore, the processes we explore in this book, which filter the presence or participation of different kinds of nonhuman animals in children's lives, also filter the presence of different kinds of nonhumans in our academic sensibility. Attention is directed towards certain groups of nonhuman animals presented in the typology (such as those represented as toys, fictional characters and 'pets'), while others are overlooked (such as those whose roles in childhood are less culturally sensible and more objectified, such as the chickens served in children's ready meals). Consequently, academic research has tended to ignore the role that relationships between humans and nonhuman animals have on the lives of the latter, rather than on the lives of children. That is, the lethal consequences for other animals of the socialization of anthroparchal relations in childhood. These relationships involve not only human children and nonhuman animals, but also human adults participating in the reflection and reproduction of contemporary childhood experience. While the importance of childhood socialization has been acknowledged by scholars of human–nonhuman animal relations (see for example Yates 2004 for a specifically sociological analysis), here too the importance of these processes has remained underdeveloped.

While many disciplines have addressed childhood, this has usually been insofar as childhood is a transitory phase rather than as a separate social grouping or important conceptual category or social position in its own right (Lezner 2001, Kehily 2009); academia has generally 'bolted' children on to studies of education, families, 'race', class, gender and so forth, rather than centred its academic concerns about childhood on children and then orbit those social structures around them. Furthermore, this disciplinary multifariousness brought along the associated diversity and disconnectedness of ontological and epistemological approaches to the study of the experiences that impacted children and their lives. While some disciplines, such as sociology and cultural studies focused on *childhood*, others (such as psychology and education) focused on *children*. 'Childhood Studies' as a field first emerged in its own right in the early 1990s (a 'Sociology of Children' section of the American Sociological Association was established in 1991). The United Nations Convention on the Rights of the Child (UNCRC) in 1989 was a crystallization of the field of children's rights, but without the emergence of Childhood Studies as a discrete discipline, the increasing interest in childhood in other disciplines merely fostered fragmentation. Childhood Studies emerged therefore as a 'genuinely interdisciplinary, multidisciplinary new field' (Lezner 2001: 183) to study and pursue a more holistic understanding of childhood, with children viewed 'in this fullness as human beings' (Lezner 2001: 183), and an entreaty that related disciplines should be contributing to this fullness, not attending to children merely as fragments of their own specialism. The gaps precipitated by the earlier disjointed approach to the study of childhood (such as the near absence of consideration of children's relations with other animals) are, with the emergence of Childhood Studies as a discrete discipline, offered a context that invites them to be closed. Foregrounding the role of other animals in childhood, and vice versa, can therefore contribute to a more holistic understanding of childhood.

Children and Childhood in Other Social Contexts

Beyond the emergence of a discrete sub-discipline of Childhood Studies there is of course a rich history of children being studied across the social sciences, as outlined above, as contributory factors to other areas of enquiry rather than focusing on children as constituting a social group in their own right. In Part II of this book, we will look in more detail at the representations of and experiences with nonhuman animals that humans encounter in childhood in some of the arenas that the social sciences have addressed. The remainder of this chapter will therefore highlight how key socialization sites relevant to the discourses and practices that we discuss in that analysis have been established as important to children and childhood.

The Workplace and the School

The withdrawal of children from the workforce and their relocation to educational establishments have been landmark developments in modern concepts of childhood, and are used as markers for wider 'social development', to the extent that education is viewed as a basic human right. The role of children, both within family and wider social networks, has changed markedly since the seventeenth century. According to Clarke (2004) this is often described by scholars as the emergence and then the spread of a 'middle-class' model or ideology of the family, which is associated with emerging commercial classes in Western Europe: this is based on the idea of the family being self-contained, with a strong male father figure at its head, and with a significant focus on the upbringing of the children in that socially and spatially self-contained unit. In this then emerging but now dominant model, children are construed as the central part of the family's purpose, insofar as their care, protection and education are a core focus and purpose of the labour of the family unit as a whole (Clarke 2004).

In England this social and physical relocation of children from the workforce to schools occurred in the late nineteenth century (James and James 2012). Other social changes relating to the period are discussed in Chapter 3 when urbanization and industrialization had substantial impacts on all walks of life including, perhaps as one of the core transformations, this re-ordering of home life, work life and school life; a process which also ran concurrently with the respatialization of nonhuman animals, and which also had particular significance for children. While industrialization in particular is often seen as a process primarily involving workers (and therefore to the modern mind, where paid work is often seen as a key marker of maturity and achieving 'adult' status), the changes it brought to both children and childhood were profound.

The Home as the Workplace

Franklin (1999) describes how preindustrial family life was characterized by a much greater conflation of family, household, workplace and physical sustenance than we recognize as normal today. In the early modern era, most of the population lived in rural locations in close proximity with nonhuman animals, who often shared the household accommodation, especially in winter. Households, on the whole, provided their own food, and although still characterized by exploitation and violence towards other animals on the part of humans, the lives and fortunes of humans and nonhumans were more immediately enmeshed, in a way that diminished and vanished as this way of life became less dominant; that is, before the typology of Figure 2.1 coalesced with its characteristic spatial and discursive distances between most humans and most other animals. Gradually then, this relationship became less direct and immediate with the growth of urban centres and the relationship between nonhuman animals and humans became much 'simpler': an increasingly instrumental model in which other animals were objectified as 'things' to be used by those in control. This meant that the place of nonhumans as directly co-located within the human family dwelling changed significantly. Initially, rural animal 'keeping' practices did arrive in towns, but these jarred with the sensibilities of the early urban dwellers who had been at the forefront of the move to new towns, which were seen as centres of civilization (Franklin 1999). Insofar as civilization entails the taming of 'nature', this aloofness towards the presence of other animals in the urban milieu also extended to the health, environmental and public order concerns discussed in Chapter 3.

The practico-discursive purification of urban space therefore necessitated the removal of nonhuman animals, excepting those who were instrumental for the functioning of the city, such as horses. Certain groups of nonhuman animals, defined as 'pets' were, of course, also allowed to remain in the city, albeit under close control in human domestic space, and often in roles closely associated with children in the household. The word 'pet' was first used to refer to indulged, spoiled human children, and subsequently came to be used for other small dependent creatures who lived as part of the family unit as well (Melson 2005). Although for human children the term 'pet' now enjoys much more limited colloquial use, the shared characteristics of children and household 'pets' in the contemporary family endures: as household members to be looked after by others, trained or educated, allowed limited behavioural lapses, enjoyed as entertaining 'spectacles' and so on, recalling the typologies of Figure 2.1 once more, and indeed the stages proposed by theorists such as Ariès (1962) and deMause (1974). So the removal of farmed or worked animals from the family's residential space, and the rise of the animal companion or 'pet', is intricately linked to the changing status of children within the family unit. The appropriateness of the concept of 'pet', whether applied to human children or appropriate nonhuman others, establishes a moral suitability for membership of the family unit: both in terms of spatial inclusion and access, and to roles with an emotional, affective focus.

During the eighteenth and nineteenth centuries, both the proportion and absolute numbers of children in the population of Britain rose, a demographic trend which, together with household poverty, fuelled an increased 'dependency burden' on wage earners in households, which in turn encouraged a process of more children entering the labour market to contribute to the family income (Kirby 2003). With larger households, children also offered 'value' through their usefulness in looking after other children in the household, freeing up older children and mothers to seek paid labour outside the home (Humphries 2010).

Redefining the Boundaries between Work, School and Family

As the spatial connection between paid work and family homes, and children and the workplace began to be loosened, schools increasingly became constructed as appropriate and important spaces for all children to spend significant amounts of their time. Social and moral fears associated with nineteenth-century urbanization, as discussed in Chapter 3, were linked to the provision of formal education for children, in that it was seen to offer one way of managing the 'unruliness' of the urban space, where issues of the cleanliness, order and productivity of the population could be addressed: biopower in Foucault's characterization of the new techniques of government of the population through this period (1998). In terms of Figure 2.1, the 'wildness' of the south-western regions of the conceptual map grated against the civilized, productive, instrumental space of the city and children, insofar as their construction as 'not humans' (see above), were no longer appropriate in this more ordered environment. Where previously educational provision and been patchy and haphazard, provided by assorted state and philanthropic efforts, order and standardization were introduced. The social differentiations used from this time to manage the population through this educational mechanism are still present in contemporary educational systems, relying on selection and segregation, whether by separate schooling for different types of children, or alternative curriculum routes for children identified as 'different' within schools (Ball 2013a, 2013b). As Ball writes, 'the school is one of those places where the body and population meet, where ability confronts degeneracy, where the norm produces abnormality' (2013a: 54).

By identifying certain places and functions as normal for children and childhood, other places and activities are by default identified as abnormal – a process not dissimilar to the spatial and social reordering of the uses of nonhuman animals in an urbanizing society around the same time, as discussed in the previous chapter; unproductive, threatening 'wildness' must be expunged. As we return to in the next chapter, 'wild' nonhuman animals continue, ironically, to be instrumentalized in terms of their function in reinforcing the spatial and discursive boundaries of urban space as human space, in which other animals only *legitimately* exist if they are subservient to human control: as body parts, 'characters' in representations, 'pets' in domestic space, 'entertainment' animals in 'zoos' or racetracks, and so on.

James and James (2012) contend that schools and schooling established not only a physical separate space for children, but also a separate identity of childhood that unified children as a social group, ostensibly downplaying other demographic differences. So the very act of removing children from the (adult) work space and putting them in a separate (child) space is important in itself (James and James 2012). As we argued in Chapter 2, the spatialization of others brings with it a discursive legitimation for segregation through the naming of others in relation to 'their' space: 'farm animals' or 'schoolchildren'. The period of their lives that children spend attending school represents an ambiguous social limbo: after the physical dependency of infancy but before they become full 'adult' agents. The advent of universal schooling contributes to the creation of a social hinterland which in turn also contributes to its management, and formal schooling provides a site which recognizes and reinforces the view of childhood being a period requiring protection, nurture and guidance (Clarke 2004). While children graduate from this process towards the privileges of adulthood, in the context of Figure 2.1, other animals in urban space are left behind both spatially and discursively, tending to remain permanently infantilized as 'pets', or having their infancy terminated in the slaughterhouse.

What happens, and how it happens, whilst children are in this school environment is also crucially important, not least in respect of how and what children learn about other animals (see Chapter 7 for a more detailed discussion of the latter). Reinforcing the unifying function of the mere creation of the child space of the school, activity structures such as national curricula, and the organization of children within those curricula suggest a uniformity of experience also (James and James 2012). Drawing on Foucault's work, Ball (2013a) outlines how schools function to normalize through the identification, modification and demarcation of the population of learners (themselves, identified as pupils or students as a distinct group) according to categories pertaining to demographic features such as (almost always) age and gender (less often formally, but still operating more informally), or markers of 'ability' or 'need'. What Ball misses from his account is the specied demarcation of children, instantiating an increasing discursive distance from other animals and further inculcating the 'logic' of Figure 2.1. The workings of the school are then broken down according to, and organized around, physical spaces within them, temporal spaces of the timetable and subject spaces of curricula, with the categorized students physically placed, labelled and tested therein. School systems then, provide mechanisms for classification and differentiation, with performance against set standards used and communicated as a marker of 'ability'.

Content of curricula vary across nations, regions and over time. The Department for Education publish requirements for the standard curriculum to be followed in all state maintained schools in England (this power is devolved in other home nations in the UK, who have their own, similar mechanisms). While, as noted, this is not universally binding in all schools in the UK, it does give an illustrative flavour of the ethos driving the provision of formal schooling to children. The National Curriculum framework states that the curriculum exists for the promotion of spiritual, moral, cultural, mental and physical development not only of pupils at school, but of society as a whole, as well as to prepare students for later life (Department for Education 2013). However, even though a degree of common experience of curriculum content may exist through policies such as standardized curricula, children's experiences of these curricula vary and they learn plenty more besides that which is laid down in the curriculum. The fostering of unified beliefs and value systems within schools can be problematic for children whose lives outside the school space do not share these values; not least for vegan children. As a result, some children will struggle to fit (or be fitted) in at school. Different approaches to schooling suit different children according to characteristics which may include their gender, class or ethnicity, or a whole range of other personal and cultural characteristics, including personal beliefs about the use of nonhuman animals, now protected under EU legislation. Schooling has a very important role in imparting knowledge and producing conformity, and inasmuch as it does this, it is there to prepare 'future adults' for the state and wider society. Children are not therefore removed from the adult world by their separation into schools, but are being marked out as different and unfinished, and prepared for it (James and James 2012). Children then, like many demarcated human groups, are marked as different not to *separate* them, but to appropriately *fit them in*, just as nonhuman animals are demarcated from humans and other nonhumans in order that they are appropriately fitted into a culturally defined, normative set of structures, which we present as the schema illustrated in Figure 2.1. These processes as they apply to human children and nonhumans are intertwined, as we will show in Part II of this book: integration processes associated with childhood necessarily involve the learning of the demarcation and integration processes and norms applied to nonhuman animals.

Play

In both school and home spheres, the recreational activities engaged with during childhood are also crucial in the socialization process. The study of play has long been an important focus of study in research involving children and childhood. Piaget (1962) argued that the use of symbols, most clearly apparent in children's play activities, facilitates problem solving and learning, and along with other theorists including Groos and Vygotsky, play was seen to offer benefits deferred until later in development (Pellegrini and Smith 1998). Erickson (1985) saw play as necessary to becoming a mature, loving adult, allowing children to experiment with the management of their surroundings and others in it. Other theorists, such as Bateson (1976) argued play to be important and beneficial to the specifics of childhood rather than as a facilitator of future skill: a difference in why and when play is important, but agreement that it is.

Sociologically, play in childhood is important in two key ways. Firstly it functions as a marker of childhood as distinct from adulthood – it is another way in which the demarcation of children as a different group is articulated (although the role of adults as playmates or play facilitators and thereby rehearsing their own socialization should not be ignored). In childhood, play is not merely defined and understood in oppositional terms to 'work' or formal study activities, but as a central, expected, core activity with inherent value. So powerful is this notion that it should be a feature of childhood that play, leisure and recreation are recognized as a right in the 1989 United Nations Convention on the Rights of the Child (James and James 2012). The second way in which play in childhood is sociologically important is the role it has as a key site for the process of interpretative reproduction, which facilitates children's learning about the social world(s) they encounter. Children develop a wide range of physical and intellectual abilities through play, such as problem solving skills, motor skills, physical exercise and creative skills, and play is also seen to cultivate social and emotional skills through enacting and testing relationships, exercising autonomy, exploring social roles, managing anger and frustration, and developing self-identity (James and James 2012, Sandberg and Heden 2011, Canning 2007). While the family remains a key site for play, children learn through play across a vast assortment of skills not only in informal and domestic contexts, but increasingly in more formal educational settings, as younger children spend more and more time out of the home in formal child care or pre-school settings, after school clubs and so forth. Therefore, play is less frequently an activity performed outside formal activities like schooling, exclusively within the relatively culturally homogenous setting of home and family life (Sandberg and Heden 2011). Nonhuman animals have a crucial, but largely under acknowledged role in children's play activities. Melson (2005) notes that between the ages of 5 and 12, children spend less and less time playing with their younger siblings as they age, but maintain the amount of time they spend engaging in the care of or playing with animal companions, so that by the age of 10 both boys and girls spend more time caring for or playing with animal companions than they do with younger siblings. Animal companions have many 'functions' in the play activities of children, including as playmates, friends, and 'props' for play activities. However, the primary presence of nonhuman animals in children's play activities is as representations on artefacts identified as appropriate for children: as toys, in games and on clothing. How nonhuman animals are represented on these items serves to classify and differentiate children firstly as opposed to adults, but then further according to other social characteristics including age and, very powerfully, gender (see chapters 5 and 6 for a more detailed analysis of the gendering of children's relations with other animals).

In the more formal setting of the classroom, nonhuman animals are seen to enrich learning, and even though this sometimes takes the form of a 'class pet', it is in a less affective role than they are afforded in the home. As we will detail in Chapter 7, while affective ties to nonhuman animals are heavily drawn on discursively, their uses in this arena are chiefly instrumental, and grow more so as children get older. As children progress through the school's age related organizational structure, nonhuman animals' roles as 'objects of enquiry' escalates until ultimately they become raw materials in science classes. The presence and use of nonhuman animals in the learning environments of children is not an uncommon practice, but it has been particularly unremarked in scholarly discourse, and there is little evidence pointing to exactly how frequently it occurs (Melson 2005).

Conclusion

Scholarly accounts of these fields of study have conceptually positioned children and childhood in ways which we recognize as resonant with the analysis of the positioning of nonhuman animals in Figure 2.1. The otherness, spectacle and disciplinarian features of theorists of the Grand Stages of childhood not only constitute elements of contemporary, complex views of children and childhood but are also comparable to our understanding of the human uses of nonhuman animals. Similarly the spatial and social positioning and repositioning of children's activities identified in this chapter and Chapter 3 is, we argue, strongly linked to the spatial and social location and relocation of nonhuman animals. In order to move forward with a comprehensive study of either children or nonhuman animals, it is crucial to address the role of each in the construction of the other.

PART II
The Contemporary Socialization of Human–Nonhuman Relations in Childhood

Chapter 5
Family Practices and the Shaping of Human–Nonhuman Identities

In Chapter 4 we discussed the importance of the family and children's place within it. Children are seen to have increasingly become the focus and indeed purpose of the modern family unit, and the family is seen as an environment in which adults protect, care for and educate children with the skills seen as appropriate for children to eventually fulfil adult roles and themselves. Family interactions and parenting practices play an important role in shaping children's empathy for nonhuman animals, and establishing and reproducing the dominant relationships described in Figure 2.1. With reference to this schematic, for children in the home environment, nonhuman animals occupying three of the zones of Figure 2.1 – animal food products, character representations (as toys and on clothing) and 'pets' – have a particularly prominent presence. This chapter will examine these areas. Firstly we will address how food designated as 'children's food' locates appropriate social norms relating to both children and nonhuman animals through the ways in which nonhuman animals are both present and represented in foods marketed for children's consumption. Secondly, using exemplary cases, we examine how toys and clothing, where nonhuman character representations are widespread are instrumentalized as both gendering and anthroparchizing symbols. Finally, the chapter discusses animal companions who in many ways are constructed as human children's quasi peers within the family.

Children's Food: Lies, Lies and Fisherman's Pies

Food practices in the home are an important site of family activity and identity work and therefore key to the socialization of children. It is both powerful and precarious in its reproduction of dominant speciesist food practices, as illustrated by this example cited by Amato and Partridge in their 1989 book *The New Vegetarians*:

> My family was sitting down to a meal of fried chicken and my young daughter brought her toy chicken to the table with her. My husband's aunt said, "Eat your chicken". My daughter seemed surprised at these words. She looked at

her aunt, her toy chicken, and then at her plate. At that moment I realized that I would have to explain to my child where meat comes from. How could I tell this innocent child who loved animals so dearly that her own mother and father actually fed on slaughtered cows, pigs, and chickens? All at once the sight of the dead chicken nauseated me. I realized that I was deeply ashamed of the fact that I ate meat. I knew the only answer for me was to become vegetarian and to raise my daughter as one as well. (Amato and Partridge 1989: 73)

From the very start of life, the food children consume in the home involves the presence of nonhuman animals with simultaneously a strong, sensible symbolic presence, and a strong but much less sensible 'actual' presence. Animals as food are ubiquitous, but as the silent realization described by the parent in the account above suggests, the presence of dead animals on a child's plate is often not explicated in family mealtime discourse. In a similar vein, Cole et al. (2009) report the feelings of guilt described by one of their participants when she deceived her child who was upset about whether a dead fish he had seen on the beach was the same as the fish meals he was asked to eat at home. This theme of the interactional objectification of other animals in the way that caregivers talk about other animals is a rich area for further research. In the remainder of this section though, we turn to representational objectification, which, arguably, aids and abets caregiver's deception of children as to the violent, instrumental process of 'producing' animal foods.

This process of obfuscation begins at the very beginning of life for many babies – with infant formula ('baby milk'). Whilst strict advertising regulations in some countries prevent infant formula manufacturers from claiming it to be superior to breast milk (see for example Department of Health 2013), representations of infant formula nonetheless emphasize the 'naturalness' of milk from nonhumans, heavily suggestive of an equivalence between human mothers' milk and milk from nonhuman mothers in terms of its fundamental, foundational role in a 'caring' dimension of parenting. Advertising regulations are therefore subtly subverted so as to enhance the status of infant formula, and lend the instrumentalization of other animals a value-rational veneer in relation to human caregiving. All mainstream infant formulas in the UK contain cows' milk, with plant-based alternatives only available through health care professionals; avoidance of cows' milk for non-breastfed babies is discursively heavily medicalized, as something required in response to allergies, and the idea of a non-breastfed vegan baby is nowhere to be found in the UK's authoritative health and nutrition advice resources such as NHS Choices. Any parent seeking information on formula feeding infants without any animal products is simply, and without further explanation, directed to the unknown, individualistic, medicalized sanctuary of a health care consultation under the assumption that only an 'unhealthy' baby would require such a product. This of course also has the effect of normalizing the consumption of cows' milk in comparison with the pathologization of ethical, or value-rational, objections to its use by humans. In the UK, there are four mainstream brands of infant formula: SMA, Cow & Gate, Aptamil and Hipp Organic. In looking at how these products are presented, it is possible to identify the early signs of representational norms that become a common feature of many of the products and cultural artefacts aimed at children that we discuss in this book. In this group of products, stylized cartoon animals and love hearts are abundant. SMA packaging is illustrated with a love heart motif, as is the packaging for Cow & Gate, which also features the image of a cuddly toy lamb. Similarly, Hipp Organic packaging features love hearts and a cartoon elephant, while Aptamil features a picture of a white teddy bear (but no love heart). The 'hearts and cute animals' imagery across this product group very much, therefore, anticipate the 'cutie' imagery also found in children's clothing, toys, books and magazines (and discussed more later in this chapter, and in Chapter 6), introducing affectivity channelled towards certain nonhuman animals, represented in certain ways, while obscuring the presence of the animals whose milk is used in the product, and their offspring for whom the milk nature intended. Cows, we might therefore speculate, are early subjects in the processes of promoting and increasing the sensibility of certain representations and supressing the sensibility of the actual animals involved. Cows are certainly absent referents in infant formula and its packaging, being both present and insensible in the very first products encountered by infants, arguably contributing to an early resilience to the dissonant treatment of cows and particularly dairy products – as both (obscured) content and cipher for maternal care.

Weaning (the introduction of solid foods) usually begins when babies are around six months old. Home prepared weaning foods are strongly encouraged (see for example NHS Choices 2013), and are both simple to prepare and overwhelmingly plant based, such as mashed steamed vegetables or fruits. However, the market for manufactured baby food is considerable. These products mimic a culturally narrow range of mainstream (anthroparchal) adult meals, and reinforce notions of the warmth and desirability of the shared family meal environment, a warmth dependent on coldness towards the killed animal others whose body parts constitute components of these meals. Examples of these include Heinz's range of baby food jars branded as 'Mum's Own Recipe', which includes 'Sunday Chicken Dinner' and 'Cottage Pie'; for the same age group Cow & Gate offer 'My First Bolognese', 'Grandpa's Sunday Lunch', 'Orchard Chicken' and 'Fisherman's Bake'. They contribute to both the normalization of a traditional omnivorous British diet and the mutually reinforcing British (and more widely Western) tradition of the ideal family unit, presenting an idealized combination of both as 'proper' childcare. Yet interestingly, although these foods are suggestive of traditional popular meals, they too are in fact primarily meals of vegetables, potatoes and rice: while the 'My First Bolognese' jar places a portion of minced beef at the fore of the picture, the recipe is 58 per cent vegetables, the 'Fisherman's Bake' is chiefly vegetables and rice with only 10 per cent content from fishes and the 'Orchard Chicken' primarily vegetables, rice and apple, despite the prominence given to a piece of cooked white chicken's flesh on the label and the descriptive use of 'chicken' in the title. It is appropriate that baby food for weaning children is primarily vegetable, fruit or rice, but it is notable that the rhetoric of popular 'meat' based adult meals is drawn into the diet so early. So through the overemphasis of the animal sourced ingredients of these meals, they serve to support food norms by introducing a small amount of real animals into children's diets, but symbolically and rhetorically a lot more. The cultural sensibility of animal's body parts is therefore elevated above that of the cultural sensibility of plant foods, reinforcing an anthroparchal dietetic hierarchy that privileges the flesh of others above all other foodstuffs (Fiddes 1991, Twigg 1983, 1979).

Both the rhetoric and imagery of food for children is therefore well established by the time children become more active participants in expressing their own food preferences; the extent to which they can exercise agency has been largely foreclosed by both gustatory and discursive habituation. In many ways the imagery of nonhuman animals in food products aligns with the imagery in other products specifically for children (such as toys and clothing discussed later in this chapter, and magazines and games in chapters 6 and 8) in terms of the sensible and non-sensible presence of nonhuman animals, and the degree of subjectivity they are afforded.

Convenience foods aimed specifically at children are simultaneously both different from and the same as their adult counterparts, reinforcing the special status of childhood but aligning it with dominant adult norms. Children are encouraged to aspire to the same eating habits as adults but not by eating *as* adults, and instead by consuming separate foods, branded to appeal to children: marking children as different while clearly signposting the behavioural 'destination'. For example, Heinz tinned pasta shapes in tomato sauce can be purchased without 'child specific' branding, or in packaging featuring a range of nonhuman characters, such as Peppa Pig, Hello Kitty, My Little Pony, or characters from the animated movie, *Madagascar* (2005). Breakfast cereals aimed at children also heavily feature representations of certain nonhuman characters – such as the Coco Pops monkey, the Frosties tiger, or the pelican on Fruit Loops.

'Little Dish' produce a range of ready meals for children, available from major UK supermarket chains, which provide a clear exemplification of these themes of sameness, difference, family values and the varying levels of sensibility and subjectivity afforded nonhumans which are common to food products marketed for children. Their website states 'All of our meals are made just as you would cook them at home ... We only ever use 100% natural ingredients, just like you'd find in your own kitchen' (Little Dish no date). Here again, products containing body parts taken from nonhuman animals confined in the south east of Figure 2.1, feature stylized imagery of different nonhuman animals, who more usually occupy more northerly and/or westerly positions in Figure 2.1, engaged in very human leisure activities. For example the cottage pie features a canoeing crocodile on the packaging, a pogoing kangaroo on the spaghetti and meatballs, and a skateboarding tortoise with a snail on their back on the cheese pasta. The representation of nonhuman animals engaging in incongruous human leisure activities is found in many media for children where nonhumans are represented. This theme is returned to in Chapter 6 with a DJing cat, amongst others, featuring in magazines targeted at pre-teen girls.

The Finest Toyshop in the World

As discussed in Chapter 4, play is important in demarcating childhood, teaching multiple social, emotional and intellectual skills, and as a medium for the process of interpretative reproduction, which facilitates learning about the social world(s) children encounter. The home and the family is not the only arena in which this occurs, but it is a key arena and the place in which early play socialization and learning takes place.

The socialization process, in respect of reproducing majority human–nonhuman animal relations, gradually and precariously tilts the balance away from an initial warm flood of affectivity, towards the inculcation of the icily detached practices of objectification. To get an overview of the ubiquity of this process in children's culture with reference to toys, we visited Hamleys toy store, on London's Regent Street: 'The Finest Toy Shop in the World' (Hamleys, 2010). The following impressionistic account is emblematic of the majority socialization process that runs through the empirical analyses in this book:

The shop is organized on five floors, with ascending levels corresponding with the ascending age of the children that the toys on each floor are marketed at. It is striking that the prevalence of animal-based toys, while always significant, gradually decreases with age. Furthermore, the characteristics of those toys shifts in line with the tilting in emphasis outlined above. The ground floor is dominated by soft toys aimed at infants and toddlers, but also at toy collectors in some cases, which hints at the enduring impact of the early socialization of human–nonhuman animal relations. The great majority of these ground floor toys are representations of other animals. Their design attracts affective practices of cuddling and stroking, which is reciprocated through the pleasant feel of the toys to children's touch and their open arms, wide eyes and happy, anthropomorphized expressions. As with the imagery presented on the packaging of children's food and clothing discussed elsewhere in this chapter, the ground floor toys are predominantly representations of animals who tend to be relatively less instrumentalized, especially 'pets' and 'wild' animals. Tellingly, these representations are also overwhelmingly infantilized: bears are cubs, dogs are puppies, cats are kittens. That is, they are represented as young children's quasi-peers, anticipating and mutually reinforcing the 'pet' relationships children may elsewhere or later encounter. Together, human infant and soft toy form a fluffy nexus of sentimentalized affectivity. Although inanimate, the rictus delight on the faces of soft toys shows their human playmates that their solicitations are always welcomed. Unlike the unpredictable, complex, reactions of their living counterparts, soft toy animals inculcate the notion that affectivity itself is a use that can be served by (some) other animals on demand. The quasi-peer status of baby soft toys gradually dissipated as we ascended the stairs of Hamleys. That is, the infantilized design of toy animals continues, but their bodies morph from the tactile comfort of plush into colder, less responsive materials, while the children's age gets further from that of the eternally-infant soft toys. Growing up means growing away from the reciprocal experience of cuddling a teddy bear and instead learning the compensatory privileges that come with distancing oneself from (some *types* of) other animals. So, instead of affectivity constituting the alpha and omega of child–other animal interaction, it recedes to take its place as one human *use* among many, for other animals.

The first floor of the store offers toys and items appropriate for babies and preschool aged children. Bright colours and cartoonized nonhuman animals appear as articulated toys, and characters in hard board books. Books with sound effects and a variety of tactile surfaces imitate nonhuman animals, very often farmed animals such as sheep, cows and chickens, in another example as with infant formula of the fostering of an early resilience to the dissonant treatment of farmed animals.

On the second floor, the intersection of anthroparchy and patriarchy begins to emerge. The toys offered here are for older children, but clearly aimed at girls: the store guide, colour coded pink for this floor, lists princesses, dolls and dress up for this floor, alongside prominent logos for brands including Barbie, the kitten head of 'Hello Kitty' and Hamleys own 'Luvley' brand (a logo with a pink love heart in place of the U): a 'boutique' of bags, nail art, makeup and jewellery for girls from three years of age. On this floor items popularly feature kittens, puppies, rabbits, birds and butterflies in a range of pastel colours, or bolder pinks and purples.

The third floor starts to dim the affective functionality of toys and focus on more explicitly educative toys, such as arts and crafts equipment, science sets and puzzles. Here, the representations of nonhuman animals begin to fulfil more objectified functionality consistent with the tone of the floor as a whole. Unarticulated model animals (listed as 'plastic animals' on the store guide) are available in a range of species comparable to those represented as plush toys on the ground floor. From the ubiquitous happy companions of infancy, they have been reduced to the status of just another manipulable object, alongside toy cars or trains. Compared with the relative freedom represented by the, often individually named, 'wild'/'pet' toys of the ground floor, the third floor houses representations of anonymous animals with a greater focus on the more instrumentalized end of the continuum of objectification, especially 'farmyard' animals. The third floor also houses the 'Build-A-Bear Workshop', where children can create their own soft toy to their own specification. While ostensibly the Build-A-Bear experience retains some of the affectivity of the ground floor plush toys, here the fluffy nexus of sentimentalized affectivity is infused with a much more overtly unequal relationship between child and toy. The child (or a buyer on their behalf) is able to 'play God' in creating, controlling and determining the exact nature of the representation as they deem it to best suit their own emotional needs.

As the child ascends to the fourth floor, colour coded blue in the store guide, toy vehicles predominate: train sets, model aeroplane kits, and toy racing cars. Among these vehicles, models of farmed animals are available, but now as little more than accessories to the mechanical toys associated with their use. The relatively realistic characteristics of animal toys on the third floor continues here and corresponds with the toy locations that children are encouraged to place them in: realistic miniatures of enclosed fields, barns, stables, or even 'livestock transporter' trucks. The draining of affect from the play experience is symbolized by the adulthood of many of the toy cows, pigs or chickens, compared with their infant counterparts downstairs. However, the full detail of the division of objectifying labour is not represented: there are no model slaughterhouses, imitation vivisection scalpels, or dismemberable plastic cow's corpses for girls and boys to play with. So, these older children's toys substitute the guilty pleasures of objectification for the innocent pleasures of reciprocal affection, but in a way that corresponds to a remorseless logic of 'growing up' being equated with being able to travel at will back and forth along the continuum of objectification, all the while without attending to the massive human violence that underpins it.

On the fifth floor, animals take on new significance as spectacles of entertainment. Rather than interacting with other animals (albeit pseudo-interactions with inanimate representations), children can delight in watching other animals perform clockwork or battery-powered tricks. In a tragic irony, the fifth floor also rewards children with a confectionary cornucopia, much of which is laced with the results of human violence which they are unlikely to be aware of: cow's milk, gelatine, etc.; the tacit lesson in violence comes sugar-coated.

We are fully aware that this critical account of the socialization process, seen through the lens of Hamleys, is monolithic. We defend this in light of the fact that this process manifestly *works*; it accustoms children to the way that things are, for the majority of human–nonhuman animal relations. It is a valuable analysis too because it is consistent, and interlaced with the other examples and processes discussed in Part II of this book. We present them together, because they happen together and they work together. While individual socialization sites operate according to their specific, contingent rationalities, their inter-textual discourses and representations entail that they mutually support each other to landscape the anthroparchal conceptual geography depicted in Figure 2.1. The opportunity for those opposing these norms, we will argue in the final part of this book, is that they *need* to happen together to work together, and as the example from Amato and Partridge's (1989) work above teases us with, if undermined in one area they can have far reaching implications for humans and nonhumans in many others. And so, therefore, we do not claim that children or their carers are passive cultural dopes. Nor do we deny that children (and adults) are capable of contesting the hegemony of human–nonhuman animal relations, which are embedded into Hamleys's layout and its toys, sweets and milkshakes. For instance, we might imagine children playing out fantasies of animals escaping or being rescued with 'farmyard' or 'zoo' toys. Such children may grow up as activists, sanctuary workers, vegans. But such fantasies are animated by values and emotions that are utterly at odds with learning and reproducing the 'correct' degree of instrumentalization of different types of other animals, which Hamleys emblemizes. In contrast with our putative resistors, we can therefore imagine an 'ideal type' of child-becoming-young adult, who descends from Hamleys's fifth floor fully equipped with the dispositions to appropriately relate to other animals, according to their discursive and material positions in Western culture. This achievement is crucial to attaining the distinction and privileges of normal human adulthood in an anthroparchal culture, a normality that depends on a curious mixture of precisely channelled affectivity, prowess in objectification and denial of its bloody details.

Clothing and the Intersection of Anthroparchy and Patriarchy

Human children, like human adults, are not viewed in their unclothed form except to their most intimate relations. Unlike human adults, who on the whole dress themselves (albeit according to powerful cultural norms), children are for the most part clothed by others, 'presented' according to prevailing cultural norms. Cook (2004) locates the peculiarity of clothing as opposed to other socially informed artefacts: it exists at the boundary of the self and the non-self, an extension of the body yet not quite part of it nor as clearly separate as other artefacts we discuss in this book. The gendered nature of children's clothing and its role in the socialization of gendered identities has been well documented in the literature (for example Crane 2012, Pomerleau 1990), with the wearing of gender inappropriate clothing seen as very negative (more so than boys playing with dolls, and almost as negatively as stealing) among younger children (Blakemore 2003). Clothing also plays a part in the socialization processes we discuss in this book, and this has been less well attended to in the literature. Human children are presented in (and to some extent as) culturally appropriate representations of nonhuman animals, which also intersects with the gendering of children's clothing and the demarcation of the stages of childhood. The clothing industry plays an important part in the creation of divisions of and within childhood (Cook 2004), and the normalizing of relationships between humans and nonhuman animals is solidly embedded within this, with clothes reproducing 'proper' human relationships with other animals.

To explore and elucidate this, we considered the catalogue of clothing offered by 'Mothercare' in late 2013 and early 2014. Mothercare, founded in 1961, is an iconic high street British chain of stores selling clothing and equipment for children. In the range of clothing they sell, only among the very youngest age group (0–12 months) are clothes marked as 'unisex' made available in addition to those identified specifically as for girls or boys. In the unisex clothing available for this age group animals familiarly also represented as 'cuddly toys' are common (teddy bears, rabbits, lambs) as well as those recognized as 'wild animals' (zebras, elephants), and named animal characters from children's fiction (particularly characters from A.A. Milne's Christopher Robin stories such as Pooh and Tigger, but not Christopher, the human child in the stories). There is therefore a recognizable consistency in the range of nonhuman animals depicted on clothing for the youngest age groups and the range of nonhuman animals depicted as soft toys for similar ages, as discussed above. Love hearts are also common in this category of clothing for infants, establishing a common ground of affectivity and dependence between human children and certain groups of nonhuman animals. When the gender categorized clothing selection is examined, differences are clear and these differences are in part identifiable by the selection of nonhuman animals depicted on items. From new-born sizes, clothes for baby boys feature bold colours, and nonhuman animals associated with the 'wild' – 'safari' animals, whales, crocodiles, insects (stylized as 'bugs') and frogs. Baby girls' clothing on the other hand feature pinks and purples, decorated with imagery of the cottage garden – fruits, flowers, ladybirds, butterflies, rabbits and chicks. Girls' clothing, from new-born, therefore reflects and anticipates the representations of affectivity and 'cuteness' found in the magazines aimed at older girls discussed in Chapter 6. These patterns start, therefore, at the start of life; associations between humans and nonhuman animals are part of how children are presented in the world and how the world is presented to children, as part of the same processes that present infancy, the stages of childhood, and girlhood and boyhood. As with other artefacts associated with childhood, the prominence of nonhuman animals diminishes at subsequent age ranges in the clothing range. For 'Toddler girls' (1–3 years) and 'Girls' (3–8 years) flowers and hearts become more common and the nonhumans less – although still from a relatively clear, narrow and gendered range such as butterflies and rabbits. For 'Toddler boys' and 'Boys', the strong colours remain and the bugs, elephants, fishes, tigers and so forth feature less and less. Returning to Cook's (2004) identification of the peculiarity of clothing, these animals move gradually away from the self–non-self boundary as children grow older as the 'normal' otherness of other animals emerges. The representations of nonhuman animals on clothing are a core part of the construction of domestic, caring activities and relationships as appropriate for girls, and strong, unbounded characteristics for boys. Anticipated through the clothing too is the expected transition of children away from the empathetic peer relationship with nonhumans we discuss elsewhere. In this context, as with some of the toys discussed above, nonhuman animals are thus instrumentalized as gendering symbols, underlining the intersection of anthroparchy and patriarchy. This is of course an important part of the construction of exploitative gendered identities for humans, but it also has profound, and hitherto under-recognized implications for the nonhuman animals: individuals on the one hand on whom these representations are built, yet on the other whose fates are built upon the norms these representations contribute to the construction of.

Living Animals in the Family Home: Pets and Threats

Living nonhuman animals located within the physical space of the family home can be seen as being both appropriate pseudo peers for children and simultaneously or alternatively a risk to them. The family home is a key site for the articulation of 'proper' human–nonhuman spatial boundaries, and especially for discourses of domestic invasion by feared others who threaten the protective environment the family is expected to provide for children. These 'rules' of transgression and protection are illustrated by the discursive shift in the presentation of 'urban foxes' in the UK in the months prior to and following an apparent fox attack on infant twins sleeping in their home in London, UK in June 2010. We undertook an analysis of UK based print media stories about urban foxes in the five and a half months before and six and a half months after the incident (that is, throughout the whole of 2010) to explore this discursive shift (Cole and Stewart 2011). Prior to the attack, the few stories in which urban foxes appeared typically framed their presence as a pleasant collapsing of the difference between town and country, with small notes of caution regarding the possible damage they could do to lawns and flowerbeds. Following the attack on the twins, the transgressive nature of urban foxes became a major feature of news stories. The main danger posed to humans was no longer simply to their flowerbeds, but that of physical threats of attack and disease to 'legitimate' human and nonhuman residents of the family space. The focus of most of this physical threat was that to children and animal companions. Newspapers reported stories of harmed 'pet' cats (themselves often largely free roaming killers of small mammals and birds on other people's property) as evidence of the unjust transgression and danger posed by urban foxes. The urban fox symbolizes both beauty and threat simultaneously, their ambiguity linked to their 'failure' to stay in their allotted symbolic and physical spaces. The suddenness with which urban foxes were recast as villains in response to this attack (at a time when popular opinion supported the 'ban' on the hunting of foxes for sport in their 'proper' place of the countryside (Toke 2010)) reveals not only the precariousness of the relatively benevolent toleration of nonhuman others in human defined milieu, but also the potency of our values regarding children and the family in stimulating these shifts.

Other species of nonhuman are seen as appropriate co-residents of the family space. Around a quarter of households in the UK are home to 'animal companions' more commonly referred to as 'pets'. Murray et al. (2010) estimate that 26 per cent and 31 per cent of UK households contain companion cats or dogs respectively. The most recent annual Pet Food Manufacturers' Association national survey puts these figures at 17 per cent and 24 per cent respectively, in addition to 9 per cent with fishes in tanks, 5 per cent with fishes in ponds, 2.4 per cent with rabbits, 1.4 per cent with hamsters and 1.1 per cent with guinea pigs (PFMA 2014).

Yet even these 'appropriate interlopers' are accepted with a degree of caution. Both breeds and individual dogs are labelled as being 'good with children' or not, euphemistically alluding to attack risk and tolerance of the close physicality expected between human children and their animal companions. This physical risk as a caution in the introduction of the 'pseudo peer pet' may be seen too as allegorical of the symbolic risk of transgressions of behaviour in 'acceptable' relationships between human children and nonhuman animals: the construction of the appropriate forms and treatment of nonhuman 'pets' in the late nineteenth and early twentieth centuries (see chapters 3 and 4) and their close association in the family unit with children denote that animal companions are seen to offer much to children's lives, but this must be viewed with caution to keep children 'safe' in many ways, both physical and symbolic.

Melson (2005) argues that animal companions are seen to offer a very different kind of relationship to others encountered in the family context, where emotional relationships can be played out, practiced and refined, supporting children's learning of care, affection, supervision, discipline and grief in a way seen to foreshadow those emotional skills they will encounter in their human–human relationships within the family and beyond. This suggests an instrumentalization of affectivity, in which emotional bonds do have value, but only, or at least primarily, insofar as they augment human–human relationships. It also begs the question as to the capacity for emotional development among children who do not share their homes with animal companions, as if nonhuman animal companions were a *necessary* conduit to human emotional maturity. Animal companions may provide a training ground for 'real' relationships, but as discussed in Chapter 6, narrative traditions in children's stories make clear that children are expected to move away to more 'mature' relationships with nonhuman animals as a rite of passage. While relationships with animal companions remain relatively privileged, in that their worth to humans remains affective, it is expected to change as humans move out of childhood as its 'emotional training' function is discarded and its affective functionality reconfigured for adults; as Ridgway et al. (2008) summarize, relationships with animal companions are akin to those with siblings for children and to children for adults. Relationships between humans and nonhuman animal companions have also been likened to being partner or parent substitutes, as a source of security (Archer 1997). Inevitably therefore, one of the ways in which the departure from childhood is marked is by the shifting in the ways in which humans relate to the animal companions in their households.

In the same way that the emergence of children's clothing as a distinct consumer sector is an important part of the concept of childhood as a distinct social category (Cook 2004), the emergence of 'pet superstores', shops where animal companions are welcome and indeed encouraged to accompany their owners on shopping trips, has brought animal companions into the consumer experience. Spending on pets doubled in the decade preceding 2007, with this expanding sector offering an ever-increasing array of accessories such as clothes, toys, holiday costumes and jewelled collars (Ridgway et al. 2008). The clothing items available for animal companions range well beyond functional or safety items for warmth, visibility or waterproofing. The 'pet' superstore PetSmart offers designs of coats and tops which are resonant of those for young children described above, especially those marketed for younger babies and girls, where hearts, flowers, pinks, soft blues and cartoon characters feature heavily. While the presence of animal characters on human children's clothing perhaps serves to apply to both human children and animal companion the common status of 'pet' as it is understood in its original form to refer to indulged, spoiled human children, and later used for other small dependent creatures who lived as part of the family unit (Melson 2005, see also Chapter 4), nonhuman fictional characters and imagery of nonhuman animals also appear on the accessories available for nonhuman companions, with zebra prints, tiger spots, feathers, Minnie Mouse and Bambi commonly found. The closing of the gap between humans and these relatively privileged nonhumans works from both directions – the 'petification' of human infants and 'babyfication' of animal companions through the use of a common language of 'pet' clothing. This comparability between children's clothing and nonhuman 'pet' accessories serves to establish a *phase* of human life (childhood), but a *fixed status* for those nonhumans granted access to a more north-westerly position in Figure 2.1. Animal companions are in many ways permanently infant, and while the same markers are present in clothing for children, they are expected to grow away from this social status (and its associated behaviours), partly through the ways in which they are presented and eventually present themselves through their outward appearance. While animal companions are permanently 'pet', for children 'pet' is a phase of early life, in part marked out by their relationships with real and representations of nonhuman animals.

Eat, Dress, Play: Our Children and Other Animals

Food, toys and clothing introduce the actual and symbolic presence of nonhumans in the family sphere and in children's lives in powerful ways. As illustrated in Figure 5.1, with the exception of animal companions, the sensibility of actual living animals is downplayed, particularly those exploited for 'animal products' in children's food, and the sensibility of representations of certain

Figure 5.1 Girls, boys, 'pets', toys

kinds of other animals emphasized in age and gender appropriate patterns. By establishing an affinity between human children and animal companions, these artefacts demarcate childhood from adulthood, but also of girlhood and boyhood as distinct kinds of childhood, and representations of nonhuman animals are one powerful way in which these messages are conveyed.

While food, clothing and play are seen as an essential part of childhood (and indeed the latter established as a right in the United Nations Convention on the Rights of the Child, as discussed in Chapter 4), 'pets' live with only a minority of families. Yet the relevance of animal companions to the processes we discuss in this book reach beyond the families with whom they live. The similarities we have explored between children and childhood, and 'pets' and 'pethood' offer insights into the status afforded both. The exclusion of certain types of nonhuman animals, such as the urban fox, from the physical space of the family is also important in articulating the home as a protected (human) family controlled space. As profound as the implications of these processes are for the children to whom we subject these messages, they are greater still for the billions of nonhuman animals whose identities as 'friend or food' are also demarcated and reinforced by these representations and roles.

Chapter 6
Cute Style: Mass Media Representations of Other Animals

The mass media constitute a vast array of different cultural forms, genres and products. Mass media representations permeate the family sphere of socialization, through animal characters on television, in DVDs, books, comics, toys and other branded merchandise, and also allow children to construct imaginary, but nonetheless powerfully affective relationships with animal characters. Recent critical accounts of mass media representations of animals have, for instance, considered living animals as characters in Hollywood films, the UK print media (Molloy 2011), or representations of 'food animals' and 'animal products' in advertising (Fitzgerald and Taylor 2014, Cudworth 2011, Molloy 2011, Adams 2004a). A common theme of these analyses is the obfuscation of what we might collectively term anthroparchal relations, especially violent practices such as confinement, mutilation or slaughter. Similarly, Anderson and Henderson (2005) point out the ubiquity of animals in children's fiction but their analysis suggests that 'pet-keeping' is communicated as the only emotionally important relationship between children and other animals, echoing our analysis of relations with animal companions in Chapter 3. As Molloy points out, 'Studies of human–animal interaction suggest that childhood experiences of animals and particularly animal narratives contribute to the formation of attitudes towards animals in adulthood' (2011: 122, also see Pallotta 2008, Serpell 2002, 1999). In common with the other empirical chapters in this book then, our intention here is to analyse some exemplars of animal representations in children's culture, with a view to understanding the mass media's role in reproducing the geography of Figure 2.1. We have chosen two examples to focus on: Hollywood feature film animations, specifically *Puss in Boots* (2011), and a UK genre of animal magazines aimed at a pre-teen female readership. Both exemplify Anderson and Henderson's argument about the centrality of 'pet' relations in children's culture, in the form of cats in *Puss in Boots* and kittens (among other 'pets') in animal magazines. The latter selection is specific to the UK, but the selection of a filmic example of a globalized animal character, or brand, also points to the importance of attending to the globalizing scope of Figure 2.1 itself; indeed the two genres and the national/ global context can be seen to inter-penetrate in the discussion below.

Puss in Boots: The Cute, the Objectified and the Ugly

Puss in Boots, a spin-off from the commercially successful series of *Shrek* films, ostensibly offers a celebratory affirmation of the positive regard that many humans hold for 'domestic' cats in contemporary Western societies. For instance, it affectionately nods towards some of the 'quirks' of cat's behaviour that probably delight many of the film's audience (see the discussion of cutie magazines below), and presents a nonhuman character as a moral agent, capable of saving himself and others through the redemptive power of community, filial and fraternal loyalty. However, anything beyond a superficial interpretation of *Puss in Boots* suggests that it acts as a repository of important anthroparchal themes in contemporary Western culture, themes which instrumentalize and objectify some, even as they sentimentalize others, and legitimate hidden exploitation. These themes distribute the film's characters in the geography of Figure 2.1 and thereby draw on familiar tropes in other children's films featuring nonhuman characters (see Stewart and Cole 2009) and other socialization contexts (see chapters 5, 7 and 8).

The film opens with adult Puss fleeing a sexual conquest, pickpocketing as he leaves. He arrives at a bar otherwise full of humans, where we learn he has a bounty on his head, but is a 'good' criminal refusing to steal from either the church or orphans. He is enticed by information about magic beans, in the possession of villainous grotesques, Jack and Jill. In Puss's attempts to steal the beans he encounters a masked cat, with whom he flees after the theft fails. In the bar they run to, they face off in contests of dancing and fencing, before the masked cat is revealed to be, in Puss's words, 'a woman': another biped cat called Kitty Softpaws. We learn that Kitty is an associate of Puss's old childhood friend Humpty Dumpty, and through flashback learn that Puss and Humpty grew up together at the same orphanage – the only nonhumans, but both described there as 'boys'. We see a young Humpty (a small egg who 'ages' into a large egg, but never hatches) obsessed with finding the magic beans, and with inventing flying machines. They embark on youthful delinquency, which matures into more serious criminality on Humpty's part and results in the escapade in which Puss is wrongly accused and outcast from the village. Reunited in the present, the three main characters embark on a search for the beans, stealing them from Jack and Jill and successfully growing the magic beanstalk. With romance brewing between the cats, they and a jealous Humpty (now disguised as a golden egg, in a 'leather' costume) climb the beanstalk and locate the Golden Goose and her golden eggs. Chased by what they assume to be the creature of lore protecting the castle, they flee with the goose and their bounty of eggs, apparently to return with them as heroes to their village. On the way, we see Puss knocked out and captured, and he wakes to discover he has been betrayed by a vengeful Humpty who intends also to destroy the village by enticing the goose's gigantic mother (the previously unseen 'creature') with the eggs and Golden Goose as quarry, blaming the escapade on a now imprisoned Puss. With Kitty's help, Puss escapes and foils the orchestrated attack. He reunites Mother Goose and her daughter, redeeming himself in the process. Humpty is also redeemed by sacrificing himself in order to save the geese. We see his broken body transformed into a solid gold egg, ascending into the clouds with the reunited geese. The epilogue shows Humpty, back in his familiar form, 'living' in the clouds with the giant goose. Exonerated and forgiven, Puss bids farewell to Kitty and the village, before being reunited with her at the end of the credits, when they finally kiss.

The Heroic Anthropomorphic Subject

Puss in Boots tells a familiar story, structurally similar to Disney's *The Jungle Book* (1967) for instance, of the eponymous wronged 'outsider', betrayed by someone close to him, finding moral and material reward and redemption through rejection of juvenile delinquency, in favour of acquiescence to the values of adult society. As he undertakes his moral journey, Puss's redemption is paralleled by the damnation of his nemeses in the film, the 'mean, greedy and ugly' (Paramount Pictures 2011) human characters of Jack and Jill, and the fall and ultimate rise of his childhood friend, Humpty Dumpty. The simple theodicic message of the film is therefore that good people prosper and bad people suffer. A key component of that suffering is the extent to which characters remain 'people' or are relegated to 'animal' status. The way in which the good and the bad prosper and suffer is therefore determined by the respective characters' shifting fortunes on a continuum of subjectification/objectification, or their positioning in Figure 2.1. That is, *Puss in Boots* hierarchically distributes the capacity to constitute the self-as-subject, to confer degrees of subjectivity on others, and relatedly, the capacity to objectify (instrumentalize) others. This fictive economy maps onto the real economy of subjectification/objectification that operates outside the cinema, and which determines and legitimates the fate of exploited nonhuman others.

The hierarchical economy in *Puss in Boots* has the moral code of society itself at its pinnacle, embodied in the norms of the village where Puss lives his early life. Those norms centre on the objectification of exploited others (nonhuman animals used for food and labour), village, familial and friendship loyalties and obedience to the law, especially laws of property; Puss's juvenile delinquencies, in cahoots with his friend Humpty Dumpty, centre on acts of theft. The village distributes its powers of subjectification/objectification to Puss when he expresses those same norms in his behaviour. This is symbolized in the film by a flashback sequence of a young Puss heroically saving the life of the human mother of the village Comandante from a rampaging, escaped bull: community, familial and species hierarchies are preserved by Puss literally putting a nonhuman other in his place, as a subjugated prisoner. Typically of the position of subjugated nonhumans in children's films (for instance the obeisance of 'prey' animals at the climax of *The Lion King*, see Stewart and Cole, 2009), the bull conspires in his own domination when he admiringly joins in a chorus of approval for Puss, while lying, defeated, on his back.

Puss's reward for this heroic act conflates the moral with the material: he is presented by his adoptive human mother, Imelda, with accoutrements that symbolize, and result from, the domination of others: a sword, a hat with a conspicuous feather and his boots, which are made of 'the finest Corinthian leather'. Triumph over the bull is therefore celebrated by the presentation of boots made from bovine skin; injury to insult. This paraphernalia simultaneously anthropomorphizes Puss, partly clothes him in the body parts of exploited nonhuman others, and invests him with the capacity to constitute himself as a subject, in that his 'character' is distinguished by his use of these objects throughout the film. Puss, as the most 'human' character in the film (more so than the dehumanized humans Jack and Jill, of whom more below), wields the greatest power to grant subjectivity to other, lesser, characters and to objectify those who are instrumentalized. This is manifested in two main themes: Puss as a proxy human with the associated capacity to both grant subjectivity and to use nonhuman others and Puss as a cipher for heteronormative masculine sexuality. These two themes are staked out at the start of the film, when Puss recounts his various names, including 'the Ginger-haired Man' and 'Frisky Two Times'.

The Ginger-haired Man: Exercising the Privilege of Subjectification/Objectification

As the Ginger-haired Man, Puss's capacity to both grant and withhold subjectivity is evident throughout the film, for instance in his ability to instrumentalize other animals (such as when he rides a horse), or his capacity to interpellate others as subjects. A striking instance of the latter occurs when Puss returns the Golden Goose to her mother with the words 'she's OK' at the end of the film. At this moment, the emphasis on Puss as protector of others is expressed through his gendering, and thereby recognition of the subjecthood of, the Golden Goose. This contrasts with the moment when the Golden Goose is taken from her home at the top of the beanstalk (which Puss does nothing to prevent). At that point, she is thoroughly instrumentalized as (stealable) property: 'it's a gold pooper, we're taking it'. This distinction subtly communicates to the audience the importance of denying subjecthood to facilitate the instrumentalization of others. But the Ginger-haired Man's powers of subjectification are most fully explored through his relationship with Humpty Dumpty. Humpty's ontological status is ambivalent throughout the film, summed up in this plaintive declaration:

'I'm not a person, I'm not a bird; I'm not even a food. I don't know what I am'. Puss replies, 'You are my brother', thereby conferring subjectivity upon Humpty purely through his relationship to Puss. At other points in the film, Puss's power to objectify Humpty is expressed through asserting that he is 'a food': 'I smell … something breakfasty'; 'I should scramble you with onions', or his threat to turn Humpty into an 'egg salad sandwich'.

Humpty's narrative in the story, and his desire for revenge on Puss, centres on his lack of belonging, his inability to find a position within the economy of subjectification/objectification. Humpty is portrayed as a keen inventor of flying machines in the film, implying a frustrated wish to 'hatch' into a bird. This aspect of the plot perhaps unwittingly opens up the possibility of critique of the film's general tendency to present eggs as abstractions from the reproductive process, but the latter abstraction is dominant throughout *Puss in Boots*. Humpty first appears in the orphanage as a smaller egg, but only 'grows up' to be a bigger egg. Post-mortem, Humpty is transmogrified into a golden egg. The Golden Goose's eggs never hatch, aren't incubated, and when Puss returns the Golden Goose to her mother, her golden eggs aren't returned as well – the 'gold' (objects) apparently remain the 'property' of the villagers. In these ways, the biological functions of eggs are obscured in the film and they are more easily objectified as 'a food' for the audience. Frequent references to Humpty as food work because the 'subjectivity' of Humpty as an egg, abstracted from the reproductive process, effaces the objectification of real (exploited) chickens.

Frisky Two Times: Intersecting Heteronormativity and Anthroparchy

As 'Frisky Two Times', and a self-described 'lover of beautiful women', Puss epitomizes cultural stereotypes of promiscuous, virile heteronormative masculinity. This is established in the implied one-night stand with a female cat at the start of the film, and reinforced throughout when Puss is depicted as both attracted, and irresistible to, human women. In all his flirtatious encounters, Puss is 'in control', but women 'can't help' but be attracted to him. Interestingly, this transgression of the human/nonhuman sexual boundary is strictly gendered. Puss declares to Kitty: 'you are a woman' (implying her sexual attractiveness), but Kitty is not depicted as attractive, or attracted, to human men (despite the anthropomorphic emphasis on her 'sexy' hip-swaying and exaggeratedly long eyelashes). Taken together, this implies a sexist/speciesist characterization of human female sexuality as more 'animalistic' in contrast to the controlled masculine sexuality of Puss. It is through Puss's relationship with Kitty that heteronormativity and sexualized gender identities are most consistently reinforced: in contrast to Puss's promiscuity, Kitty remains 'faithful' and monogamous, only flirting with Puss. Frisky Two Times asserts his virile credentials to Kitty through familiar speciesist/sexist posturing, inviting her to think of him as 'beefcake, stallion, tiger'. The traditional gender roles in *Puss in Boots* extend to Puss heroically saving Kitty's life as they tumble from the beanstalk. Puss finally 'claims' Kitty as his sexual partner in the film's epilogue, providing a 'satisfying' culmination of their flirtation throughout the film. Just as Humpty's subjectivity depended on Puss's gift ('you are my brother'), so Kitty's sexual fulfilment only lies in relation to Puss's pursuit of her.

While Frisky Two Times is the heteronormative centre of *Puss in Boots*, some other instances are striking. The most notable is Humpty's 'joke' about rape when contemplating his potential imprisonment: 'you got any idea what they do to eggs in prison? Let me tell you this, it ain't over easy'. Homophobia also runs through *Puss in Boots*, expressed in the way the film jokes around the theme of viewing male genitalia: Puss displays revulsion at the prospect of a human showing him the 'golden eggs' implicitly tattooed on his genitals; Puss and Kitty express comic distaste when Humpty undresses in front of them. Puss reacts with disgust to Beanstalk Jack, who is depicted as enjoying watching Puss lick himself. In this last example, a stereotypical 'dirty old man' has the distinction of being the only character to express non-heteronormative sexual desire in the film. Finally, heteronormativity asserts itself through the hierarchy of attractiveness of its characters. Puss and Kitty are the beautiful people, while Humpty, the tattooed tavern customer, and the 'dirty old man' are grotesques.

The distinction of the beautiful and the grotesque also intersects with the class politics of *Puss in Boots*. Puss and Kitty are established as eloquent and refined through their physical attractiveness, 'well-spoken' accents and the stereotypical cleanliness of cats, alluded to in their 'well-groomed' appearance in the film. Puss's 'refinement' is specifically reinforced through his clothing: the 'dandy' feathered hat, and especially, his boots of 'finest Corinthian leather'. For the adult audience, in North America at least, this reference to 'finest Corinthian leather' recalls the famous marketing slogan for Chrysler Cordoba cars used in the 1970s, voiced by Mexican actor Ricardo Montalbán. This reference, combined with the voicing of Puss by Antonio Banderas, most famous for his role as Zorro, articulates 'positive' stereotypes of both 'Latin' and feline temperaments: laid back, vain, promiscuously virile. In contrast Jack and Jill's status as 'bad' people is equated with physical unattractiveness, non-normative body shapes (conceptually linked to their description as 'greedy', in contrast to Puss's moderate lapping of milk), non-middle class accents and their 'animalistic' association with pigs. The latter has a dual aspect: their literal harnessing of the 'demonic' (labour) power of the red-eyed boars who pull their wagon, and their implied affective relationship with their captive piglets. Cultural associations of pigs with 'dirt' therefore taint Jack and Jill as 'dirty' characters, and their 'animalism' is compounded by Jill grunting/growling at Puss when gagged after her capture. Beanstalk Jack's inept handling of the magic beans is similarly linked to an ageist and ableist characterization of a sleepy, feeble and senile old man, whose forgetfulness is contrasted with Puss's youthful and vigorous impatience to act on the basis of the story that Jack recounts.

Constructing the Consumable Other

The final, and arguably most important theme of *Puss in Boots*, is the cultural reproduction of instrumentalized nonhumans as exploitable objects. The superabundance of Puss's names, noted above, stands in marked contrast to the namelessness of most of the nonhumans in the film (naming and the withholding of names is elemental to the economy of subjectification/objectification – see chapters 2 and 8). Nonhumans who are objectified to different degrees outside the cinema, do not have names, cannot use human language, and are not clothed – all key markers of Puss's subjectivity (non-character 'prey' animals are similarly represented in *The Lion King*). Examples include the rampaging bull mentioned earlier; the team of boars (depicted with demonic red eyes) who pull Jack and Jill's wagon; a group of piglets captive inside the same wagon; a group of chickens who scatter in fear and confusion during the climactic action sequence of the film; horses, used to pull the heroes' cart and ridden by Puss in the final shot of the film; a lamb (as in 'Mary had a little ...') who appears in flashbacks to the orphanage where Puss grows up; the Golden Goose and her mother; a cow appearing in the (G)litter Club who has her bell rung by a musician in the cat band, which accompanies Puss and Kitty's 'dance fight'. These examples refuse subjectivity to animals who are functional, that is who are instrumentalized, in *Puss in Boots*. Even those animals who are not explicitly (e.g. horses, boars, bull and cow) or implicitly (e.g. chickens, piglets) exploited in the film perform symbolic functions for the viewing audience, facilitating value-rational and affective practices. For instance the permanently infant lamb acts as a 'cute' repository for the self-congratulatory capacity to 'care' for lesser (because dependent) nonhumans. The latter discourse of humans 'protecting' vulnerable nonhuman others echoes justifications for nonhuman exploitation that are deployed in a formal educational context (see Chapter 7 and Cole 2011).

While a more positive message of humans giving sanctuary to abandoned nonhumans can be found in the depiction of Imelda's 'orphanage' in *Puss in Boots*, the film re-inscribes nonhuman dependence on humans, even in the case of its more 'independent' characters. When Puss recounts his early life to Kitty, he describes being blown into the village in a basket and being 'a kitten with no milk, no mama' before being saved by Imelda. His wish to make his human 'mother' proud is a central motivation for Puss's moral direction. In a rare critical moment in the film (of 'real' human–nonhuman animal relations), Kitty recalls that 'a nice couple took me in', but when explaining why she was de-clawed (hence the 'Softpaws' element of her name), she speculates that this was a result of 'playing too rough with the hamster' or damaging the 'nice couple's' curtains. Kitty wistfully reflects, 'cat people are crazy'. Puss and Kitty then are contrasted by their respective experiences with 'responsible' and 'irresponsible' 'pet owners', but the fundamental status of cats as 'pets' is stabilized in these shared experiences. In this context, it is also important to note a hierarchy of subjectivity among the cats in *Puss in Boots*. Apart from Puss and Kitty, cats also appear as unvoiced, unclothed, are quadrupedal, and drink milk from bowls, contrasted with Puss drinking from a glass. But, they are granted a partial subjectivity through their performances as musicians and dancers in the film, or as sexual beings in the case of Puss's partner in a one-night stand. That partial subjectivity mirrors the status of cats as 'pets', protected from the worst effects of instrumentalization but still subject to extensive human control, for instance of their movements, diet and reproductive process, and still instrumentalized for their capacity to amuse and entertain (see the discussion of cutie magazines below). Puss himself, when stripped of clothing after his imprisonment, reverts to cat-like behaviour (e.g. licking himself) and uses feline wiles to attempt escape (fixing the gaoler with wide, big-pupilled eyes to attempt to persuade him to let him go), and is shown as easily distracted (and thereby has his 'human' subjectivity temporarily suspended) by a moving light, shone by Kitty after the playful dance/fight scene. Puss and Kitty playfully provoke each other in the dance fight by using desubjectifying 'catlike' moves. These break the anthropomorphic spell, exemplified by their bipedal gait, human speech, and clothing, that they depend on for their status as 'subjects' in the film.

Puss in Boots *in the Context of Figure 2.1*

Puss in Boots then, grants different levels of subjectivity to its characters corresponding to their symbolic and material uses of humans outside the cinema (i.e. as 'cared for', but entertaining, animal companions, or as 'food'). At the same time, it facilitates non-sensibility to the material exploitation of nonhumans (with the exception of Kitty's de-clawing story, which is 'safe' from an anthroparchal perspective because cats are not exploited for human food and are constructed as ideal recipients of affectivity). As the characters that the audience are invited to identify with, Puss and Kitty's carnivory is suppressed in the film. The human audience therefore never have to confront their own complicity with the objectification of 'food' animals. These cats never kill, and subsist only on milk; an ideal food to resonate with the young viewer for whom the drinking of other animals' milk has been normalized since infancy (see Chapter 5). The milk drunk in the film is implicitly cows' milk, which, unsurprisingly, is not problematized in relation to the separation of cows and calves, the killing of infant male calves, the 'veal' industry, etc. This is indicated by the presence of the cow with a bell in the (G)litter club (viewers are presumably to infer that the cats milk 'their' cow!), Puss's ordering of a 'leche' in the tavern at the start of the film, and his virile declaration that he only drinks 'whole milk' at the film's climax. There are only two, weak, allusions to cats as killers/carnivores. The first is in the form of a fish's skeleton used as a musical instrument in the (G)litter Club (which could be imagined as having been scavenged from human refuse). The second is a bird brought as a 'gift' by Puss to his 'mama' Imelda at the end of the film. But, crucially, the bird is only playing dead – she/he opens her/his eyes to camera to reassure the audience that Puss doesn't really kill.

While Puss (and the other cats) normalize other species' milk-drinking for the human audience, another incident reinforces the 'food' status of the voiceless piglets: when discovered attempting to steal the magic beans from Jack and Jill's wagon, Kitty distracts their human antagonists by throwing a piglet at them and shouting 'sausage bomb!' This joke only works because the piglets are already objectified, and never granted subjectivity, in *Puss in Boots*. By way of contrast, Babe, a human voiced pig subject in the film of the same name (1995), is taunted by Duchess the cat with the 'food' status of pigs: 'Pork, they call it – or bacon. They only call them pigs when they're alive [...] Believe me, sooner or later, every pig gets eaten. That's the way the world works. Oh, I haven't upset you, have I?' This disturbs the audience's positioning of pigs as 'food' as it invites empathy with Babe's fear of this violent potential fate, but only because Babe has been constructed as a subject in the film (Stewart and Cole 2009).

Like many children's films featuring nonhuman animal characters, *Puss in Boots* has been promoted through a tie-in with McDonalds. An accompanying television advertisement is telling. It opens with children in a village square, recalling that of the film, being invited by Puss to follow him up the beanstalk that emerges from a 'happy meal' (*sic*) box. At the top of the beanstalk, Puss and the children find themselves in a McDonalds restaurant, where the 'happy meal' box is shown to contain a 'milk jug', 'chicken nuggets' and 'apple dippers'. This particular construction of a meal of course resonates with *Puss in Boots* and the film has provided nothing to trouble the child's consumption of these specific products of exploitation. The emphasis on cows' milk-drinking invites peer recognition between the child targets of the advertisement and Puss himself ('apple dippers' are accompanied with a 'caramel' dip that contains, alongside the ubiquitous corn syrup and sundry additives, 'sweetened condensed milk' and 'cream'), while, as noted above, chickens only appear in the film as startled (and implicitly unintelligent) non-characters. The focus of the child consumer's affective sentiment for nonhuman animals is drawn towards Puss and the other characters from the film, represented in the meal as plastic toys, and therefore away from the real nonhumans objectified to 'provide' the 'happy meal' (see Figure 6.1 below). It is worth noting that for some of the 3-D screenings of

Puss in Boots, children were provided with glasses shaped like cats eyes, lest there be any confusion about who they are intended to identify with in the film.

From a critical vegan perspective, the advertisement and film are a tragically missed opportunity to promote plant-based food – we might imagine a vegan restaurant at the top of the beanstalk, naturally selling bean burgers, not least as a 'tie-in' with the orphanages' residents having been depicted as largely subsisting on beans in the film (though beans are thereby stigmatized by association with material deprivation, a familiar trope that devalues plant foods – see Adams 2004b, Fiddes 1991, Twigg 1983, 1979). Furthermore, we might indulge ourselves with an image of Ronald McDonald as the terrible giant of the Jack and the beanstalk story, and McDonalds restaurants, with their egregious, obfuscatory, ideology of human–nonhuman animal relationships, as the epitome of castles that float in the sky. More seriously, *Puss in Boots* exemplifies the cultural reproduction of anthroparchal norms that legitimate the exploitation of nonhuman others, intersected with heteronormative, sexist, racist and classist stereotypes.

Cutie Magazines: The Gendering of Affectivity

Another area of children's culture in which other animals feature prominently is in magazines, especially those marketed towards pre-teen girls. As will be seen below, the 'cutification' of feline representations is a theme in common with *Puss in Boots* in this genre. At the time of writing, there are four monthly titles published in the UK, all aimed at a pre-teen girl cohort and all widely available in newsagents and other outlets: *All About Animals*, *Animal Cuties*, *Animal Friends* and *Animals and You* (henceforth referred to as AAA, AC, AF and AY respectively, and as 'cutie magazines' collectively). In this section we discuss our analysis of an issue of each of these four titles, all published in Spring/ Summer 2012 (the most recent editions at the time we began our analysis). This enables us to present a contemporary snapshot of the way that other animals are constructed for children in this form of mass media. It also illuminates the strongly gendered construction of children's identities in this age group, on the basis of idealized relations with other animals.

The key characteristic shared by all of these titles is their focus on anywhere but the south-eastern region of Figure 2.1. That is, all of them engage readers with other animals in ways which do not explore or disturb the most exploitative forms of human–nonhuman animal interaction. This can be illustrated with a simple content analysis of the images of animals depicted on the front covers of each title, which we've represented in Table 6.1 below.

Table 6.1   Content analysis of cutie magazine covers

Title	Humans	'Pets'	'Wild'	'Representations' (toys)	'Representations' (art/graphics)
All About Animals	0	10	5	10	11
Animals and You	3	10	0	3	3
Animal Cuties	0	11	0	4	11
Animal Friends	5	5	5	0	1
Total	8	36	10	17	26

Of the 89 images of nonhuman animals on the covers of the magazines, none are of the most commonly 'farmed' animals likely to be consumed by the magazines' readers (cows, pigs, sheep, 'poultry' or fishes). Collectively, the images therefore illustrate the logic of Figure 2.1 in microcosm, in that the vast majority are either 'live' images of 'pets' (36, or 40 per cent), or representations in the form of photographs of toys or cartoon/graphical images (43; about 48 per cent). A minority are 'live' images of 'wild' animals (10; about 11 per cent). The north-east and north-west regions of Figure 2.1 are therefore thickly populated, the south-west less so, and the south-east not at all. In addition, there are three photographs of eight humans in total: it is immediately striking that the two titles which directly imply a relationship between humans and other animals – *Animals and You* and *Animal Friends* – are the only two which feature humans on the cover. On AY, this comprises a photograph of two girls, dressed for riding, holding the harnesses of two ponies, and a photograph of a girl cuddling a puppy, with all the children smiling into the camera. On AF, this comprises a photograph of a safari vehicle, driven by a black man, and containing a white family of mother and father, son and daughter, excitedly looking at a rhinoceros in the foreground of the picture. So, normative forms of relations are valorized in these magazine covers, in which other animals are presented as inspirations of affection and or excitement among children: as 'pets', as toys, as graphical 'characters', or as exotic spectacle. Furthermore, the images of humans interacting with, or spectating, other animals, graphically demonstrate these relations, and the pleasures to be derived from these relations, for the reader.

In this section, we argue that this genre of magazines provide a set of resources for children to rehearse these forms of relations with other animals, and to incorporate them into their own identities as very particular kinds of animal lovers. The dominant theme here is a symbiotic process of the manufacture of sentiment and its infantilization-feminization, the leitmotif of which is magazines' construction of 'cuteness'.

Constructing Cuteness

The 'cuteness' of certain other animals is emphasized throughout these girls' magazines, to the extent that it could be argued to be the definitive characteristic of the genre. As we discussed in Chapter 2, representations of other animals play a key role in the childhood socialization of the value of caring for others. However, other animals tend to be constructed as worthy of care and affection only because of a combination of their aesthetic appeal and their relative helplessness compared with children. 'Cuteness' is the characteristic that synthesizes aesthetics and infantilism, which thereby signifies that the animals represented in these magazines are worthy of girls' care and affection. In this section, we examine the exemplary construction of 'cuteness' in our sample of cutie magazines, and especially the May 2012 issue of AC: the magazine is dominated by photographs and stylized representations of nonhuman animals, whose cuteness is constructed through the deployment of a plethora of contextual, symbolic and lexical markers.

'Pets' and 'Characters'

Cuteness is a defining characteristic of the *types* of animals who are most often depicted in cutie magazines. That is, the categories of 'pet' and representations of 'animal characters' from Figure 2.1 pre-date the cutie magazines genre and are already available as pre-scripted cultural resources for the magazines' editors and authors (see Chapter 3). The categories presented on the magazine covers therefore straight away communicate that the content of the magazines is 'safe', in respect of not overtly troubling the south-eastern killing zone of our relational map. The self-evidence of the meaning of these categories is also reinforced in the magazines themselves: 'Who wouldn't want one of these supercuties as a pet? They're gorgeous!' (AC 2012: 4). At the same time, animals who typically occupy other regions of Figure 2.1 are largely absent from cutie magazines, and when they do appear, it is never in ways which trouble instrumental human–nonhuman animal relations. The suffering of 'wild' animals is represented to some extent, through advertisements for conservation charities and features about endangered species (of which more below), but farmed animals only appear as honorary cuties, that is, as cartoon representations that echo those of kittens or puppies, presented as 'pets' or pseudo-pets, or as toys, none of which make reference to the bloody fate of the majority of 'farmed' animals.

Infant Animals

The animals depicted in AC are almost exclusively infant, or baby animals; that is puppies, kittens, foals, kits (infant rabbits), pups (infant guinea pigs), ducklings and chicks. Puppies, kittens and kits are by far the most numerous, echoing their popularity as 'pets' for children (see Chapter 5), as well as suggesting that infant nonhumans are suitable companions for infant humans. The infancy of the animals plays a number of important roles. Firstly, it is a key to their consistently 'cute' appearance in the magazine: soft fur and dewy eyes. The infancy of the 'live' images is compounded by the anthropomorphized appearance of the cartoon animals that often appear on the same page. Especially notable are the outsized heads of cartoon animals, which recall the proportions of human babies but not real puppies, kittens and so on. Secondly, infancy emphasizes these animals' vulnerability and need for care and protection. Children are therefore constructed as carers, or at least vicarious carers for these infants, although the infancy of the 'pets' in cutie magazines also suggests the transience of this kind of 'infantile' affectivity. This is in line with the attenuation of affect described in Chapter 5, for instance in the increasing prominence of instrumental-rationality in animal-related toys in Hamleys. The construction of children as carers is reinforced by the rarity of depictions of infant animals being cared for by their own parents or by other members of their own species; generally, the reader is explicitly or implicitly placed in the situation of looking after the needy cuties, at least vicariously. Most images are of individual animals, though more unusually pairs of sibling animals are depicted together. Very occasionally parents are depicted with their offspring, as in the case of a guinea pig and her pup in AY (2012: 9). Most adult animals depicted in cutie magazines are 'wild', for instance present in advertisements for conservation charities (more on this below). The chid reader-as-carer is also more directly expressed in the invitation for readers to, 'Draw a cute picture [...] or send in photos of your gorgeous pets'. Successful contributors win a prize of 'Hello Kitty buildable figures' (a set of heavily stylized and anthropomorphized plastic kitten toys, outfitted in a range of human costumes). In the pages of AC then, the lines between 'real' animals and their representations are blurred in a dizzying oscillation between the north-eastern and north-western regions of Figure 2.1. This relationship between living animals and consumable representations has important consequences for the construction of readers' identities, which we explore in more detail below. Thirdly, infancy ensures innocence in two respects: asexuality and the absence of violence. The uniform depiction of infant animals in AC allows the reinsertion of a sanitized other into human experience: the puppies don't fuck, the kittens don't kill and consequently their own innocence marks them as worthy recipients of the ministrations of innocent child readers. There is an interesting contrast here with the sexuality of 'Frisky Two Times' in *Puss in Boots*: the humorous allusion to sexuality (arguably aimed at the parents in the film's audience more than the children) confers subjectivity on Puss as an anthropomorphized and racialized cipher; he is a very different species of animal to the kittens in cutie magazines. AAA includes a competition to win *Puss in Boots* 'goodies' (2012: 30), again illustrating the interpenetration of anthroparchal representations in children's culture.

Cute Style

In addition to their infancy, and the associated anthropomorphism of the giant-headed cartoons discussed earlier, there are a range of design features in AC that stylize animals (real and representational) as cute. Firstly, a distinctive photographic style, exemplified by the 'pin-up' image: full-page photographs of archetypically cute animals. The AC issue we examined included three such examples (similar examples can be found in all of the other cutie magazines): a foal named Blossom, pictured in a green field with buttercups; a puppy named Billie, looking at the camera with head cocked, and in extreme close-up; and a pair of tabby kittens named Holly and Ben, apparently sleeping. All three images are framed by a stylized floral border and include the AC logo as well as the animals' names. The pin-up is a special case of the more general emphasis on close-up photographs of posed animals, which feature on almost every page. Most frequently the animals are posed with their gaze directed into the lens of the camera, or else looking into a distance that's absent from the photographs, or more unusually with eyes closed, apparently sleeping. These poses communicate that the animals' interest and affection is focused on the reader, or, if their attention is directed elsewhere, that attention only functions to capture them in a cute pose for the enjoyment of the viewer. Secondly, a cute lexicon for describing animals: this includes cuteness itself ('Kitten cuties' 'your little cutie', 'they're super-cute'); a set of adjectives that emphasize a cute aesthetic appeal ('beautiful bunnies', 'really gorgeous animals', 'sweet pup', 'adorable little kitty') and exclamations of affection ('... puppies can spend quite a long time asleep! Bless'). Thirdly, the liberal deployment of love hearts and floral motifs, also discussed in chapters 5, 7, and 8. These function as ubiquitous symbols of sentimental affection in UK culture, notably associated with the commercialization of Valentine's Day. In *Animal Cuties*, love hearts appear as decorative motifs scattered on most of the pages of the magazine. For instance, AC invites the reader to 'spot the cuties!' (AC 2012: 3) elsewhere in the magazine by matching thumbnail photographs of a kit, foal, puppy and pup with their full-size images elsewhere. Each thumbnail has a pink-edged white heart next to it, with the task being to 'Write the page numbers in the heart shapes when you find them!' Representations of flowers are similarly abundant throughout cutie magazines, and the sentimental motif shades into a romantic one in an AY poster featuring a photograph of an unnamed puppy gazing into the camera while gripping a plastic red rose between her or his teeth (AY 2012: 10).

Super Furry Animals

Visual and lexical markers of cuteness are combined with assertions of the tactile pleasures offered by animals: 'These two cheeky pups [...] have really soft, shaggy fur' (AC 2012: 4); 'Cocker spaniels have really soft floppy ears. Don't you just want to give them a tickle?' (AC 2012: 5). The furriness of pets recalls the already-established furriness of soft toys a little earlier in the socializing process (recalling the ascent of the floors of Hamleys, discussed in Chapter 5). Soft toys are still present in cutie magazines, for instance in a competition to win 'Puppy in my Pocket So Soft goodies' (AC 2012: 23, more on this example below). AC also contained an insert from the World Wildlife Fund (WWF), promoting an 'adopt a leopard' scheme for 'the world's most endangered cat', the Amur leopard (WWF no date: 2). WWF is well-known for its cute-panda logo, and in this case, offers a soft toy version of an Amur leopard as an incentive to sign up to the scheme. In common with other representations of animals, the Amur leopard toy appears more like a cub than an adult, with an outsized head and posed sitting upright on her or his haunches (see Figure 6.1 below). The human baby-like pose and stylization fits with the campaign to *adopt* leopards, that is, to take on a caring, protective, parental role. This sits comfortably with the form of child relation encouraged with both pets and with representations of animals (especially toys) in cutie magazines. The human–nonhuman hierarchy is subtly set in motion through the construction of vulnerability and dependence in other animals, with girls being encouraged to assume the responsibility and power that comes with the human role of carer for the animal other. The WWF's choice of a soft toy promotion is also ironic in the context of its report that 'its beautiful fur is highly prized by poachers' (WWF no date: 2). This reference to violent, instrumental relations with other animals is rare in animal cutie magazines (in fact it is only manifested in the context of protecting 'wild' animals in this and similar features), but it is a 'safe' exposé of violence because it is perpetrated by criminal outsiders against an ideal (because furry) victim. This contrasts with the 'legitimate' violence of farming, vivisection and so on, which remain hidden from children in the magazines. A striking reinforcement of this fluffy segue between representations and real animals is given in a double-page poster in AF of a kitten photographed apparently sleeping on her or his side, with a soft toy rabbit under her or his leg, as if being cuddled (AF 2012: 14–15). This image suppresses the more likely predatory relation between cats and rabbits (likewise the Amur leopard insert doesn't mention their prey animals, or the fact that they are carnivorous predators), but also reinforces the anthropomorphic character of 'pets' by showing them enjoying the same pleasures as enjoyed by the children reading the magazines (which decidedly do not include killing and eating other animals and eating their raw flesh). This construction also recalls the innocent framing of cats as cows' milk-drinkers in *Puss in Boots*, discussed above. This theme is continued in the next section.

From Playmates to Dependents

While the infancy of animals is the dominant theme in cutie magazines, animals are also often represented as children's peers, through speech or thought bubbles attached to photographs of live animals, through giving voices to cartoon representations, or through the context of their representation. Peer recognition between animals and children forms a bridge with the more exclusive focus on animals as peers earlier in the socialization process, especially in the form of soft toys (see the discussion of the ground floor of Hamleys and our discussion of infant socialization in domestic space in Chapter 5). As Cosslett writes, voicing animals in writing for children is a tradition in British literature that gathered pace in the Victorian era (Cosslett 2006). Cosslett argues that for some authors at least (for instance Anna Sewell in *Black Beauty*), this device was deployed to encourage empathy with animal characters on the part of readers, by using human language to establish animals' subjectivity. While from a contemporary perspective, this might be critiqued for eliding animals' own means of communication and expression, this technique remains salient in animal cutie magazines (as well as in literature that is critical of anthroparchal relations, discussed in Chapter 9). However, voicing other animals often functions to demonstrate *their* empathy for children, and therefore their status as appropriate playmates. For instance, AC features a range of activities for readers, including a cut-out template for a 'super-cute' 'Treasure box' (AC 2012: 12–13). The box itself is faced with four cute images (of a rabbit, a kitten, a pair of puppies and a pair of guinea pigs respectively) and love heart and floral graphics. It is accompanied with a photograph of a dog 'thinking', 'Can I put my toy in there too?' and a rabbit 'thinking', 'I'm putting carrots in my box'. Another activity, to make a magazine holder, features a photograph of a kitten 'thinking' 'I'm going to stick some wool on mine' (AC 2012: 16). Wool-toying elevates kittens towards the north-west of Figure 2.1, enjoying the privileges of exploiting other animals, in this case sheep, alongside their human playmates, although this is of course obscured within cutie magazines themselves.

AAA takes the anthropomorphized playmate theme further by using photoshopped images of animals enjoying, and voicing their enjoyment of, human activities in a 'pop pets' feature (AAA 2012: 4–5). 'Pets' are therefore discursively positioned as sharing in, but also providing, children's recreation and entertainment. Similar to the packaging on the 'Little Dish' meals discussed in Chapter 5, this includes a cat operating a turntable ('Pump up the volume'), a puppy listening to an iPod ('I [love heart] pup music [*sic*]'), a kitten singing into a microphone ('I'm miaow-sical') and a pair of guinea pigs playing a guitar and conga respectively ('This is heaps better than going on that wheel'). AAA's 'Pups'n'Pals' feature (2012: 6–7) is a photo strip story of friendship between two girls, Megan and Bille and their puppies, Mabel and Scramble. The story in this issue, 'Doggy Diva!' is about Billie and Scramble starring in a television advertisement (itself a meta-reproduction of the categorization of animals as instrumentalized 'entertainment'), becoming starstruck, but then realizing their folly and reuniting with Megan and Mabel for a happy ending. The story imputes human speech and anthropomorphized desires to the puppies, for instance in one frame Mabel wears the same pair of pink love heart sunglasses as Megan and 'says', 'I'm going to dream of fame and fortune' (AAA 2012: 7). AY similarly voices puppies, but this time representations of puppy characters (Poppy, Daisy, Maxie and Coco) in a comic strip called 'Poppy's World!' (AY 2012: 4). The heavily cutified female characters (e.g. with large humanized eyes, long lashes and a sparkling purple bow for Coco) are depicted comically bickering as they prepare a picnic of sandwiches (apparently salad and cream cheese), chopped fruit and a dessert (the dessert is not depicted or specified).

Alongside these forms of peer recognition though, are more 'grown-up' discourses that reaffirm the positions of animals in Figure 2.1, that is, without the human zone of the far north-west. This largely consists of informative features about animals as pets, or as 'wild' animals, albeit the latter may well be captive in 'zoos' and therefore shade into the position of 'entertainment animals' in Figure 2.1 (see Chapter 3 for a discussion of the emergence of 'zoos' as edificatory and/or entertaining socialization sites). For instance, AY reports on three new-born 'mini meerkats' at Bristol Zoo Gardens (accompanied with a photo captioned 'sweet!'), who have been named Timon, Pumbaa and Rafiki, 'after characters from The Lion King, as the musical of the Disney film will be heading to Bristol later this year!' (AY 2012: 4). The cutification of the meerkat triplets shifts them towards the north-east of Figure 2.1 through the inter-textual reference with fictional animal characters, two of whom are not even meerkats (Pumbaa is a warthog and Rafiki a mandrill in *The Lion King* film). Cutie magazines therefore transmit more or less straightforward education/ socialization about the proper place and treatment of other animals (albeit always utilizing a cute style) alongside the more subtle constructions described elsewhere in our analysis. To illustrate further, a common instructional technique is to insert editorial assertions about the desires and needs of animals, to implicitly educate readers about caring for them. For example, an AF feature on puppies takes 'a look at how a puppy sees the world!' (AF 2012: 4) and voices a series of photographs with the following captions: 'Play with me!'; 'I'm hungry!'; 'Is it time for walkies yet?' (AF 2012: 4–5). Some editorial assertions about other animals' needs still emphasize the cuteness of animals and also reinforce the notion that their overriding need is care or affection from a human: 'Awww, this cutie [kitten] wants someone to tickle his tummy!'

(AC 2012: 25). Moreover, this kind of voicing asserts that the needs of other animals happily intersect with the tactile desires of children. Another example is given in a feature on interpreting guinea pigs' vocalizations in AY (2012: 8–9). Alongside an interpretation of 'wheeking' as an eager anticipation, 'especially if you're about to feed it!', the feature interprets 'shrieking' as a communication of fear, which is 'translated' as 'Help! I need snuggles!' in the speech bubble appended to the relevant photograph of a guinea pig.

While editorial translations of nonhuman vocalizations and other forms of expression may be critiqued as somewhat self-serving, in that they reinforce the dominant interests of human 'owners' in the pleasures offered by 'pets', the recognition that other animals do have their own ways of communicating are obviously an important step in fostering empathy for other animals on the part of children. A (restricted) subjectivity is thereby constructed for other animals in cutie magazines, but its tight parameters assert their inferiority to, and dependence on, humans. As we argued in Chapter 2, knowledge claims about other animals instantiate a discursive distance between 'them' and 'us' which is mapped on Figure 2.1. In the mass media, children are gradually socialized away from peer recognition and towards discourses of ownership and control, a process that accelerates in the context of formal education and digital media, discussed in chapters 7 and 8 respectively.

Consuming Cuteness

As noted above, cuteness is not only attributed to infant animals, but is a characteristic that girls can absorb into their own personas (for clarification, no boys were depicted in any of the issues we analysed for this chapter, except the front cover of AF mentioned above). Just as the meaning of animal categories like 'pet' pre-exists cutie magazines, so too does cuteness as part of the 'meaning' of children, and especially pre-teen girls, the primary target market for these publications. So, the magazines appeal is inter-textual, recalling a cutifying process to which many children, especially girls, will have been exposed since their own infancy. In the magazines, two complementary cutifying routes are present: through encouraging readers' rehearsal of cute style in the pages of cutie magazines themselves and through encouraging readers' conspicuous consumption of cute products. The former is encouraged by invitations to submit 'pet' photographs, artwork depicting animals or stories about readers' animal companions. For instance, AAA's 'Pets Corner' feature carries the subheading, 'Aw! Look at your cute pets and fab pictures!' (AAA 2012: 32), while AY's 'Post It!' feature is hosted by Poppy, the smiling cartoon dog wearing a love heart collar mentioned above. Contributors' captioned photos illustrate children's pleasure and skill at using the cute style of the magazines themselves.

For example, one 8-year-old AY reader writes, 'These are my baby guinea pigs after they were born last summer. Aren't they the cutest ever?' (AY 2012: 28).

The conspicuous consumption of cute products is manifested in the provision of material resources for the construction of a cute gendered identity, centred on the display of a sentimental attachment to cute infant animals. Cute materials take a variety of forms. Firstly, free gifts attached to the front covers of the magazines. For example, the May issue of AC offers a free gift of two 'bag tags' attached to the front cover, featuring a stylized plastic kitten and puppy respectively. The kitten tag is also attached to a pale pink love heart, adorned with a deep pink bow, and the word 'cute' in blue lettering. The package containing the tags is stickered with the legend 'Best Friends', which is surrounded by five love hearts. Finally, the cardboard backing to the package is decorated with cartoon drawings of a puppy and kitten, with smiling, anthropomorphized expressions. Taken together, the package exerts a powerful emotional pull for the intended reader, with the wording and imagery combining to offer girls the opportunity to display their cute-caring identities by using the tags.

Secondly, there are advertisements and promotions for animal-based toys, which can explicitly instruct girls in conspicuous cute consumption. For instance, AC includes a half-page competition with items from the well-known brand Hello Kitty as prizes, which is captioned thus: 'Show your friends how much you love Hello Kitty with these cool Tagz Styling Sets. Decorate your clothes, nails and jewellery or try out some temporary tattoos!' (AC 2012: 23). 'Love' is communicated here as an appropriate feeling for both real animals and for animal characters/material goods. Hello Kitty and the like facilitate girls' expression of their loving identities, their care for vulnerable, infant, others (the Hello Kitty 'Kitty White' character is a kitten, gendered as female by a pink bow worn askance over her left ear). It is easy to see a connection here with a wider socialization process in which caring roles are encouraged in girls, with other animals and animal representations providing practice for childcare in later life. This is illustrated in another half-page competition, this time with the Puppy in my Pocket brand supplying the prizes. Readers can win 'a Newborn Nursery plus Mums and Babies set', which 'features two puppies with special nappies; dip them in water and watch the colour change to find out if it's a boy or a girl' (AC 2012: 23).

Thirdly, the consumption of sweetness, materially and symbolically and coming in the form of free gifts of sweets, or the inclusion in the magazines of recipes for sugary foods. The consumption of sweetness functions as an ironic metaphor for the logic of Figure 2.1 as a whole, because 'animal products' typically feature in the gifts and recipes, from gelatine in a packet of Haribo chews, to eggs and butter in a biscuit recipe. The latter example is especially striking: the biscuits are in the archetypal shape of a bone chewed by 'pet' dogs, and the ingredients include 'unsalted butter, 1 [hen's] egg [...], [cows'] milk, Smarties or chocolate buttons [both of which also contain cows' milk]' (AF 2012: 17). The products of violence therefore come sugar-coated, literally and metaphorically, and moreover in a symbolic form that masks and thereby normalizes the dismemberment of animal corpses to provide 'toy' bones for 'pet' dogs. AF could, of course, have included a vegan biscuit recipe, taking any shape it wished (the bone shape is provided by cutting out a cardboard template), but the conspicuous absence of 'normal' animal products could raise difficult questions about anthroparchal relations. In our view, AF could, and should, be raising just such questions, although that would make it a very different kind of publication. Doing so would be a step towards articulating the affectivity it stimulates and the value-rational action of vegan-activist practice, in opposition to the remorseless instrumental action that it conceals. We return to this theme of anti-anthroparchal mass media in Chapter 9.

Conclusion

On the face of it, films like *Puss in Boots* and cutie magazines might be taken to contradict a Weberian theme, explored in Chapter 2, of the progressive triumph of instrumental rationality and the associated displacement of traditional, affective, and value-rational action in Western culture. However, in light of our discussion of Foucault's emphasis on the contingency of specific rationalities, these instances of anthroparchal mass media make sense in the context of their interconnection with the other regions of Figure 2.1. To that end, Figure 6.1 illustrates how the mass media examples that we have considered direct attention towards the northern and western sections of our conceptual map, where other animals are relatively protected by affectivity.

Access to the (relative) safe zones of Figure 6.1 however, is only granted on the basis of the cuteness of animals' representations; even Amur leopard's protection from poachers is mediated by their cutification, which ironically (and perhaps dangerously) reproduces the aesthetic appeal of their hair. Therefore, the *prima facie* reading of a re-enchantment of human–animal relations in children's mass media may itself be contradicted on two levels. On the one hand, these mass media representations facilitate the continuation of exploitative instrumental relations by burying them beneath an avalanche of sentimental imagery; they do not disturb the oppressive business-as-usual of the 'factory farm', et al. In Figure 6.1, the common cuteness of otherwise disparate felines mixes up the real and the imaginary; it is no longer possible (if it ever was, in light of the socialization of children already described in Chapter 5) for children to remain sensible to the discourses and practices that condemn the non-cute beyond the borders of Figure 6.1.

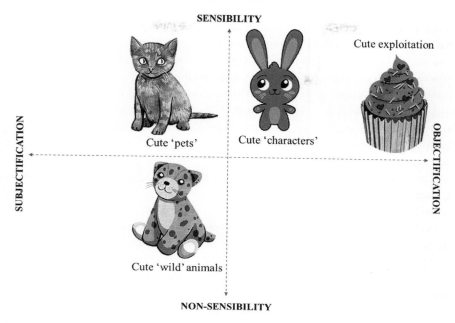

Figure 6.1   Cutification as protection and denial

On the other hand, these film and print cute representations reinforce our Foucauldian position that a sociological analysis is enriched by attending to the *specific contexts* of different human–animal relations, even though we might conclude that they ultimately take their place in an anthroparchal network. The examples considered in this chapter illustrate the importance of affective relations with other animals in children's, especially pre-teen girls' lives, but also the association of affectivity with immature femininity, thereby setting up the precariousness of affective relations in adulthood whenever they come up against instrumental imperatives. *Puss in Boots* and cutie magazines therefore miss the opportunity to engage children with a critical questioning of instrumental relations by denying their existence, while foreclosing the critical potential of empathy through channelling it towards cute representations and away from the most intensely objectified victims of anthroparchal relations. This direction of attention above the equator of Figure 6.1 is, tacitly at least, predicated on the construction of childhood innocence (see Chapter 4), the notion that children are protected from harm by being lied to about the reality of the majority of human–nonhuman animal relations. So, while these magazines might engender emotional attachment to specific *categories* of other animals, they avoid taking the crucial next step of articulating those feelings with actions that can challenge and transform violent human–nonhuman animal relations. That is, they may themselves be understood as instrumental in the continuance of exploitation, rather than offering any challenge to it, despite superficial appearances to the contrary. The *apparent* inversion of Weberian disenchantment in the endearing antics of the Ginger-haired Man and in the pages of cutie magazines, demonstrates its success; viewing other animals as magical and wonderful is a childish, and especially a girlish, pursuit. This construction undercuts opposition to exploitation for children and adults alike; it is a manifestation of sentimental, effeminate, childishness that has no place in adult (male, rational) debates about human actions towards other animals. As Molloy (2011: 27–31) makes clear in her discussion of the marginalization of feminist opposition to vivisection in the nineteenth century, the 'feminization of sentiment' in relation to other animals has a long history in Britain. This trivializing discourse continues to be manifested in the attribution of stereotypes of sentimental feminine naïveté to opponents of exploitative relations in the UK print media (Cole and Morgan 2011b, Morgan and Cole 2011). In the next chapter, we explore how children's formal education about other animals manipulates the stock of affective discourse and practice that we have seen built up in chapters 5 and 6, while accustoming children to the 'truth' of instrumental-rational relations with other animals.

Chapter 7
Education: Making Anthroparchal Domination Reasonable

By the time children enter formal education, they have already been immersed in the practico-discursive spaces of family and mass media socialization outlined in chapters 5 and 6. This chapter considers how the UK education system builds on that prior learning by a combination of tacitly and explicitly teaching the normality of human dominance over other animals. As discussed in Chapter 4, schools provide processes of demarcation of both physical and conceptual spaces which mark children as different in order not to separate them, but to appropriately fit them in. In this chapter we will look at how the processes represented in Figure 2.1 interweave with this physical and conceptual demarcation in order to reproduce and reinforce the dominant power relationships that involve both human children and nonhuman animals. We do so by looking at a number of distinct areas where the school environment involves human children in the lives and deaths of nonhuman animals. On a daily basis, children are exposed to messages about the consumption of nonhuman animals as food though the food practices engaged with during the school day, which clearly have important links and overlaps with practices in the home environment, discussed in Chapter 5. However, the management of school meal times in the school context supports the normalization and favouring of eating certain animals but not others, whether as school meals or in packed lunches brought from home. We also discuss some of the practices embedded within the formal school curriculum which position particular animals according to Figure 2.1, affording different levels of subjectivity and sensibility according to not only dominant constructions of different nonhuman animals, but also the perceived appropriateness of these activities according to the age of the children involved. These practices, broadly speaking, can be divided into three areas: firstly the use of live animals to meet curriculum goals where affective or *apparently* value-rational relationships are emphasized through a discourse of care and welfare, and which are more commonly found in activities for younger age groups; secondly, the use of (usually parts of) dead animals as objects for experimentation by older children; thirdly, we discuss a set of practices involving the transformation of living animals into dead animal products in projects located in schools and how these often controversial exercises consolidate uses and practices already present elsewhere in school activities. The chapter concludes with an analysis of a Europe-wide curriculum initiative that brings together these anthroparchal messages through online gaming and associated classroom materials, resonant of the recreational digital gaming activities discussed in Chapter 8.

The Hidden Curriculum: The Socialization of Anthroparchal Food Practices, Part 1

The tacit reproduction of human dominance includes education about food practices in schools, which reproduces the normality of consuming other animals and compounds the marginalization of vegan food practices; processes which are further entrenched by the formal catering provided by school canteens and snack shops. The issue of meals eaten by children while at school reveals the tensions between the integrity and inexorability of the school and home spheres in children's daily lives, with parental (and student) resistance of schools' attempts at determining food intake over home based norms, habits or preferences. Yet at the same time there are increasing attempts at state control of food habits in the school space, couched as a public health issue. This can be seen through the promotion of policies implementing breakfast clubs, free school meals for infants and recommendations such as the School Food Plan (Dimbleby and Vincent 2013), trying to encourage greater uptake of school provided meals over 'substandard' packed lunches or other 'off premises' food practices during school hours. Public health therefore provides an apparent value-rational orientation to such policy interventions, although the instrumental biopower imperative for a healthy, productive population that is not a 'burden' on public finances might undermine that positive interpretation. However, these initiatives remain insensible of the ethical, environmental or indeed health consequences of remaining committed to the inculcation of consuming other animals as 'normal' for children; apparent ruptures between home/'private' and school/'public' socialization sites remain articulated through their anthroparchal assumptions.

In Fletcher et al.'s (2013) qualitative study of school food practices, meals eaten at school provide school students (and to a lesser extent their parents or carers by proxy) with the opportunity to perform identity work, through which children can create, perform and establish or resist images of themselves. The study identified a resistant culture to what were seen as the 'prohibitive' restrictions of meal content determined by schools (in the form of school meals). Yet on top of these social control issues around determining what is eaten, the researchers also found that resistance to school meals was informed by students' desire to avoid the 'chaotic' environment of the school canteen, and instead create their own social spaces with peer groups of their own choosing through the practice of taking meals. Ludvigsen and Sharma's (2004) study of 174 British school children aged 4, 10 or 15 found food choices in the school environment to be strongly influenced by gender and income related stereotypes, enforced through subtle peer pressure that had a strong influence on food choices. Furthermore, the authors found these stereotypes were often portrayed in the media and advertising, which, they argued, also had a strong influence on children's choices. The children's accounts suggested a much more permissive environment of food choice at home, and by comparison school meals were disliked for being limited and repetitive. In this context the ability to bring the eating rules (or apparent lack of rules) of home into the school space is an understandable logic.

This jostling for position for the governance of food intake during school hours between school and home rules, together with the influence of media, advertising and peers, emphasizes the importance of considering the sites we analyse separately in chapters 5–8 as being interconnected in the lives of children. What happens in schools, which we describe in this chapter, can only be fully understood in the context of what we also describe elsewhere in the other chapters of Part II of this book. What happens in schools recalls and reinforces what also happens at home, in the media and at play, in distinct interconnected ways which vary according to the 'appropriate' rationality of each context and medium: a jigsaw puzzle of different practices and discourses that piece together to form a picture of oppression and exploitation of other animals, with children being drawn into complicity with its assembly. So, despite resistance to schools' 'control' over children's eating practices, the average take up of school-provided meals in England schools was 46.3 per cent in the primary sector and 39.8 per cent in the secondary sector in 2011–2012, a figure which has shown a slow but marked increase over recent years (Nelson et al. 2012). Both school meals and home prepared packed lunches, therefore, retain important roles in the reproduction of food practices in childhood.

Lunchbox Norms

Formal advice about the appropriate content of lunchboxes is provided through a broad spectrum of commercial and non-commercial organizations. The role of vested, animal exploiting interests in the form of commercial producers (or their representative bodies) in the production of materials targeted at and disseminated through schools is not always immediately apparent, and indeed often obscured. Through partnerships with, and cross referencing to, materials from non-commercial bodies such as the NHS, a veneer of objectivity is arguably afforded to what sometimes amount to little more than sophisticated advertising campaigns aimed at children and distributed through the state funded school system.

The NHS public health campaign 'Change4Life' provides food preparation tips and recipes across the life course, including advice specifically aimed at children's diets, and advice specifically on packed lunches. Despite an explicit focus on the UK Government's 5 A DAY policy (which advocates the consumption of a minimum of five portions of fruit and vegetables every day), this advice tends to treat plant foods as additions to already existing meals, rather than as integral to them. In a section of their website devoted to 'Healthier lunchboxes and picnics' (Change4Life no date), eight 5-day weeks' worth of packed lunch ideas are provided (two for 'kids aged 5–8' and six for 'kids aged 9 and over, or adults'). Of these 40 meals, all contain animal products, and none are wholly plant based. Suggested meals tend to begin with a 'meat' or dairy based component and furthermore, with a tendency to 'bolt on' fruit and vegetables as isolated 'extras', rather than forming the basis of a meal or a meal component. For example, suggestions for including fruit or vegetables in packed lunches for the younger age group include, 'Tomato' or 'Carrot sticks' on their own, not as a sandwich or wrap ingredient for instance (Change4Life, no date).

The 'Food for Life Partnership' (Food For Life 2013) is a National Lottery funded network of non-commercial organizations which produces teaching resources for primary and secondary schools in the UK, which fit within National Curriculum goals in subject areas including geography, science and Personal, Social and Health Education (PSHE). Among its materials is an acknowledgement of the role of 'food' and farming on the environment, but these do not specify the harmful effects of animal use (see Chapter 1), instead emphasizing and encouraging 'Seasonal, Local, Organic' approaches to eating. One of the partner projects, 'Food a Fact of Life', provides a website resource for 5–11 year olds, exploring 'healthy eating, cooking, and where food comes from'. An interactive exercise aimed at 5–8 year olds engages the user in an activity where they construct a packed lunch from a series of options by dragging and dropping images of food into a frame to complete a meal. If a lunchbox is compiled free from animal products (using the single vegan-suitable sandwich filling offered: hummus), when the exercise is complete a summary appears explaining that there is no cheese or yoghurt included, and to remember to include them next time. The website materials are created by the British Nutrition Foundation and DairyCo, a levy funded organization of the dairy industry, whose aims include the promotion of a positive perception of dairy farming with the general public.

School Meals

The 2013 Department of Education backed report 'The School Food Plan' makes recommendations for the provision of meals eaten during school hours, and is strongly in favour of school provided meals over home provided packed lunches. Couched chiefly in terms of the health issues associated with food intake, the report also explicitly sets out school meals as a means to achieving improved academic performance, as well as social skills within the school and the wider community (Dimbleby and Vincent 2013). The report provides the same subtle, insidious damning of plant based meals common in health related dietary advice elsewhere, such as the packed lunch advice discussed above. The report presents an early draft of the new standards it claims are needed, and like many dietary advice sources, these guidelines still put 'meat', the bodies of fishes and eggs top of the list as protein sources: 'Red meat should be provided at least twice per week and fish at least once a week' (Dimbleby and Vincent 2013: 143). While beans, pulses, soya products, nuts and seeds are recognized as a protein sources for non-'meat' eaters which should also be given at least twice a week for all children, an additional category of 'Milk and Dairy' is presented as a *necessary* food group without any suggestion of alternative sources: 'A portion of food from this group should be available on a daily basis, for example as cheese or yoghurts. In addition, reduced fat milk for drinking should be available as an option every day' (Dimbleby and Vincent 2013: 144). Whatever the wrangling over private/public food provision for children then, the anthroparchal baseline remains intact.

The Formal Curriculum: The Socialization of Anthroparchal Food Practices, Part 2

Within the formal curriculum, children are more explicitly educated about different forms of nonhuman animal use, and norms of nonhuman animal 'care' in ways which build on the affectivity and empathy cultivated in the family and mass media. However, affectivity and empathy are themselves exploited, or instrumentalized, to normalize extant violent and exploitative practices while simultaneously masking questions of the morality of using other animals. This echoes the nineteenth-century legislative process in which 'protection' of other animals amounted to outlawing exceptional, 'irrational' cruelties while allowing the routinization and normalization of exploitation, as discussed in Chapter 3. Both living and dead animals are enlisted to facilitate learning anthroparchal norms in schools, considered respectively in the next two sections.

Living Animals

'Hatching programmes', are commercial organizations which provide hatchery equipment and eggs shortly before they are due to hatch, and target schools and residential care homes for business. One such programme, the Living Eggs company, supplies portable chick hatcheries to schools and 'provides life cycle education programmes that enable children to see chicks hatching from their eggs' (Living Eggs 2013a). At a cost of just under £300 charged to the school, a single 'kit' includes 10 eggs a few days before they are due to hatch in a specially designed incubator with large viewing windows to enable as many children as possible to watch the eggs, plus a brooder box to house the hatched chicks, similarly designed for optimized viewing. The eggs are sourced from vaccinated 'breeding stock' at commercial hatcheries, and fumigated and sanitized in bacterial wash before delivery to schools (Living Eggs 2013c). The programme is advertised as of two weeks duration, with the hatched chicks becoming the property of the participating school. If schools are unable to house or rehome chicks themselves, the company undertakes to rehome all chicks with 'hobby farmers' or 'free range egg growers'. The focus of the programmes is clearly around the origin and production of eggs rather than chicken's flesh, yet scant mention is made of the fact that half of the chicks will be male despite the fact that the companies do undertake to rehome both hens and cockerels if schools are unwilling or unable to keep the hatched animals. Opposition to schemes such as Living Eggs (including Animal Aid (2013) and Oppose Living Eggs (no date)) have claimed that 'rehomed' cockerels have minimal life expectancy before being sent to slaughter. Living Eggs acknowledges that rehoming cockerels is problematic because they have no commercial value alive, and couch it as an issue of fairness that schools should not return more males than females to them, but do not comment on the life expectancy of any of the chicks once they have been 'rehomed' (Living Eggs 2014a). A similar company (The Happy Chick Company (2009), sponsored by supermarket egg producers The Happy Egg Company) acknowledges that the fate of their cockerels may not be as rosy as the rehoming discourse paints: 'we understand that many males are destined "for the pot". But up until that point, they also deserve to run in the sun, chase the insects and feel the grass under their feet'. Thus the scheme reinforces the leitmotif that humans have a duty of care to nonhuman animals that are identified as 'farmed' animals, but that ultimately to use them is normal and proper, in fact an unavoidable 'destiny'. The language of destiny elides human responsibility for deliberately killing cockerels and constructs human violence as beneficent, as if its victims ought to be grateful for their time 'in the sun' prior to execution. Likewise, the formulation, 'we understand' makes it seem as if the Happy Chick Company had discovered an unfortunate truth, rather than being directly culpable for the needless confinement and death of the animals they exploit for profit.

The Living Eggs website provides materials for classroom activities according to different student ages (Living Eggs 2013c). The focus of the suggested activities broadly align with the processes we have described elsewhere, with emotional relationships and functions of the chicks giving way to 'thingification': the instantiation of ever greater distance between humans (in this case children) and other animals, under the direction of adult educators and commercial interests. The class activity materials aimed at 5 to 7 year olds include headings such as 'Personal, Social and Emotional Development', 'Community Cohesion' and 'Expressive Art and Design' (Living Eggs 2014b), while suggested activities for 11 to 14 year olds include 'Bungee Egg Drop', 'The Great Egg Drop' and 'Investigate a Frozen Egg' (Living Eggs 2014c). These activities, therefore, move from a focus on affective relationships in the younger age groups, to a more explicitly instrumental use of the eggs as objects of investigation in the activities for older children. Tellingly, Living Eggs also claims that it 'promotes socialisation and caring' (Living Eggs 2013b). The theme of 'caring' through controlling other animals is key to the maintenance of human dominance, the construction of other animal dependence on humans, and the attenuation of the subjectivity of other animals (see Cole 2011). Rather than encouraging 'caring' then, school hatcheries duplicitously train children in moral indifference to the instrumentalization of other animals and therefore inculcate amorality in general: the opposite of what the UK education system ostensibly intends for its young citizens under the aegis of PSHE.

The RSPCA provides guidance for schools on the topic of using living nonhuman animals in school activities (RSPCA no date). They discourage keeping animals in schools, instead advising that animals should be seen by children in what it refers to, apparently without irony, as their 'natural environment': 'Giving young people access to farms is potentially a good way of teaching them about farm animals and where their food comes from' (RSPCA no date: 6). As we argued in Chapter 2, the appending of spatializing adjectives to 'animal' discursively naturalizes their confinement in 'appropriate' locations in Figure 2.1. The report concludes by promoting the RSPCA's 'Freedom Food' farm assurance produce labelling scheme, used on 'animal products' which meet the organization's welfare standards, and encourages schools to adopt 'animal friendly' menus for school meals, 'e.g. using Freedom Food-labelled products' (RSPCA no date: 14). So the report seeks to reinforce two of the key processes we identify throughout this book: to confine certain types of nonhuman animal use to particular spaces and for specific instrumental purposes, purposes which inevitably terminate in the killing of those animals; hardly the act of an animal's 'friend'.

Melson's (2005) research indicated that although poorly documented, the keeping of living nonhuman animals by schools is not uncommon. Figures from the Royal Society of Chemistry in 2005 found that 18 per cent of primary and secondary schools (ages 5–18) in the UK keep small mammals, and 14 per cent keep giant African land snails. The use of woodlice in choice chambers, an experimental method where live woodlice are given a choice between two chambers of contrasting controlled environments in order to see which they prefer, is reported by 89 per cent of schools (Royal Society of Chemistry 2005). This final, widely used practice involving nonhuman animals anticipates later school activities in which nonhuman animals are subjects (or more accurately objects, as they are used after death) of scientific experiment and enquiry, ultimately anticipating the activity of vivisection as appropriate in the accumulation of human knowledge.

CLEAPSS, formerly known as the Consortium of Local Education Authorities for the Provision of Science Services, is an advisory service controlled by its membership, which is made up of Local Authorities (formerly Local Education Authorities) throughout the British Isles (excluding Scotland). It provides advice services to schools across the 4–18 age groups. Their resources for schools include 'Student Safety Sheets', covering health and safety issues relating to procedures conducted in school science lessons, written in a format designed to be directly accessible to children. The Safety Sheet on 'Animals (living)' states:

> It is illegal to treat vertebrates in a manner causing pain, suffering, distress or lasting harm. Such cruelty might result from some experiments, poor handling, unsuitable housing or inadequate feeding. Some animals may bite and some people may be allergic to hairs, skin, scales, feathers, droppings, etc. Some animals can present a health hazard, although the risk of diseases being passed to humans is usually low but may be higher for farm animals. Wild animals can harbour diseases and parasites, especially if injured. Obtaining animals from *reputable sources*, preventing contact with wild species and adopting good hygiene practices will usually make the risk insignificant. A few species present higher risks and should be avoided. Bees and farm animals need special facilities and specialist knowledge. Some native species are protected and must not be brought in from the wild. It is illegal to release any non-native species into the wild. (CLEAPSS 2013: 89, emphasis added)

Here we see the issue of space become an important determinant of use, not just a consequence: confinement of nonhumans in other contexts or for other purposes ('reputable sources' vs 'wild animals') becomes a marker of appropriateness for use of nonhuman animals in schools. Furthermore, the commercial exploitation of nonhuman animals for experimentation is constructed as a 'reputable' activity, as a contribution to the education of children; anthroparchal instrumentalization underpins the value-rational rhetoric of educative practices.

Dead Animals

The use of nonhuman animals in primary and secondary school science curricula is still widespread: 28 per cent of schools in the UK carry out dissections of rats' bodies, 52 per cent carry out eyeball dissections, 70 per cent demonstrate the inflation of sheep's lungs and 87 per cent carry out heart dissections (Royal Society of Chemistry 2005). Restrictions on which animals' body parts can be used in school science experiments are detailed in the Specified Risk Materials (SRM) regulations which address BSE (Bovine Spongiform Encephalopathy) risk, and which are defined in EC Regulation 999/2001. Eyes from sheep, goats and cows must come from animals under 12 months old, although other animals are not covered by these regulations. Regulations mobilize concerns resulting from the infectivity risk of a specific agent, but contribute to separation and demarcation processes of animals in the school space, and therefore their role in children's lives. Other animals' body parts are highly sensible in these educative practices, but the killing practices that led to those parts being in the classroom are non-sensible, mirroring the relation between 'farmed' animals and the cultural ubiquity of 'animal products' in Figure 2.1. CLEAPSS's advice suggests that schools cultivate relationships with local butchers for the supply of 'bits' that retain all the parts of organs deemed necessary for classroom dissections, but caution that availability and 'intactness' of organs may not be the only consideration teachers should address:

> Thus anything that you can obtain through *normal channels* should not be SRM and could therefore be used. However, you may get more hassle than you need if eyes from cattle are dissected, students go home and tell their parents what they were doing in science today and parents freak out, complaining to the principal, chair of governing body, local newspapers etc.! You also need to consider the suitability of pigs' eyes if you have pupils with religious/cultural objections to handling material from pigs. (CLEAPSS 2013: 1, emphasis added)

The CLEAPSS Safety Sheet 'Animals (dead) and animal parts' (CLEAPSS 2013) echoes this demarcation of the appropriateness of this particular use of animals using criteria relating to their species and source – so their use by humans in the context of these school experiments is, again, as with the use of living nonhuman animals, determined to a great degree by whether they had previously been deemed appropriate for other types of human use which also occupy the south-eastern 'killing zone' of Figure 2.1:

> Whole animals obtained from a *reputable biological supplier* should be safe to use; but road kill, for example, might be infected. Items intended for human consumption, available from butchers, abattoirs and fishmongers, should

also be safe … Some people have cultural or religious objections to handling particular species. Some people object to killing animals, whether for food, medical research or dissection in schools. Fewer people object to the use of material intended for human consumption available from butchers, abattoirs and fishmongers. (CLEAPSS 2013: 88, emphasis added)

The CLEAPSS guidance then, tacitly works with the logic of Figure 2.1 in order to further the specific rationality of dissection as an educational practice. It negotiates the complex terrain of the conceptual map to ensure that dissection can proceed without disturbing the positioning of animals elsewhere. This has the further consequence that the difficulty of the 'some people' who object to any instrumental killing of other animals can be marginalized.

Killing Animals: School 'Farmers'

In recent years there have been a number of high profile media stories in the UK (e.g. BBC 2013c, 2013e, *The Guardian* 2009, *The Daily Telegraph* 2009) about school activities which involve the keeping of live animals on school premises in order that the animals are then slaughtered and consumed by some members of the school community. Below, we discuss three examples of this phenomenon, and the common themes it raises in terms of the processes we describe throughout this book.

In 2009 Eastfield Primary School in Leicestershire raised pigs in order to be made into sausages, which were then sold to students' parents to raise school funds. Similarly in 2013 Peasenhall Primary School in Suffolk raised three pigs to be slaughtered and sent to a local butcher to be made into sausages (BBC 2013c, 2013e, *The Daily Telegraph* 2009). In 2009 Lydd Primary School in Kent reared a 'wether' (a castrated male lamb) who they named Marcus, who was slaughtered, dismembered and offered as 'meat' products in a school raffle (*The Guardian* 2009, *The Independent* 2009).

These examples share a number of common features which illustrate many of the practices and norms discussed throughout this book and represented in Figure 2.1: that the activities educate children with complete information about food production, that the deaths of these animals are sad but necessary, and that resistance to them chiefly revolves around the appropriateness of these activities in the physical and conceptual space of the school.

Firstly, all of the examples were partly justified by claims of children 'knowing the full story'. The head teacher at Lydd Primary was quoted in *The Guardian* newspaper as saying 'The aim was to educate the children in *all aspects* of farming life' (*The Guardian* 2009, emphasis added), a Peasenhall Primary teacher claimed the students would be involved in '*every stage* of the pigs' journey from making a home for the pigs to marketing the meat' (BBC News 2013e, emphasis added), and Eastfield Primary's head teacher similarly justified their project, which also involved the farming of sheep, ducks and chickens in addition to the pigs that attracted media attention, by rhetorically asking 'do we want children to grow up in ignorance, or do we want them to grow up making informed choices?' (*The Daily Telegraph* 2009). This veneer of openness, honesty and completeness of information is, of course, a careful and delicate falsehood. Lydd Primary's local County Council, for example, strongly refuted suggestions that children visited an abattoir as part of the project, to see Marcus or any other animal killed (*The Guardian* 2009). The children involved in these exercises do not see the slaughter of the animals they are encouraged to care for, with the only parts of the process visible to them being those parts which were already apparent in terms of the equatorial line in Figure 2.1: the affective relationships forged with 'pseudo pets' during their lives on school premises and the 'meat' products they consume. The zone in the south easterly region of Figure 2.1 remains non-sensible, unattended and unchallenged. Under a banner of 'teaching them everything' these projects transmit through a different means, all that children either already know, or learn elsewhere (*and no more*), through the socialization processes discussed throughout this book (see for example, the discussion of Hamleys toy store in Chapter 5, and games such as Farmville and Family Farm in Chapter 8).

Secondly, these care-and-kill school projects present the deaths of these animals as both inevitable and necessary if perhaps emotionally uncomfortable, but that the necessity should overcome the discomfort; instrumental rationality must triumph. As such it can be seen as part of the process of emotional detachment and loss of sentimentality for other animals that we have identified as being a part of growing up elsewhere in this book (see also Stewart and Cole 2009). These school projects also bear comparison with Jovian Parry's (2010) analysis of the slaughter of nonhuman animals in popular television 'celebrity chef' programmes, such as the two UK shows *The F Word* (2005–2010), presented by Gordon Ramsay and *Jamie's Great Italian Escape* (2005), presented by Jamie Oliver. Parry argues that, within a patriarchal framework, these shows trivialize affective concern for other animals through its feminization, while asserting the instrumental imperatives of slaughter through its masculinization. That is, they discursively reinforce the non-sensibility of the south-east of Figure 2.1 at the very moment that they purport to reveal it, because what they 'reveal' are other animals who *must be objectified*. A similar process can therefore be argued to be at work in school care-and-kill projects. For instance, the deaths of the pigs at Peasenhall was necessary, according to one 6-year-old boy's account of the project 'so the humans stay alive for longer' (BBC 2013e) and according to one teacher there 'We've discussed that we're going to feel very sad … But they've all said "we like eating sausages"' (BBC News 2013e). Similarly, one Eastfield parent acknowledged that the process was both difficult and necessary: 'Children have to learn where their food comes from, but this seems insensitive' (*The Daily Telegraph* 2009). Lydd teachers were reported in *The Guardian* newspaper as claiming that the exercise taught students the 'reality' that meat comes from animals (*The Guardian* 2009). Apart from the extremely dubious claims of 'honesty' that these practices use as legitimation, this elevation of gustatory pleasure over the pain of complicity with killing the innocent is a bizarre lesson in emotional maturity: eat your way past sadness. The 6-year-olds' account also suggests some quite blatant lies have been taught about the necessity of animal products for human survival. It is also worth noting that the impact of these discourses and practices on existing vegan or vegetarian children at these schools does not apparently feature in the thinking of the staff at the schools involved. As we discuss in Chapter 9, vegan children themselves can and could be excellent educators about the 'reality' of human use of other animals.

The third common theme in all of these incidents is that opposition to the schools' plans is very much couched in terms of the appropriateness of the practices in the school space. Paul O'Grady, the television presenter, made a well-publicized offer (which the school refused) to purchase Marcus from Eastfield Primary and rehome him on his land with 11 other sheep he owned, and keep the Eastfield students updated on his well-being (*The Independent* 2009): 'The sheep that go to slaughter are not made pets of ... But a lamb that you hand-rear, that you personalise, that you give it a name and then announce that is going off to the abattoir is wrong. You can't do that' (*The Guardian* 2009). O'Grady here expresses what we might interpret as discomfort resulting from the disturbance of the organization of Figure 2.1: the repositioning of animals from the north-west towards the south-east. A parent of a student at Lydd was quoted by the BBC as saying: 'I feel this is the same as my daughter coming home from school to find her pet rabbit bubbling away on the stove in a stew. My daughter was told it was no different to buying lamb from the supermarket. I really don't think this is the same thing' (BBC 2009). Of course, in almost every sense the scenarios this parent describes are the same as the school projects – the confinement, killing, dismembering and eating of nonhuman animals. What is different are merely the places in which these activities are occurring, and the actors involved: the school rather than the farm or factory, and children and teachers rather than farm and shop workers.

Replacing Living Animals with Virtual Counterparts: Farmland

Echoing the farming simulation games discussed in Chapter 8, educational materials designed as games, or including a gaming element provide one alternative to the use of living or dead nonhuman animals, but without offering an alternative educational message to those practices involving actual nonhumans. One such example of this type of material is Farmland (European Commission no date b), an online video game, developed by the European Commission, which claims to educate children between the ages of 9 and 12 about 'animal welfare' on a 'livestock' farm. The website is translated into 23 European languages and produced with the support of the Directorate General for Health and Consumers. The game and information is supported with downloadable materials for school teachers and students.

A series of web pages prepare children for playing the game in which they take charge of a virtual 'livestock' farm. These pages are illustrated with human characters who reappear in both the game and the classroom activity materials. All of the human characters are Caucasian in appearance, and conform to a number of phenotypical, gendered and other social stereotypes. There are three female characters: Bérénice, Amandine and Jaqueline. Bérénice guides the player through the game, is 'in charge' of the 'broiler chickens', and introduces a supermarket game. She is depicted as a young blonde female wearing her long hair in pigtails. When the game was first launched, she was dressed in denim shorts and a white shirt exposing her midriff, and although her physical shape remains the same she is now depicted in a long sleeved jersey and full length jeans, apart from in the final supermarket game where her original costume remains. Amandine manages the pig pen, and is also depicted as a young female with long hair, and an accentuated slim waist and broad hips. Jaqueline does not appear at the farm, but in the supermarket task. She is an elderly thick set woman with white hair, a shawl and spectacles. There are five male human characters: Marc, Bertrand, Miguel, Paolo and Lionel. Marc is associated with the pig pen in the game, and is portrayed as being in charge of maintenance, wearing a tool belt over his clothes and carrying a toolkit. Bertrand is in charge of cleanliness, and cleans the cowshed in the game. He is a thick set red haired youth dressed in baseball cap, dungarees and a T-shirt which recalls the Nike sportswear logo. Miguel, who 'trains' the laying hens, is of large build, with overly emphasized broad shoulders and muscular arms. He is described as a former paratrooper and wears camouflage trousers and a green beret tucked into his shirt. Paolo, who works in the cowshed, is an elderly man wearing half unfastened dungarees and carrying pitchfork and bucket. Finally, Lionel is of similar broad, muscular build to Miguel, and is described as a former Formula 1 driver: he is in charge of the transport of animals. These depictions recall the gendering of humans, and their 'appropriate' relationships with nonhumans, described in Chapter 5, in addition to employing the 'cute', cartoonish style of representations described in Chapter 6. Information pages introduce illustrated by these characters introduce pigs, 'broiler' chickens, laying hens, 'dairy calves' and 'dairy cows', with each human character described as being in charge of the animals and processes described.

Throughout these information pages, the messages emphasize to children that the food functions of the animals are 'what they're for', and the necessity of guardianship of them by the farmers 'for their own good'; human practices determine the meaning of nonhuman animal life. For example, the 'laying hens' page states that 'Laying hens are reared to produce eggs' and 'Each hen is usually kept one year for the production of eggs' (European Commission no date g). These extracts unquestioningly reinforce the notion that the production of eggs for humans is the only purpose of hens' lives. It also elides the radical foreshortening of those lives as a consequence of 'the production of eggs'; that is, human responsibility for killing hens' who have only been permitted to live for a fraction of their natural lifespans. Furthermore, the farmers who are confining, controlling and in collaboration with the slaughter industry, ultimately prematurely ending the lives of these animals are presented as being responsible guardians who are needed in order for those animals to live. This is achieved through statements such as 'Pigs rely on humans to provide them with the housing conditions and materials necessary to develop properly' (European Commission no date h) and 'Dairy calves are separated from their mother soon after birth and are artificially fed so that the mother's milk can be used for food production. Soon after calves are born they are fed colostrum, which is a liquid containing all the vitamins and minerals needed to fight disease' (European Commission no date e). Both of these themes, of purpose and guardianship combine to present human involvement in the form of farming as a natural and necessary process: dairy cows 'need to give birth to calves on a regular basis, so that they can produce the necessary milk ... Farmers need to be attentive to dairy cows which are producing a lot of milk because they can be prone to many diseases' (European Commission no date f). These knowledge claims instantiate a hierarchized distance between children and farmed animals, legitimating the latter's instrumentalization but all the while euphemized as value-rational 'care'. So, even when some of the exploitative practices of farming are finally exposed to children (after systematic obfuscation in family and mass media socialization practices), their discursive construction reasserts their non-sensibility as exploitative, or as ethically questionable, from children's perspectives.

The 'Transport of Animals' information page, illustrated with a picture of 'Lionel' the truck driver, also emphasizes the guardianship of humans over nonhuman animals, highlighting how stressed, thirsty and tired the animals get during transportation, and the need to attend to these issues, but not questioning the purpose of their transportation for slaughter, talking instead in only vague terms of a 'destination': 'Once the animals arrive at their destination, great care must be taken in getting them off the truck' (European Commission no date i).

With no interim stage between transport and shops described, the next stage of the game process covered by Farmland is the supermarket, introduced by Jaqueline. Corresponding to this stage of the resource, the educational materials explain how consumers can shop their way to a clear conscience: 'So remember – be aware, and check the labels when you go to buy food. By doing this, you too can help make a real difference to animal welfare' (European Commission no date a). Remaining uncritical about the constructed food function of nonhuman animals, the materials reinforce the ubiquity of animal products in food items: 'In shops, all types of food, from pizza to ice cream, contain these products' (European Commission no date a). Living without dependence on these products is therefore unthinkable within the world of Farmland; the boundaries of anthroparchal discourse are vigilantly guarded.

The game itself opens with an aerial view of the locations of all the gameplay activities. In the foreground, and occupying the largest area of the screen, is the 'farm' and its buildings where the different 'livestock' animals are confined, with a single transporter truck at the side of the 'farm' site. All of these items can be clicked to open up a different game activity (described below). In the background of the opening vista are two other areas, joined to the 'farm' by a road. One is the supermarket which can be clicked to play the shopping activity with Jaqueline. The final area, located on the road between the 'farm' and supermarket, is a large white building with no signage and several transporter trucks parked outside. This area cannot be clicked on, has no description, and has no depictions of either humans or animals. In Farmland, the abattoir is literally unmentionable.

The activities in the farm area involve different 'goals' for the player. In the 'broiler chicken' game (described as a henhouse, despite it housing the only named nonhuman in the entire game, Théodore, apparently male and therefore not a hen), the goal is to raise Théodore to maturity as quickly as possible, as the farm have received an order for three crates of chickens. This is achieved by guiding Théodore around the screen to food and water supplies, taking care not to bump into other moving chickens 'Or Théodore will lose a life' (European Commission no date b). If such a collision occurs, there is a flurry of feathers on screen and Théodore lies motionless on the floor as if dead for a few seconds, before resuming his chase around the screen. In the 'laying hens' game, introduced by Miguel the former paratrooper, the goal is to get the hens fit so that they can lay as many eggs as possible. In the cowshed game, introduced by Paolo, the 'Dr in bovine dietetics', the task is to ready a calf for the butchers by feeding him and making him grow as quickly as possible with appropriate nutrition in order that 'it produces good quality meat' (*sic*) (European Commission no date b). A second cowshed activity focuses on the management of viral threats to the dairy herd, with the player cleaning the shed in order to 'save the cows' (European Commission no date b). In the pig pen, the player is told they can care for multiple needs of the pigs by improving the physical structure of the barn in order to make an environment from which they can supply good quality 'meat' to the supermarket. The mission of the transporter game is to take the animals from the 'farm' to their vaguely framed 'destination' in the most comfortable conditions possible in the shortest time possible. The clock on the game runs down, and as long as the 'needs' levels are maintained (water, food, sleep, straw), the player succeeds, without an actual destination being depicted. All of the games therefore focus on the food production uses of the animals rather than their well-being as an end in its own right; instrumental action trumps value-rational action. Despite Farmland's rhetoric of respect and care, and the frequently repeated tagline of 'Respect, health and quality for a happy farm', animal welfare is only given value inasmuch as it contributes to productivity of animal products. The lives of the nonhuman animals represented in Farmland ultimately have no inherent value.

The game is accompanied by classroom materials for teachers and students, which include class plans and activity suggestions, reinforcing, often much more explicitly, the processes covered in the game which position the consumption of nonhuman animals as normal, natural and responsible. Mollified by a recurrent reinforcement of the importance of 'respect' towards farmed animals, the handbooks combine images of the game's human characters, red love hearts, animal food products and farmed animals. They explicitly state, and emphasize, that farmed animals are 'not pets', but reared for the purpose of the production of their meat, milk or eggs for human consumption. For example, a 'True or False' quiz activity for 10–12 year olds includes the statements 'There are calves reared for beef production and dairy calves' and 'Calves reared for beef production are kept with their mothers and are often raised outdoors' as 'true', but 'Calves reared for dairy production can also stay with their mothers' as 'false' (European Commission no date d: 8) without any acknowledgement that the dichotomous taxonomy of 'beef' and 'dairy' calves or the co-habitation of mothers and calves are imposed, human constructs: objectifying knowledge that legitimates the domination of farmed animals. 'Our Food: Dear meat diary' is a group activity encouraging children to discuss how often they eat 'meat', and asks children to think of alternatives that they could substitute 'meat' for once a week (European Commission no date c: 34). So while it raises the issue of 'meat' reduction, the exercise clearly establishes regular 'meat' eating as the norm, with the teacher's notes clarifying 'This exercise is not intended to support a vegetarian diet' (European Commission no date d: 37). Reading the materials as a whole, we would go further and say that none of the exercises even acknowledge that any of the students might already be, or consider being vegetarian or vegan at all. Children are reminded, before doing these exercises that potentially open up animal consumption practices to question, to 'Always have fun' while engaging with the work. This deliberate trivialization of ethical issues as 'fun' might be read as a powerful distraction from the instrumentalizing direction of children's learning and a suppression of potentially more threatening affective responses from children, such as sadness or anger at the exploitation of other animals; responses that are explored in some of the vegan socialization materials discussed in Chapter 9.

Conclusion

Taken together, the educational discourses and practices that we have described in this chapter serve to position farmed animals, their representations and 'animal products' according to our model, illustrated in Figure 7.1.

School food practices, despite the friction with the privatized food practice of the home, recall and reinforce domestic food socialization in respect of the primacy of 'animal products', which are highly sensible in school canteens and snack shops. At the same time, living nonhuman animals in schools purport to provide a means towards making the 'reality' of the south-eastern regions of Figure 7.1 sensible. However, as we have argued, in practice they are exploited in order to legitimate the continued exploitation of their farmed counterparts, as well as being exploited as ('meat'), or for (eggs), human food themselves. Dead animals' body parts as educational tools in the classroom similarly depend on

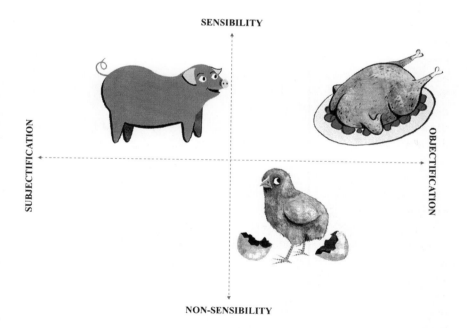

Figure 7.1 Exploitation as destiny: Educating children in the 'proper' positions of other animals

'farm' exploitation and on the taken-for-granted acceptance of 'farming' other animals as legitimate, a legitimacy already established for children across the socialization sites considered earlier in this book. Meanwhile, the Farmland game and its associated information focus subjectivity on the human characters and the animated representations of the animals, and emphasize the guardianship of the farmed animals by the human characters, and by association the activities of 'livestock' farming. Thus, the representations of humans, nonhuman animals, the fictionalized image of the farm, and animal food products are made sensible in the northern regions of Figure 7.1, masking the realities of the treatment and experiences of nonhuman animals farmed for the production of food in the south-eastern regions, most notably through the total absence of reference to the slaughter process. Education practices and discourses as a whole serve to objectify the nonhuman animals represented, by identifying animals as little more than machines for the generation of 'useful' body parts (whether food or experimental tools). Value-rational action for children in respect of farmed animals in their educational practice is therefore reduced to being enjoined to assist in preparing them for slaughter in school food projects, or searching for labels on food as the alpha and omega of human 'care' for farmed animals.

Chapter 8
Playing with Power: Virtual Relations with Other Animals in Digital Media

In this chapter, we discuss the practice of manipulating digitized representations of other animals, particularly those found in social media and console games. The chapter focuses on representatives of two genres: farming simulations on Facebook, such as Farmville and Family Farm, and Nintendogs and Nintendogs + cats, a group of 'pet'-ownership simulations that run on the Nintendo DS handheld games console. These were chosen because of their representational style which echoes that highlighted in the family, educational and mass media sites that we have discussed so far: anthropomorphism, infantilism and 'cuteness'. The two genres focus on two distinct types of 'real' human–nonhuman animal relations: farming and 'pet'-keeping. However, the style of representations, the discourses in which they are embedded and the modes of gameplay, echo each other and synergistically reproduce extant anthroparchal relations, while simultaneously enjoining players to rehearse those relations. Digital games therefore integrate practice and representation, continuing a theme noted in relation to the display of 'cute' animal character paraphernalia from cutie magazines in Chapter 6. 'Practice' is pertinent in two senses in digital games, in that the manipulation of digital representations is itself a practice through which human–nonhuman animal relations are reproduced, while also being practice, in the sense of training or rehearsal, for non-virtual human–animal relations, especially eating animals and owning animals as 'pets'. Both of them foreground animals' dependency on human control, euphemized as care; their willing complicity in subordinate roles to humans; and concomitantly the unthinkability of nonhuman agency without hegemonic human–nonhuman animal relations. Finally, both genres, and especially farming simulations, make vegan alternatives to exploitation unplayable as successful strategies. This produces a powerful normalizing effect in respect of (euphemized) exploitation being represented as 'just the way things are'.

The significance of digital games is that they enable players to put into practice (in both senses) many of the lessons from other socialization sites that were discussed in chapters 5–7 in the course of gameplay. Of course, these games are not exclusively played by children. Just as adults may persist with their affection towards soft toys, or retain an emotional connection with animal characters from favourite stories and films, so too they may find pleasure in the way these games recall some of the affective glow of human–nonhuman animal relations in childhood, as well as their intrinsic rewards for 'successful' gameplay. Unlike console games, farming simulations also depend on players having the ability to make online payments to generate revenue, thereby entangling the pleasures of consumerism with the pleasures of human supremacy. This motif, of humans being rewarded for successfully manipulating and controlling other animals, and converting their bodies and secretions into consumable 'products', brings into focus the defining *privilege* of anthroparchy. Ultimately, what separates human players and characters in digital games from the nonhuman animal representations is the multiplicity of rewards and satisfactions for agential behaviour that are on offer to humans, compared with the paucity of automatized behaviours that are prescribed for other animals. In spite of their anthropomorphization, digitized animals display a much narrower range of actions than their living counterparts, so that there is a roughly inverse relationship between human privilege and nonhuman animal constraint; in fact a good approximation to hegemonic human–nonhuman animal relations in the non-virtual world. This relationship between privilege and control exemplifies the distance between subjectified humans and objectified animal others that we mapped out in Figure 2.1 and will be further explored in our analyses of digital representations below. Continuing our theme of an idealized chronological socialization narrative, we begin with a discussion of the Nintendogs series of games, which is designed to be playable by younger children ('made for ages 7+'), before turning to the farming simulation genre, which is pitched at a teenage and upwards audience, given Facebook's policy of only making accounts available to people aged 13 and over.

Nintendogs: 'It's love in a box!'

Nintendogs and Nintendogs + cats are a series of games for the hand-held Nintendo DS console that simulate 'pet'-ownership. Despite the use of dogs and cats in the games' titles, the series specifically simulates the ownership of *puppies and kittens*: 'There's nothing quite like taking home an adorable puppy or kitten. Teaching, caring for, and loving your furry new friend is an experience unlike any other' (Nintendo 2011a). Promotion of the games foregrounds 'pet'-ownership as an affective practice, exemplified in the slogan 'It's love in a box!' However, at the same time, affective practice is instrumentalized in relation to the rehearsal of non-virtual human–nonhuman animal relations. As one player puts it on the Nintendogs + cats website: 'It's a great game for all ages. Good for teaching people to be responsible pet owners, and good for those who can't keep real pets. I highly recommend this series!' ('Sandura', cited in Nintendo 2011d). As we explored in chapters 4 and 5, 'pet'-keeping is constructed as perhaps the most benevolent of all human–nonhuman animal relationships in Figure 2.1, not least because of its edificatory function for children, providing a testing ground for the development of empathy and care for a more vulnerable other. However, as we discussed in Chapter 6, childhood empathy is carefully disciplined and directed away from the most vulnerable other animals: those confined to the south-east of Figure 2.1. In this section, we explore the construction of 'pets' in Nintendogs and the more recent Nintendogs + cats, through a description of some key elements of gameplay, and the promotion of the series on the Nintendo website.

Cute Capitalism 1

Representations of puppies and kittens within the Nintendogs series tend towards realism, but the 'pet' as a type of animal in Figure 2.1 is always already a cutified icon (see Chapter 4), and especially so when they are infants. As we examined in Chapter 6, puppies and kittens are especially potent cute symbols and a crucial aspect of the gameplay in the series is the eternal youth, and eternal life, of the puppies and kittens. This temporal ossification of animals within a perpetual present disembeds them from the biological-chronological life course, which in turn enables their objectification as edification, as entertainment or as repositories of sentiment for players. In common with the construction of animal cuteness throughout the socialization process, Nintendogs + cats are always ready to respond with affection to the ministrations of the player. Uncomfortable truths about animals' ageing, illness and death, or 'deviant' behaviour that resists codification in accordance with their objectified 'uses', are written out of existence by the games' programmers. In these ways, the agency of Nintendogs + cats is tightly circumscribed: they can never contest the knowledge that constructs the 'pet' category in Figure 2.1, and furthermore they reproduce that knowledge in every aspect of their interactions with human players.

The game series exemplifies the disciplining of empathy: the naïve utopia of human–'pet' interaction that they construct obliterates the exploitation that is inherent in the non-virtual 'pet' industry, and the misery of the farmed animals whose abominated flesh ('unfit for human consumption') feeds the loved puppy or kitten, notwithstanding the minority of cats or dogs fed with a vegan diet. While the denial of this violence is absolute within the games, commodification itself is highly visible, and integral to the facilitation of affective practice; the players' relationship with puppies and kittens is mediated through capitalism as they are obtained within the game through being purchased from a kennel, and of course the games and consoles themselves are commodities. The tacit rhetoric of the games invites us to reflect on how else might a child enjoy a pleasurable and loving relationship with another animal, without the mediation of capital: 'The game also teaches children about how to take care of another living thing and how you have to earn money to buy new things' ('Courtney', Nintendogs 2011d). As well as encounters with free-living animals, many children and adults *do* enjoy enduring relationships with other animals liberated from the south-east of Figure 2.1, from factory 'farms', vivisection laboratories and other places of confinement as well as abandoned animal companions exiled from the safe zone in the north-west of Figure 2.1. However, these non-commoditized, and arguably value-rational relationships (see Chapter 9), are not the ones that are celebrated in Nintendogs + cats. The human privilege of spatially and discursively locating other animals is exemplified in the ownership relation; puppies might be played with in the kennels, but there they must remain until purchase, because they are owned by the kennel. After purchase, the correct location of the puppies is in human-defined and controlled domestic (in-game home) or recreational (in-game park and urban) space. After buying a puppy, the player takes her or him to their virtual home. It is only in this context, at this time, that the puppy comes indoors from the garden/kennel set-up. The player is then informed that she or he is nervous in unfamiliar surroundings, and stroking settles her or him down; affective practice is trained in the player. But before any other of the puppies needs are tended to, the training of the puppy begins, as the player is informed that now would be a good time to teach her or him to sit. From the beginning of the gameplay therefore, the inequality in the relationship is clear: puppies exist for the pleasure of the player, but their representations indicate that they are perfectly content in that relationship, displaying no regret for the loss of contact with their erstwhile kennel playmates. Meanwhile, the player can enter into or leave interaction with the puppy at will, just as can non-virtual human owners.

In a familiar motif from other socialization sites, Nintendogs + cats cutifies the consumption process itself, as well as the representations of animals within the games. Taking an example of the gameplay in Nintendogs, the game begins with a choice between 'Buy' and 'Look' in the idyllic surroundings of idealized kennels, with background sounds of running water, bird song and playful barking. If the player chooses to 'look' (or perhaps, window-shop), she or he sees three puppies in a fenced back garden. The puppies are playing together until the player arrives, then they run barking to the screen. If the player does not respond they retreat, sit or lie down, walk around, but do not resume playing together; the human–animal interaction is paramount and analogously to cutie magazines and soft toys, Nintendogs are represented as focused on satisfying the desire of the human player. The puppy that the player chooses to interact with (by touching the screen with a stylus) scrabbles at the screen, jumping and wagging her or his tail furiously. The player can use the stylus to 'stroke' the puppy, who rolls over and presents different parts of her or his body for attention. Sometimes 'stars' appear to come out of the puppy, training correct affective practice on the part of the player with a glittery reward. Eventually the other two puppies approach the fourth wall and vie for the player's attention, but not each other's. If the player chooses to 'buy', she or he begins with a £1,000 budget, with puppy prices starting at £510. The only puppies available are pure breeds; icons of human manipulation of the reproductive process of other animals, such as 'Miniature Daschund', 'Shih Tzu' and 'Siberian Husky'. The puppies, who appear on screen in threes ready to be bought (in assorted colours and genders), must be separated from each other; the player can only start the game with an individual puppy. The puppies also appear with a brief description of their characters, and after purchase, they are named by the player. These individualizing features exemplify the relative subjectification of animal companions in comparison with other types in Figure 2.1. By contrast, representations of animals in farming simulations are not named and have no individualizing characteristics. However, the puppies in Nintendogs are only individualized through their commodification; buying and owning carries with it the privilege of naming, recalling the Gnat's discussion with Alice, discussed in Chapter 2.

The privilege of naming is echoed in the privilege of regulating access to social space. The DS console is a hand-held and therefore portable device, so that the players 'pet' can be carried around as a more or less constant companion, which also allows a merging of a real human walk with a virtual walk for the Nintendog within the console. The developers of Nintendogs + cats have taken further advantage of this capacity by embedding a 'StreetPass' feature within the game, so that players carrying their console who pass each other can automatically exchange game data. This facilitates the appearance of each other's 'pets' within an in-game park. In a conversation between Nintendo's Global President, Saturo Iwata, and the games' developers, it is reported that this makes it possible for players to 'give presents or send short comments bragging about your pet' (Konno, cited in Nintendo 2011b) and to 'brag about your pet on a worldwide scale!' (Iwata, cited in Nintendo 2011b). Players are also encouraged to 'Pose with your pet!' via an in-game camera feature, and to take in-game photos of their puppies and share them with other players: 'Did you teach it [sic] a new trick, or are they just acting cute? Don't miss out on the magic moment! Any time the inspiration strikes, you can fire up the Nintendo 3DS camera in-game to take a photo of your pet' (Nintendo 2011c). Therefore, the console technology now fosters the performance of affective practice towards (representations of) other animals, deepening the motif of the performative cute identity facilitated by cutie magazines (see Chapter 6). Furthermore, it illustrates the potential of digital media to disseminate anthroparchal relations, enhancing the potential profitability of Nintendo and the anthroparchal culture industries more generally. This theme of the performativity of anthroparchal relations is pursued in our analysis of the Facebook farming simulation genre.

Facebook Farming Simulation Games

Farming simulation games form a distinctive subgenre in digital media. Titles include Farmville, Farmville 2, Family Farm, Gourmet Ranch and Happy Farm (aka Pocket Farm). To give a sense of the popularity of the genre, Farmville is the longest established of these titles, with over 40 million 'likes' on Facebook at the time of writing, while Farmville 2 can boast over 10 million 'likes', Family Farm about 2 million, Gourmet Ranch over a million and Happy Farm over half a million. The number of games players is also likely to considerably exceed the numbers of 'likers' of their Facebook pages. Farming simulations are not limited to Facebook as a platform, but their presence on social media is especially interesting because of the way this facilitates the quasi-*public* rehearsal of human–nonhuman animal relations. This happens in a number of ways: the encouragement to share in-game achievements with Facebook friends (whether or not those friends are players of the game); gameplay incentives to recruit Facebook friends as new players; 'community' features which reward networking with other players (such as by virtually visiting each other's farms); Facebook pages for the games themselves, which Facebook users can 'like' and where they can post comments about the games; and game-specific forums, also linked from Facebook, where players can network and share tips and game information. Farming simulations also attract fan/player websites with wiki-style information and/or forums for the exchange of tips, tactics and comments about the games. In the subsections which follow, we analyse the representational style and language used within the games. For instance some simulations embed messages to players, which are frequently presented on screen, as the words of in-game characters who talk players through their experience and encourage continued gameplay. We thereby explore how farming simulations 'enchant' instrumental rationality with discourses of affectivity, tradition and value-rationality. Taken together, this makes the bars of Weberian cages that confine the 'real' animals whose experiences make these games possible, very difficult to see.

Cute Capitalism 2

Capitalism is, of course, the impetus behind the production of farming simulation games. These games, aimed at older age groups, make much more explicit reference to profit than the subtler references found in Farmland, discussed in Chapter 7. Income generation is derived not from the sale of the games themselves, which are free to begin playing for any Facebook user, but from the sale of in-game items and shortcuts for real-world currency. The games share an open-ended gameplay experience, which therefore makes the potential income-stream open-ended too. Likewise, the gameplay itself mimics this never fulfilled capitalist ideal of endless profit generation, reinvestment, and business expansion: 'The more animals you have, the more animal products you can sell for a good price' (excerpt from Farmville 2 gameplay). While farming simulations offer myriad 'quick wins' from in-game tasks and missions, they are not apparently designed to be 'completed' as were examples from many older computer game genres, before the flourishing of online multiplayer gaming. The games also offer increasing in-game rewards for daily playing, incentivizing habituation to the games themselves, and by doing so, to the daily rehearsal of anthroparchal human–animal relations. Open-ended gameplay in this genre reveals an imaginary vista of infinite expansion, wealth and control. But, the purposelessness, or irrationality, of that process in respect of any value–rational action is obscured, especially by the integration of affective action with instrumental rationality. This is starkly evident in the cutification of capitalism itself in farming simulation games.

The capitalist instrumentalism of farming simulations is embedded in their gameplay, which is centred on the generating of profit in various in-game currencies. This happens through the trading of the products of players' farms, for instance selling foods manufactured in an in-game kitchen, or utilizing 'products' derived from plants and animals on the players' farms. The celebration of capitalism within farming simulations is not a tacit ideology, but written across the gamer's screen. For example, in the early stages of Farmville 2's gameplay, an in-game farmer character (Walter) greets the human player thus: 'Now that I'm in the business, know of any tricks of the trade? I'm new to this but, oh yes, you look rather new to this as well. Well, no harm in a little competition! Capitalism is king, they say!'

Another Farmville 2 character (Marie) makes clear the instrumental purpose of farming animals: 'Feeling the cycle of farm life yet? Crops and animals form a virtuous cycle … that ends in coins! Let's go!' Marie also invokes nonhuman animal exploitation as a metaphor for capitalist accumulation itself, under a heading 'Milking it', she says 'Feed animals to get their goods to sell for coins!' Meanwhile, Family Farm directly equates the profitability of farmed animals with the cute characteristic of corporeal softness: 'Oh my, these Ostrich Feathers are truly beautiful and soft. I wonder what their market value is. And who knows, maybe we can start thinking about what to make of them later … ?' As this last example suggests, there is not a straightforward revelation of instrumental rationality in the celebration of capitalism within farming simulations; capitalism itself is cutified and wrapped in a cuddly affectivity. To illustrate this further, the 'cycle of farm life' bears inter-textual interpretation in light of the 'circle of life' motif as a song lyric and character monologue in the hit Disney cartoon, *The Lion King* (1994). In both the film and the game, the invoking of cyclical processes (that involve the killing of animals) inscribes their inevitability, so that ethical choices are elided. In *The Lion King*, the device is used to explain away any nascent ethical discomfort with eating animals for the lion cub, and future king, Simba. Affective discourses also layer an emotional pull over (pun intended) the 'naked self-interest [... of] callous "cash payment"' (Marx and Engels 1985: 82) that drives gameplay. In previous work, we have argued that the emotive message of the circle of life can assuage potential discomfort for the audience about their own non-vegan eating practices (Stewart and Cole 2009). In Family Farm, a similar process is at work: the metaphor of a virtuous cycle alludes to innocent and benevolent natural processes, which the human player is just helping along; the implication is that they continue into perpetuity in any case. Invoking cyclical processes helps to naturalize capitalistic exploitation of animals as normal and inevitable, at the same time as dressing it up in the non-threatening garb of nature and tradition. We return to this theme in the next section.

The Rural Machine

The iconography of farming simulations recalls the naïve rural idyll celebrated in farm-related toys and games, advertisements for animal products in the mass media, and educational resources, which we discussed in previous chapters; none of these communicate the experience of most nonhuman animals in the animal-industrial complex (Twine 2012, Noske 1989). The rural idyll in farming simulation games is further contextualized as North American, in that players' farms are typically called 'ranches'. Farm/ranch settings are rural, in verdant green 'natural' surroundings, and in game-characters (including players' avatars) are dressed in stereotypical US 'country' garb. For instance, Farmville 2's Marie is dressed in a 'cowgirl' outfit and rides bareback on a horse into the player's ranch at the start of the game, while Family Farm's Little Darryl wears a cowboy hat, plaid shirt and denim dungarees. Characters in other farming simulations are similarly attired, and ranches across the genre may be decorated with rural icons like straw-stuffed scarecrows or hay bales. The trope is completed with the use of barnyard sound effects (clucking hens, lowing cows, and so on) and country and western style in-game music playing on a loop. The overall effect is to conjure a traditional image of farming and thereby to construct farming itself as traditional social action. In Farmville 2, the timeless tradition of farming is made more explicit, when Marie reports: 'Look what turned up! A page from the old [player's ranch name] Farm Almanac! It's full of lost farm wisdom!'

As Weber argued, traditional social action may be characterized as the least rational in his typology, as it is the closest to automaticity, involving little conscious thought on the part of social actors. The discourse of farming as rural tradition is therefore especially effective at subduing critical reflection about the exploitation of other animals. Paradoxically, the invocation of tradition may be interpreted as a technique for suppressing cognizance of instrumental-rational action at the same time as the latter is celebrated as the *raison d'être* of the gameplay. Capitalism itself is embedded as 'traditional' by the in-game world and the instrumentalization of other animals is likewise traditionalized and simultaneously connected to capitalism. This process ironically carries the ring of historical truth, in light of David Nibert's analysis of the relationship between the historical 'domesecration' of other animals, capitalism and violence in the Americas and beyond (2013, and see Nibert 2002). In the British context, Marx's assertion of the importance of large scale sheep farming and associated violent dispossession of the rural human population in the development of capitalism is also salient (Marx 1887: 667–96). Deforestation as a result of animal farming also transformed the British landscape. However, the celebration of denuded hillsides and a depopulated countryside, from Victorian landscape painting such as Mark Thompson's (1812–1875) *Sheep Walk Cronkley Crags, Teesdale* (1866), up to the present day iconography of the rural tourist industry, collapses tradition and capitalism into the 'natural' order of things. This is exemplified in the conflation of 'traditional' capitalist land use, such as sheep farming and 'nature' in the discourse and practice of Natural England, a governmental body charged with protecting and improving 'England's natural environment' (Natural England 2013). The automaticity of tradition is therefore closely aligned to discourses of 'nature' as unreflexive, timeless and inevitable (which also recalls the cyclical discourses discussed above). So, rural iconography facilitates the misrecognition of exploitative human action as harmonious with nature both within and without farming simulations. 'Farmed animals', in spite of their discursive distinction from 'wild' animals inhabiting 'wild' nature (see Figure 2.1), are therefore 'naturally' to be found on the players ranch, despite the fact that players *actively place them* within the game. This recalls the rhetoric of RSPCA school guidance discussed in Chapter 7, referring to the importance of children seeing other animals in the 'natural environment' of the farm. The objectification of farmed animals that farming simulations perpetuate is therefore simply an acknowledgement of their (constructed) nature; they cannot logically exist without the ranch. Ethical choices about the use of other animals are thereby effaced in farming simulation gameplay, just as they are in the naturalization of non-virtual farming. This is illustrated in a reminder from 'Big Mart' to the Gourmet Ranch player that, 'When planting and raising animals it's important to realise that everything has its [*sic*] proper place'.

The 'proper place' of animals in farming simulations is, fundamentally, on the ranch, but beyond this, their 'proper place' is also defined according to their location within a grid of objectifying knowledge about their operation and function as productive units. For example, Farmville 2 requires a specified quantity of 'feed' to be given to different species of animal in order for them to 'produce' commodities for the player. Family Farm goes further by specifying different feedstuffs for different types of animals, such as clover for 'dairy' cows, pasture for 'beef' cows, or, bizarrely, sweet potatoes for pigs. This knowledge is tabulated in files which players can access from links embedded within the game. Animals' needs are reduced to precisely quantifiable feed requirements, which in turn yield precise and therefore predictable quantities of commodities. In other words, animals' biological processes are reduced to simplistic mechanical models of input-output, facilitating the calculation of their profitability; ironically, a reasonable approximation to the treatment of factory-farmed animals (see Coppin 2003). The animal machine motif is perhaps most extreme in Family Farm, in which the player can switch on an 'automation' feature, which applies equally to machines and nonhuman animals on the farm: 'automated' animals eat and 'produce' continually, without the human labour of a mouse-click, as long as sufficient species-specific feed is available. Big Mart's reminder is fulfilled in the infinitesimal division of labour here: the alpha and omega of animals' lives is to consume one specific foodstuff and to produce one specific product. Crucially however, any questions this might raise about whether any sentient being could really be fulfilled by such a circumscribed range of experience is defused by the manifest contentment of farming simulation animals.

Happiness in Slavery

The 'naturalness' of instrumentalization is reinforced in the stylization and programmed behaviour of animal representations in farming simulations, as well as the ways in which the games deal with the issue of their animals' confinement. As illustrated in Figure 8.1 below, 'farmed' animals in the farming simulation genre share stylistic characteristics with cute animal representations elsewhere in children's culture. They typically have large eyes, outsized heads, often wear a rictus smile, and never refuse or resist their positioning and treatment by players. In Family Farm players are also reminded of the entertainment uses of other animals, as long as they are sufficiently 'cute': 'The Ostrich is so cute! Tell your friends so they can come and have a look!' As established in infancy with the stylization of soft toy animals, cute representations not only invite affective responses from children, but also construct animals as always eager to please with their open 'arm' poses (the redrawing of legs as arms is a common technique of anthropomorphism), wide eyes and so on. Farming simulations draw on this representational style to establish animals' contentment with their own instrumentalization within the games. Constructing the willing complicity of exploited others is a key legitimation of anthroparchal human–animal relations, notably in welfarist discourses discussed in Chapter 7, but also in 'adult' representations of 'food' animals on restaurant menus, butcher's shop windows, animal product packaging, and so on. For example, our local shopping centre houses a butcher's shop with a smiling cartoon pig in the window; a short distance away the window of a café trading in ubiquitous British café fare (bacon, sausages, etc.) is adorned with a similar cartoon pig. Between 2006 and 2011, the blog Suicide Food documented the ubiquity of these kinds of representations in everyday Western food culture, with ironic commentary:

> … we've logged and chronicled more (way more!) than a thousand images of animals delighted to be killed, and sometimes despoiled and tortured, for you. Our goal when we started the Suicide Food blog was to reveal just how horrifyingly absurd (and repetitive!) meat culture is, and just how much it depends on bizarre beliefs for its legitimacy. (Suicide Food 2011)

These more adult-orientated representations retain some elements of cute style, such as large eyes, smiling, anthropomorphized expressions or even human clothing. This invokes the care-affect iconography of childhood representations, reinforcing a message that nonhuman animals have been cared for, even as they confirm that they exist for human satisfaction, and that they are perfectly happy with that ontological doom. While this genre of animal representation looks bizarre when abstracted from the wider cultural context, it makes sense when understood from the perspective of someone emerging from the ideal-typical socialization process documented in this book. Indeed, Richard Scarry (1919–1994), one of the most successful children's authors and illustrators of recent decades, depicted butchers as cartoon pigs, who, incredibly, sell bacon and pork, in his book *What Do People Do All Day?* (2010).

Returning to Family Farm, most animals are not depicted as tethered or confined within pens, but many animals do remain almost motionless and all of them remain exactly where the player places them on their ranch. They also bear a frozen demeanour, except for their animated munching of 'feed'. Occasionally, for instance in the case of pigs (three of whom can co-exist within a fenced 'coop'; a relatively unusual example of animals being fenced in the game), the representations look through the fourth wall and grin even more delightedly at the player when fed. Some of the representations exhibit what we might interpret as recalling stereotypies (repeated behaviours indicative of distress) in real confined animals, but in farming simulations, these are supposedly meant as endearing character traits. For example, a Family Farm turkey repeatedly 'bounces' on the spot, while raising and lowering her wings. In contrast with the mostly static animals in Family Farm, in Farmville 2 animals wander around the players 'ranch', though despite this apparent freedom, they never choose to leave it. The reason is their absolute contentment in their 'proper' physical and discursive location on the ranch, and their eagerness to reward players with their 'products' in return for being fed: 'Now she's happy! She gave you an egg! Grab it!' (Marie commenting on a fed chicken in Farmville 2); 'She gave you milk! That will fetch a good price' (Marie commenting on a fed 'wild goat' in Farmville 2).

The Farmville 2 representations are notably more animated than their counterparts in rival farming simulation games, for instance gambolling excitedly after being fed, and Marie's comments on their behaviour echo that animation by imputing pleasurable reactions from animals. Marie also expresses concern for the happiness of the players' animals through in-game comments, albeit instrumentalized to undercut the possibility of a value-rational concern with their well-being for its own sake: 'We've been paying the chickens a lot of attention, but the goats are the real money-makers. Let's make them more comfortable'. The theme of animals' contentment being directly related to their productivity recalls and reproduces the ideology of animal welfare education, discussed in Chapter 7. In farming simulations, animals' contentment is boiled down to an even narrower set of concerns than the five freedoms: being fed, and, in some cases, being spectated by human admirers. Despite her apparent concern for the animals' well-being, Marie directs the player to, 'Hit the feed mill for a Pavlovian reaction from the cloven-foot set [goats]', simultaneously reinforcing instrumental human–animal relations, human agency and nonhuman non-agency. While Farmland determines players' success by being able to meet animals' corporeal needs in real (game) time, the animals in farming simulation games never suffer from hunger (despite the reference to Pavlovian reactions), still wearing their rictus grins (Family Farm) or playfully gambolling (Farmville 2) without virtual sustenance for days on end (a partial exception in Gourmet Ranch is discussed below).

By contrast with the happy 'freedom' of Farmville 2, Gourmet Ranch depicts its animals as confined within pens (albeit outdoors), and as more expressionless than those in either of the examples discussed so far; they constitute a notably less smiley menagerie than either Family Farm or Farmville 2 for instance, though they retain the distinctive large eyes and heads of cute representations. The expressions of animals in Gourmet Ranch is notable for imputing low intelligence and sensibility to 'farmed' animals, for instance by drawing on cultural tropes of goggle-eyed expressions or droopy eyelids. Interaction between the player and the animals is much more limited. In the case of Gourmet Ranch's pigs for instance, the player is only required to 'click' on pigs to 'harvest' them when they are 'finished'; even feeding animals is removed as a minimal aspect of 'care' for their well-being. Instead, they are automatically content in their allotted pens. Unlike their counterparts in other farming simulations, Gourmet Ranch's pigs are replaced by a representation of bacon when 'harvested' (of which more below). The language of 'finishing' and 'harvesting' is the most direct allusion in the farming simulation genre to the euphemistic language of 'real' farming, as documented by Joan Dunayer (2002) for instance and as discussed in the discourse used in animal welfare education in Chapter 7. As the title of the game suggests, the central gameplay concern is more immediately focused on preparing meals in the game kitchen and serving them up to in-game customers in a diner, rather than with the animals themselves. These elements combine to maximize the objectification of the represented animals in Gourmet Ranch, compared with other examples. Taking the three examples of Farmville 2, Family Farm and Gourmet Ranch together, they form a rough and ready descending scale of cutification, coinciding with their relative amplification of agency and inverse attenuation of instrumentalization. From Farmville 2, through Family Farm, to Gourmet Ranch, the scenario is more nakedly instrumental for animals, but even at its worst, it remains thoroughly euphemized. This obscuration of suffering and killing is explored further in the next section.

The Non-sensibility of Killing, Suffering and Sex

The most blatant denial of the non-virtual farming practices in this genre is the absence of the slaughterhouse, the human actions of violence and confinement and anything other than comic reference to animal's physical or mental suffering. As noted above, Gourmet Ranch flirts with the reality of dismemberment when pigs are 'harvested', but there is no expression of fear or pain on the part of the game's pigs, nor any representation of the firing of the captive bolt pistol into their heads, the shackling of their trotters, the cutting of their throats, or the immersion of their corpses in the 'scalding tank' and subsequent evisceration, skinning and butchery. Most farming simulations avoid getting even as close to reality as Gourmet Ranch. In Family Farm, animals used to 'produce' commoditized flesh never die: their products materialize next to them, already conveniently processed, when they have eaten their species-specific feed: the pasture-fed bovine produces a neatly wrapped packet of 'beef'; the rice-fed turkey produces a de-feathered, decapitated, footless turkey carcass; the sweet potato-fed pig produces a tidily butchered pork chop. Meanwhile, the animals keep contentedly munching and smiling as if nothing had happened. The same is true of animals used to 'produce' hair or feathers, sheep and angora rabbits, are sheared; ostriches and peacocks are plucked, all by unseen hands and without any hint of distress on the part of the animals. As discussed above, the needs of other animals are limited to feeding, at most, and lack of feeding has no apparent material affect. Happy Farm depicts animals as thinner when awaiting food, and in the case of pigs, they stand on their hind legs, rubbing their stomachs and giving a 'comically' pained look through the fourth wall. Therefore, an affective pull incites the player to produce feed for Happy Farm's animals, but as with the other examples of the genre, nothing appears to happen if feeding ceases, other than that the generation of profit also ceases. The pathetic 'behaviour' of Happy Farm's animals further reinforces their absolute dependence on the human player/carer; once again instrumental-rational action is dressed up as affective action, or even value-rational action given the desperate portrayal of hungry animals. For instance, the painfully hungry pigs cannot fend for themselves; they must appeal to the player to feed them. After being fed, they eat and gradually fatten over several hours, until they appear bloated and unable to move, with uncomfortable anthropomorphized expressions, unless they are relieved of their 'excess' flesh. The relief of flesh (which then appears in the player's storehouse as 'bacon') occurs in bizarre fashion: a mouse click on a fattened pig calls down a hot tub, in which the pig is immersed, emerging a moment later thin and hungry once again; a perverse echo of the slaughterhouse scalding tank. As a whole, the farming simulation genre blatantly denies the inherent violence of instrumental-rational practices which objectify animals. Arguably, in farming simulations we are closer than in any other socialization site to the south-eastern region of our conceptual map, but the cultural form can only bear this proximity through a representational style that is the most phantasmagorical of all the representations we have considered.

Another striking absence from farming simulations' phantasmagoria is intimate relations between other animals and sexual relationships and activity in particular. Reproduction, parenting, sibling or companion relationships are entirely removed from the simulated farming experience, echoing the discursive lacuna about animals' intimacy, especially sexuality, in most of the other socialization sites that we have examined in chapters 5–7. A partial exception is the role of animals' parental or sibling affectivity in the cutification process (see Chapter 6). In farming simulations, despite their deployment of cute style, nonhuman animal to nonhuman animal intimacy is apparently purged entirely. In Farmville 2, goats 'give' milk after being fed; there is no account of lactation being at all connected to pregnancy and birth. Likewise, 'dairy cows' in Happy Farm stand on two legs, with 'arms' crossed over their chests, as they 'impatiently' await their feed, before eating contentedly on all fours when supplied with it by the player. When they've eaten their fill, they sit back on their haunches, with swollen udders, looking expectantly through the fourth wall at the player to milk them (an instantaneous process that happens at the click of the mouse). Unsurprisingly, the only function of eggs in farming simulations is to sell or as an ingredient in more profitable food products (of which more below). Animals in Family Farm and Happy Farm appear as fully productive adults when bought by players. On Gourmet Ranch, animals appear as mini-adults who grow automatically over time, until they are ready to be 'harvested'. On Farmville

2 however, infant animals do appear, but, likewise, when purchased, not as a result of birth and not with their mothers but as individual orphans. The genre as a whole then eliminates the reproductive process, and in particular the role of commercial hatcheries and breeders in the animal-industrial complex. The Farmville 2 orphan is constructed as an investment opportunity, intermingled with affective discourse that enforces animal dependency on human care: 'Feeding grown animals takes feed, but growing baby animals into adults takes a nurturing hand'. Baby animals must be fed with 'baby bottles' by the player, in to order to grow into productive, profitable, adult animals: 'Baby animals need to drink special Baby Bottles to grow up'. The baby bottle, which appears to be filled with milk of an unspecified species, is fed to animals regardless of their mammalian status or otherwise; baby chicks are fed the same way as kid goats, by the human player's avatar. On Family Farm, the obscuration of sexual reproduction is taken to absurd lengths: the milk producing buffalo is referred to as 'he' within the game, while egg-laying ducks are depicted as colourful drakes, not hens. In the latter case, the cuteness of the representation apparently trumps biological veracity as the primary consideration of the games' designers.

Animals' intra-species intimacy is arguably profoundly disruptive for the socialization process, unless it can be fitted into the logic of cutification, such as cuddling kittens in cutie magazines. This is because it is incompatible with the construction of nonhuman animals as existing purely to satisfy human desires. This is particularly the case in respect of the disruption of mother–infant bonds in the 'production' of milk from cows, goats, sheep and so on (in Family Farm, horses, camels and pandas can also be farmed for their milk, illustrating the precariousness of particular animals or species in the conceptual map; in an anthroparchal culture, all are at risk of discursive and physical annihilation in the south-eastern death zone). The killing of 'unproductive' infant male offspring in the milk industry is potentially one of the most upsetting realities of farming that is carefully screened from children throughout the socialization process, but the severing of the connection between reproduction and lactation in farming simulations facilitates its denial. The gendered experience of suffering and death in the farming process are also removed from consideration by farming simulations: an early death for male calves, kids or chicks on the one hand, versus a truncated life of forced pregnancy and as near-as-possible perpetual lactation or egg-laying for their female siblings. The farming simulation genre is expert at fostering non-sensibility to the gendered messiness of sex and death on the farm, at the same time as it generates highly visible, distracting and absorbing fantastical representations. As a consequence, opposing farming on the grounds that it is exploitative appears logically absurd within the virtual world of farming simulations, because the game's player has no evidence that it is exploitative; in fact quite the contrary, thanks to their careful merging of affect, tradition and instrumental rationality.

The Unthinkability of Veganism in Farming Simulations

The logical absurdity of vegan discourse and practice is reinforced by its absence from farming simulations. The key to in-game success is the profitable exploitation of the farm's 'products' through combining them in machines, workshops, kitchens, and so on. The relative difficulty of obtaining the ingredients determines the in-game price of the finished product, so players are invited to consider cereals, vegetables or fruits as ontologically equivalent to flesh, milk, eggs or honey; that is, as commodities. In fact, the games take this further by constructing nonhuman animals themselves as commodities; while their biological reproduction is effaced, their capitalist reproduction is self-evident, as new animals are acquired through purchase using in-game currency. Returning to in-game recipes, there is no room for creativity on the part of the player; each game determines a menu of permitted recipes. This means that attempting a subversive gameplay style as a virtual vegan who refuses to 'own' animals on their ranch is impossible, because recipes are dominated by animal products, even recipes that in reality are entirely plant-based. So, aside from the predictable fare of flesh-based hotdogs, burgers, and so on, Family Farm decrees that hen's eggs and cow's milk are essential ingredients in the manufacture of *bread*, and even more bizarrely, that goat's milk is essential in the manufacture of plant 'milks'. Similarly, it is impossible to bake a vegan cake, prepare egg-free pasta, or make a vegan jam (all jams must contain honey in Family Farm).

Within the world of farming simulation games then, it would be very difficult to imagine survival without animal products because of their ubiquity in manufactured food products and prepared recipes. Ironically, this facilitates the reproduction of non-virtual stereotypes about dietary veganism as being impossible to sustain because of an impoverished range of available foodstuffs (see Cole and Morgan 2011). Contesting that stereotype has been a central concern since the inception of the modern vegan movement (Cole 2014). But, farming simulations exemplify how difficult that contestation is when veganism is made to appear as an unliveable and therefore unthinkable lifestyle in popular culture. It is perhaps understandable that the existence of veganism needs to be suppressed in order that the relaxed acceptance of anthroparchal relations is not disturbed within the game world. Although we cannot claim to have exhausted the gameplay of any farming simulation in the course of our research, at the time of writing, we have not encountered any mention of veganism, or of explicitly vegan products (besides automatically vegan items such as fruit juices) in any farming simulation game. The closest to a broken silence about veganism comes in Family Farm, where Darryl mentions vegetarianism in the course of a mission to manufacture 'beef': 'Produce more meat. Nobody can live without meat! Well, except vegetarians of course'. And then later: 'Good work! Be sure to sell your beef only to the non veggies out there though!' In these examples, vegetarians are constructed as if they were a species apart from 'non veggies', who for unspecified reasons do not need to eat meat; perhaps the player is being invited to think of vegetarians as having a 'special' diet analogous to the monotonous eating habits of the in-game animals. That interpretation gains some credence in light of the only explicitly named vegetarian food item (as far as we are aware) on Family Farm being a 'veggie burger', that is solely manufactured, unappetizingly, from 'wheat bread' (which contains cow's milk and hen's eggs) and cabbage. The concomitant of the absence of vegan dietary practices is the normalization of the consumption of animal products as a pleasurable experience; 'I can already smell the salami! Quick, I'm starving!' (Darryl, Family Farm). The nutritional necessity of animal products is also reproduced and embedded within affective and traditional practices: 'Bobby's parents ordered Beef Burgers for all of us. Ol' Macdonald will be pleased: we'll all have our daily dose of proteins!' (Darryl, Family Farm).

This absence of vegan diets is only part of the story. Farming simulations also embed the notion that (willing) captive animals themselves are essential to farming as a practice. Of the examples we have looked at, Farmville 2, Family Farm, Gourmet Ranch and Happy Farm all begin with at least one animal already captive on the player's ranch. Not only is the range of available products to the player severely limited by eschewing nonhuman animal exploitation, progress in the game (gaining 'experience' and 'levels') would also be near impossible, because generating profit is so bound up with in-game animals and their products. In Farmville 2, players expand their ranches with the aid of a herd of goats who clear land by eating the grass on overgrown plots adjoining the players ranch, though the goats are under the control of Marie: 'Need more land? I can arrange to have a landscaping service clear space for expansion'. Family Farm also represents animals in 'working' roles: in-game dogs are fed 'beef' and in return find truffles for the player (albeit without moving from their allotted space on the ranch). While most games avoid the issue, Farmville 2 deepens the sense of farming depending on nonhuman animals by the in-game production of 'fertiliser' from animals on the ranch, such as sheep or horses. Although it is obviously implied that this fertilizer is animals' manure, this is delicately skated over and the product appears on screen ready bagged up for the player to apply to her or his crops, after feeding the appropriate animals. Vegan farming methods are as unthinkable within the genre as are vegan dietary practices. Furthermore, nonhuman animals only exist as 'useful' animals in the conceptual map. Most of them are 'farmed' animals, though there are also some examples of 'worked' animals (for instance truffle hunting dogs, or a donkey-powered mill on Family Farm) or 'entertainment' animals (such as a decorative Aviary on Family Farm and the more general cutification in the Farmville series).

This positioning of nonhuman animals within the genre exemplifies the coalescing of knowledge and power, or representation and practice; animals are known, and only knowable, according to their uses in a world that is utterly determined by human supremacy and privilege. Therefore, to countenance a vegan player within that world would be to imagine a ranch, and therefore a world, devoid of any nonhuman animals whatsoever. This fantasy equation of veganism with the annihilation of other animals is present within 'real world' anti-vegan discourse, for instance in Simon Fairlie's reactionary assault on veganism in *Meat: A Benign Extravagance* (2010), or in Donna Haraway's similarly stereotypical dismissal of veganism (or rather a house of cards that both authors respectively label 'veganism') in *When Species Meet* (2007) and arguably for very similar reasons: the construction of knowledge of other animals as dependent on human 'care' and control in the socialization process, makes it extremely difficult to envisage those same animals existing, let alone thriving, without anthroparchal human–nonhuman animal relations. Being human has been so thoroughly enmeshed with the privileges of domination for so long (see Nibert 2013, 2002) that to imagine being otherwise is apparently beyond the pale of a non-vegan culture.

Conclusion: Mapping the Powerplay

One reason for the ordering of the empirical analyses in this book (family to mass media to education to digital media) was to trace an ideal-typical socialization narrative, as children move chronologically into different socialization sites (see Chapter 1). The sites themselves interpenetrate, for instance in the playing of digital games in the home or at school, or the embedding of mass media in the form of on-screen advertisements alongside Facebook games. As the example of Farmland shows in the previous chapter, from the perspective of an 'ideally' socialized child, the farming simulation genre itself has additionally been validated as an educational-socialization resource in schools. So, this narrative is not intended as a veracious account of any particular child's experience. Instead, it functions as a metaphor for an idealized socialization process, which is crowned by the figure of the child exploring Hamleys's representational zoo and learning human–nonhuman animal relations as she or he ascends its floors (see Chapter 5). In that context, digital games are the culmination of that process: they allow children a final rehearsal of all that they have learned, at the point just before they go on to reproduce exploitative relations in earnest as adult anthroparchal consumers, while for adult players they add a 'fun' veneer to the banality of enjoying everyday exploitation in the 'pet' shop, butcher's shop, or fast food restaurant. For adult players, farming simulations also facilitate a revision of childhood socialization and a celebration

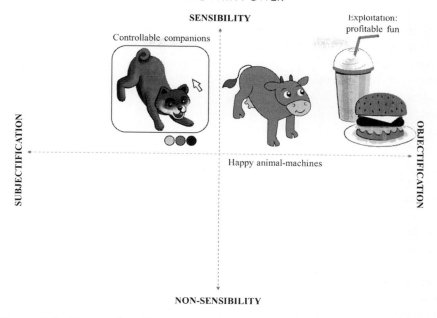

Figure 8.1   Powerplay: Representing 'pets', 'farmed animals' and 'animal products' in digital media

of their habituation to normal human–nonhuman animal relationships. The celebratory tone of games playing as such is apposite as the culmination of anthroparchal socialization. The north-eastern corner of Figure 2.1 is a space for human recreation and pleasure, a smorgasbord of the fruits of exploitation. We illustrate these celebratory practices and representations in Figure 8.1 above.

'Pet'-owning and farming simulations exemplify the differential intensity of the objectification of other animals, according to the human pleasures that they serve. Nintendogs tend towards the north-west of Figure 8.1, thanks to the individualizing characteristics of the gameplay, while the anonymous farmed animals of Facebook tend towards the north-east, anthropomorphic grins notwithstanding. By being positioned so far to the north, these representations facilitate the sensibility of animal products by obliterating sensibility to human violence; by making a game of exploitation. As Figure 8.1 illustrates, digital game representations are themselves highly culturally sensible, but the further these representations take us towards the north pole of Figure 8.1, the further we are from the other country of pain and death. Farming simulations constantly risk exposing exploitation to critical reflection, which might undermine the pleasure of the games if the prior socialization process had not been sufficiently robust. Therefore, as we have documented in this chapter, farming simulations draw on affective, traditional, and to a lesser extent value-rational, discourses at the same time as they stimulate the reproduction of instrumental-rational action. At this point, socialization of the irrational, paradoxical, simultaneity of sentiment and violence is complete; the child has fully grown into the contradictions of the anthroparchal dystopia.

PART III
Reconstructing Children's Relations with Other Animals: Vegan Practices and Representations

Chapter 9

We've Got to Get Out of This Place: The Utopian Vehicularity of Vegan Children's Culture

The intertextuality of anthroparchal practices and representations across the social institutions of the family, education system, mass and digital media weaves a thick comfort blanket of affectivity that simultaneously cloaks violence and exploitation. The empirical analyses in chapters 5–8 have documented an 'ideal' process through which a child can grow to feel emotionally attached to animals while simultaneously enjoying the vicarious privileges of their domination through consuming their bodies, their bodily secretions and the objectifying knowledge extracted from them. However, the socialization of anthroparchal relations is a precarious process; the tight weave of the comfort blanket is necessitated by the irrationality and buried emotional trauma resulting from 'loving' one's victims in the animal-industrial complex (see Luke 1996). It is therefore always at risk of fraying, unravelling or in some cases, being entirely cast aside; children can and do go vegan (Amato and Partridge 1989). Veganism is understood here as a process that synthesizes a value-rational, rather than instrumental-rational, orientation towards other animals with socio-emotional healing and reintegration consequent to the renunciation of violence and exploitation; the renunciation of anthroparchal socialization. This understanding of veganism is at odds with that which is generally evident in popular culture. For instance, a content analysis of coverage of veganism in UK national newspapers showed that they tend to represent veganism as ridiculous, impossible to sustain, pleasure-denying, faddish or even as a repository of embittered hostility (Cole and Morgan 2011b). This is unsurprising if we consider veganism as a threat to a fundamental aspect of the hegemonic socialization process in the contemporary West, which we have documented in this book. When veganism is partially rehabilitated in mainstream culture, it tends to be as a faddish quirk of consumer culture (Cole and Morgan 2011a, Cole and Morgan 2011b), i.e. its presence is at the cost of the defusing of its radical threat to anthroparchal relations. Veganism is notably absent in the examples of children's culture discussed in chapters 5–8, but vegan cultural resources for children are increasingly available, tugging at the threads of Figure 2.1. In this chapter, these cultural resources are considered as constituting a counter-discourse, which repositions other animals in Figure 2.1 and furthermore, destabilizes its entire 'logic' and in so doing, promises the fulfilment of a Weberian dream of the re-enchantment of human–nonhuman animal relations: both humans and other animals are thereby offered a way out, or at least the beginnings of a way out, of Figure 2.1. We begin this chapter with situating vegan children's culture in its anthroparchal context; this is key to understanding the apparent 'failure' of veganism to take hold on a mass scale in the contemporary West to date, as being because it is tacitly and relentlessly *opposed and marginalized* by anthroparchal culture. We then move on to consider vegan literature as a rich and exemplary site for the contestation of anthroparchal culture through foregrounding an ethical reconfiguration of both human–other animal relations for children, and children's understanding of human ontology itself.

The Cultural Context of Vegan Children's Culture

The overarching theme of vegan children's culture is that it repositions other animals, moving them westwards in the context of Figure 2.1, by deconstructing the objectification of animals in anthroparchal culture and facilitating the sensibility of animals as agential beings in children's experience. However, the vegan counter-discourse is massively under-resourced compared with the financial might of the animal-industrial complex that underpins the anthroparchal cultural artefacts documented in chapters 5–8. Therefore, a neat correspondence between forms of discourse and counter-discourse is not (yet) possible. While criticism of some aspects of anthroparchal culture can be found in some 'mainstream' cultural artefacts, such as the film *Babe* (1995), which goes some way towards critiquing the exploitation of other animals for human food (see Stewart and Cole 2009), vegan cultural interventions generally have to find their way into children's experience via ethical entrepreneurism, grassroots activism and third sector organizations and, to pursue the Weberian theme, are more evocative of vocational (value-rational) works than commercial (instrumental) enterprises. That is, they are orientated towards the value of reconfiguring human relationships with other animals among their consumers, rather than towards using representations of animals as a means to profit-generation. In a consumer capitalist context, dominated by instrumental-rationality, it is unsurprising that cultural interlocutors, such as vegan children's cultural artefacts, currently operate at a miniscule scale relative to Disney et al.; the heavyweights of the anthroparchal culture industry. The products of the latter fit into the 'logic' of Figure 2.1 in a mutually sustaining web for multiple aspects of the animal-industrial complex: from the 'pet' industry to the cultivation of animal-food preferences in children. Bearing in mind this inequality of scale, resources and tone between anthroparchal discourse and vegan counter-discourse, rather than offer a like-for-like analysis of vegan cultural interventions in the socialization sites of the family, mass media, education and digital media, to match chapters 5–8, we have chosen to focus primarily on interventions in the field of children's literature. This is a particularly rich site for vegan culture, illustrating the potential to destabilize anthroparchal socialization within the socialization process itself.

A common objection to discourses for social change, especially insofar as they aim to shape and re-shape children's thoughts and actions, is that they are merely indoctrinating propaganda. The argument goes that they therefore run counter to the dominant cultural value of freedom of choice, in the context of a democratic consumer society (see Bauman 1988). However, vegan cultural interventions, as with cognate interventions into other forms of oppression and violence, are highly conspicuous only because they run against the grain of the taken-for-granted indoctrination that continues remorselessly throughout children's upbringing. As chapters 5–8 illustrated children have scant opportunity to engage in 'choice' about how they relate to other animals without those proscribed by Figure 2.1 (although hope remains in the fact that despite the odds, children can and do break free of Figure 2.1, discussed in Chapter 5). Anthroparchal children's culture rarely has to expend effort undermining veganism, apart from defensively on occasions (for example in the backlash to Ruby Roth's vegan children's books discussed further below), because it occupies the hegemonic cultural terrain. Therefore, the extent to which it shapes children's thoughts and practices typically goes unrecognized from a non-vegan perspective. It is therefore inevitable that vegan culture has to engage critically with its other while anthroparchal culture has the luxury of remaining largely silent about its own operation, and thereby silencing its interlocutor in most circumstances. This is the context into which a new genre of children's illustrated books advocating veganism has emerged in recent years.

Ethical Critique in Children's Vegan Literature

The highest profile examples from this genre to date are three books illustrated and written by US author Ruby Roth: *That's Why We Don't Eat Animals* (2009), *Vegan is Love* (2012) and *V is for Vegan* (2013). In relation to countering the anthroparchal socialization process Roth's books may be argued to pursue twin strategies. On the one hand, she reveals other animals' exploitation and counterpoises that with a narrative of other animal's agency and a concomitant vision of their lives lived free of human intervention. On the other hand, she reconstructs human animals as capable of being motivated by values of compassion and peaceful co-existence with other animals, who can flourish with the renunciation of anthroparchal privileges. In Weberian terms, Roth reconfigures human animals as primarily value-rational rather than instrumental-rational beings, on the basis that other animals are agents and not exploitable resources. With Foucault in mind, we can consider that Roth constructs knowledge of other animals that does not facilitate their objectification and exploitation; rather, it constructs empathic knowledge that facilitates respect and a sense of wonder. These twin strategies of reconstructing both nonhuman and human animals will now be considered in turn.

In *That's Why We Don't Eat Animals*, Roth effectively juxtaposes the south-east with the south-west of Figure 2.1. Sometimes on facing pages, and sometimes on consecutive pages, Roth illustrates and writes about members of the same species either enjoying their natural habitats, or incarcerated by instrumentalizing technologies. For example, pigs are shifted south-westwards in Figure 2.1, thus: 'Free pigs live with their families and friends. Snorting and whistling, they recognize each other's voices from far away. They root for food, wrestle, and play ball in the sun …' (2009: 20). They are then shown in the south-east of Figure 2.1, thus: 'A factory-farm pig may spend her whole life alone, fattened in a pen so tiny that she won't even be able to turn around. A free pig never poops where she eats or sleeps, but on a factory farm she has no choice' (2009: 22). In the case of birds, Roth explicitly breaks the barrier between the south-east and south-west of Figure 2.1: 'Birds raised for meat, called poultry, are just like the birds we see outside our windows' (2009: 17). Confinement versus freedom as in this case is the clearest contrast being drawn in Roth's work, but the subjectivity of other animals is also asserted through their relational capacities, contrasting with the individualizing practices of 'factory farms'; 'Just like we do, many baby animals stay close to their parents long after they're born […] On factory farms, there are no animal families. With no mama in sight, these babies live without a sense of family or safety. Animals belong in families […]' (2009: 7). Other animals are drawn in affective combinations, either familial or friendship-based, with the text emphasizing animals' tactile pleasure, comfort and security. For example, Roth illustrates an adult pig with two piglets, laying in an open grassed space under a sunset, and writes, 'Sometimes they snuggle so close that it's hard to get them apart. Love is part of their nature' (2009: 20–21). These intra-species affective tableaux are striking for the absence of representations of human animals; Roth depicts a nonhuman utopia free of human exploitation in *That's Why We Don't Eat Animals* that contrasts with dystopian extant anthroparchal relations. There is a striking contrast here with the construction of nonhuman pleasure and security as being dependent on their 'domestication' which we have seen repeated throughout the anthroparchal socialization process. For instance, soft toy animals reach out for human infants, not for each other (see Chapter 5). The cutie magazine genre constructs other animals' as being dependent on human affection, and tellingly, tends to sever familial connections between the infant animals they favour and those animals' parents or siblings (see Chapter 6). Educational representations and practices involving other animals abstract them from their natural environments and intra-species relational contexts and construct them as only existing to serve human interests (see Chapter 7). Finally, both 'pet' and 'farming' simulation games all but abolish intra-species relations in favour of representing nonhumans as being devoted to serving human interests to the exclusion of all else (see Chapter 8).

Roth's illustrative style also contrasts with anthroparchal representations, utilizing different strategies in different books. In *That's Why We Don't Eat Animals* and *Vegan is Love*, Roth eschews both photorealism and anthropomorphism. The latter is evident in the depiction of animals with small eyes, and the absence of mouths in many cases (such as in drawings of pigs and cows), foreclosing the anthropomorphic trope of the loving dewy/baby-eyed gaze and the rictus grin directed towards a human viewer/consumer. Instead, Roth's illustrative motifs include emphasizing snouts or tails; less 'human' aspects of other mammal's embodiments. Roth's animals then, are drawn attractively, but are resolutely 'other'. This has a dual consequence: the illustrative style asserts their inscrutability, that is, their inaccessibility to objectifying knowledge but also their fascination; their capacity to inspire wonder. Children are tacitly enjoined to take lasting pleasure in the living beauty of other animals, rather than the ephemeral pleasures of ingesting their (misrecognized) dismembered corpses. The wondrousness of free-living animals is emphasized through a vibrancy of colour that contrasts with the drabber palette colouring animals depicted in captive situations, such as laboratories, in *Vegan is Love*. While other animals are sometimes drawn looking out of the page, the impression evoked is more of mild curiosity directed towards the reader, rather than the adorational cute style, and often the gaze of the animals is directed towards each other as they are depicted playing, foraging, or otherwise interacting. They are also written about and depicted as enjoying their lives in ways that are analogous to human experience (for example enjoying playing or cuddling) but in order to emphasize their self-sufficiency as fully formed communities of subjects, and not in order to emphasize their affective utility as *partial* subjects awaiting human ennoblement as 'pets', and so on.

Vegan is Love uses a similar representational style to *That's Why We Don't Eat Animals* in its depiction of other animals, but adds depictions of human animals too; it therefore forms a segue between the twin strategies of revealing/problematizing other animals' exploitation and reconfiguring humans as non-anthroparchal beings. By writing directly about veganism, Roth is concerned in *Vegan is Love* with representing a radical difference between the way in which vegans and non-vegans experience their relations with other animals, and this is reflected in the relative subjectification/objectification of human representations. The only example of eye contact between a human and nonhuman animal in the book is that between a human boy (implicitly vegan in the context of the accompanying text that ends with the book title, 'Vegan is love' (2011: 4)) and two sheep, encountering each other on a rocky hillside. By contrast, other humans in the book have their privileged subjectivity undermined through being deindividualized. This is pursued through a number of techniques: shadowy crowds spectate a pair of giraffes at a 'zoo' or an elephant at a circus, problematizing the construction of 'entertainment animals' in Figure 2.1; a masked vivisector inspects stacks of caged monkeys, problematizing the construction of 'laboratory animals' in Figure 2.1. Both examples illuminate for the reader the practico-discursive extraction of objectifying knowledge from other animals; their physical 'framing' by the bars of cages, the walls of laboratories, or the fences of zoo enclosures abstracts them and forms them as cultural artefacts, that is, as exploitable material in the instrumental pursuit of human self-interest. But the humans involved in these processes (including silhouettes of children in the 'zoo' and circus crowd) are depicted as emotionally distanced from the animals they consume as spectacle or experimental tool. Humans' capacities as affective, empathetic subjects are therefore shown to be stunted through their very engagement with objectifying practices. The implicit message is therefore that we confine and kill some part of ourselves as we confine and kill others. This is further emphasized by the contrasting immiserated subjectivity of the giraffes, elephant or monkeys in the respective illustrations. Another set of illustrations de-aestheticize the instrumental use of other animals for human aggrandizement. A jockey is drawn as fixated on the winning post that lies beyond the page (coincidentally the horse is being ridden eastwards, thinking in terms of the doom of Figure 2.1 and the lethal outcome of 'horse-racing' for many horses; see Animal Aid 2014), or a 'bull-fighter' is drawn posturing to the crowd through the fourth wall. In these cases, other animals are made to appear as adjuncts to human 'achievements', foreclosing empathic engagement between the species for the human 'achievers'.

Roth's most recent book *V is for Vegan* explores a different representational strategy, eschewing conventional 'cute style', but also experimenting with anthropomorphism in order to show other animals' objecting to their positioning in Figure 2.1. For instance, a chicken is drawn wide-eyed in alarm at the prospect of being eaten by a boy: 'A is for animals, friends, not food. We don't eat our friends, they'd find it quite rude' (2013: 3–4); and a calf is drawn with eyebrows to facilitate an angry expression directed towards a boy holding a glass of cow's milk; 'D is for dairy. Moo! Milk is for cows' (2013: 7). In *V is for Vegan* then, other animals are depicted in relationships with humans. However, these are problematized partly through the subjectification of other animals, who are implicitly questioning their exploitation at human hands. The implication is not only the reconstruction of other animals, but once more, a questioning of the

156

self-construction of humans through anthroparchal relations being contrasted with non-anthroparchal relations. For example, *V is for Vegan* depicts a self-satisfied looking woman (with eyes closed so as not to see the bird at the bottom of the page) wearing a feather boa (2013: 6). Far more common in *V is for Vegan*, though, are 'positive' depictions of humans enjoying non-exploitative relations with other animals, or enjoying vegan practice (although these shade into each other). The former includes a girl gazing appreciatively at an insect while lying on a sunny hillside (2013: 5); another girl releasing a beetle from a jar (2013: 13); or a third girl adopting a cat from a rescue shelter (2013: 24). The latter includes a smiling boy and girl balancing bowls of vegetables, 'V is for veggies, which ones will you taste?' (2013: 28); a group of children enjoying preparing fresh plant foods such as smoothies and salads (2013: 15–16); or iconically, a baby in a superhero-style romper suit with cape and chest-emblazoned 'V', triumphantly holding a carrot and cuddling a puppy; 'Y is for you, because your choices matter' (2013: 31). Taken together then, Roth's books ironically pursue a strategy to empower readers through critiquing a central privilege of human being within an anthroparchal cultural context, reconfiguring the 'privilege' to exploit as *dependence* on self-abnegating estrangement from other animals. In this way, Roth's work sits firmly in a tradition of vegan writing that advocates humility vis-à-vis other animals as a key to a more fulfilled human life, relieved of the moral and emotional confusion attendant to anthroparchal relations (see Cole 2014 for a detailed discussion of this theme in the early writings of The Vegan Society in the UK in the 1940s–1950s). Humans are booted off the throne in the north-west corner of Figure 2.1 by Roth's work, instead taking our place in 'the same web of life' as other 'earthlings' (Roth 2009: 42). The contrast between the metaphor of an interdependent web and a hierarchical model of power in Figure 2.1 is striking.

As noted earlier, Roth's work, unsurprisingly given its disturbance of the anthroparchal order, has not gone unchallenged. A story in *The Mail Online* (the internet version of a popular tabloid newspaper in the UK, *The Daily Mail*), ran under the headline, 'New children's book promoting veganism sparks outrage for graphic images and unhealthy diet message' (2012). The article went on to quote Nicole German, 'a registered dietician in Atlanta', thus: 'The main problem I have with this book [*Vegan is Love*] is that children are impressionable, and this is too sensitive of a topic to have a child read this book […] It could easily scare a young child into eating vegan'. Although the article as a whole was not implacably hostile to the concept of children going vegan, the headline and citation of an 'authoritative' source constructs a negative appraisal of the book as a whole, which aligns with earlier research on the overwhelmingly negative representation of veganism in UK newspapers (Cole and Morgan 2011b). More pertinently in this context though, is the illustration of the privilege of silence about influencing 'impressionable' children with anthroparchal cultural messages. However, German's opinion also suggests an impoverished view of the ethical-agential capacities of children, certainly one that is at odds with the construction of empowered children in Roth's books themselves. That theme of empowering children's ethical agency is pursued in other examples of vegan children's literature.

Two Stevens, an Alien and a Flying Pig

While Roth's books have arguably gained the greatest notoriety to date among the genre of vegan fiction for children, there are several other notable examples, each taking a different approach to the issue of critiquing anthroparchy and (literally) sketching out an alternative relational environment for children to imaginatively inhabit, and, the authors clearly intend, to manifest in daily practice. While German's anxiety focuses on the conversion of children, the eponymous character of Dan Bodenstein's *Steven the Vegan* (2012) focuses on empowering children who are already vegan. The narrative accompanies Steven and his class on a school field trip to a farm sanctuary: 'a special place where animals can run, play, and live their lives in happiness' (2012: 5). On arrival at the sanctuary, Steven uses the occasion of being questioned about his vegan packed lunch to explain his veganism: 'animals are my friends, not my food' (2012: 10). In common with Roth's approach, Bodenstein juxtaposes images of factory farming with images of freedom and Steven's not-yet vegan friends react with shock and then empathy in response to Steven's revelations: 'Marion and her classmate Andrea knelt down to pet the baby calves. "I don't want to take milk away from this little guy"' (2012: 14). Steven goes on to metaphorically collapse Figure 2.1 by pointing out the inconsistencies of eating flesh from some species of other animals and not others, 'What's the difference? [...] Why eat any of them?' (2012: 27). The book follows up the critique with the vegan alternative, driven all the while by questions from Steven's inquisitive classmates: 'Just because I don't eat meat doesn't mean I just eat salads. I eat rice, pasta, even veggie burgers with French fries' (2012: 29). The nutritional value of plant-based diets are bolstered by Steven enrolling iconic nonhuman species as exemplars of robust health: 'Many dinosaurs were vegans ...' (2012: 32); '... hippos, elephants, rhinos, giraffes, buffalo and gorillas' (2012: 33). In the context of Figure 2.1, Bodenstein thereby reverses the usual cultural hierarchy in which carnivorous nonhumans are afforded a greater measure of subjectivity and cultural reverence than herbivores (see Fiddes 1991). A striking example of this aspect of the anthroparchal hierarchy comes in Disney's *The Lion King*, in which herbivorous nonhumans are characterless, massified, voiceless objects, in sharp contrast with the heroic carnivorous subjects that drive the narrative of the film (Stewart and Cole 2009). Bodenstein's characters are happy to accept herbivorous nonhumans as their role models, 'I love giraffes' (2012: 34). The book ends with Steven having employed a combination of exemplary vegan practice (his lunchbox), rational argumentation (revealing facts about farming and pointing out the illogicality of selective consumption of other species) and affective/empathic persuasion ('I'm sure they don't like it [factory farmed cows]. It's more crowded in there than a school bus' (2012: 13)). The outcome is the conversion of his classmates to plant-based diets, 'I'm telling my mom and dad that I'm not eating animals anymore' (2012: 35). The negotiation and renegotiation of appropriate behaviours is, as this suggests, not just a part of the socialization and learning which occurs in childhood; as the discipline of Childhood Studies has emphasized, children are full social agents and childhood a full category of social life, not simply an incomplete adultness under construction.

Steven therefore provides a resource for vegan readers, a scenario in which their ethical practice is respected and not ridiculed, 'He was very proud. He imagined this is what his teacher felt like when she taught the class something new' (2012: 36), but also a scenario in which veganism can become the basis for enriching human friendships, integrating the classmates' social group rather than isolating Steven as 'different'. Steven also provides an aspirational figure for not-yet vegan readers, as iconic as the gorillas and dinosaurs who he celebrates. However, an arguable limitation with Bodenstein's construction of veganism, is that vegan practice within *Steven the Vegan* is more or less limited to dietary practice; although Steven's motivations are centred on renouncing anthroparchal privileges and ending exploitation, they are expressed principally through his food choices. Two caveats to that interpretation though, are firstly the inclusion of a somewhat broader definition of 'vegan' on the title page: 'a person who doesn't use animal products for food, clothing, or any other purpose' (2012: 2), and secondly the crucial role of empathic experience with other animals in building Steven's case: he doesn't win the day purely through abstract argument, but in large measure through the way in which experiencing other animals brings home the full consequences of Steven's accounts of exploitation. The context of the narrative would arguably also make it difficult to insert the panoply of vegan objections to the exploitation of other animals (although issues such as using sheep's hair or cow's skin for human clothing might have fitted in). For example, in an earlier children's book, *The Tale of Eartha the Sea Turtle* (2011), Bodenstein critiques human impacts on 'wild' animals by fictionalizing a real account of a sea turtle who was entangled by a fishing line, before being helped and untangled by human rescuers. In other words (no pun intended), different stories can and do highlight and critique different forms of anthroparchal relations and/or celebrate vegan (that is, anti-anthroparchal) praxis. As further examples, Jenny Hall celebrates the role of other animals in maintaining soil fertility, within the context of vegan-organic horticulture, in *Organic Alice and the*

Wiggly Jiggly Worms (2008). A pair of short illustrated books for young children written by Mary Brady and illustrated by Steve Hutton respectively critique the exploitation of 'pets' (*The Umpteenth Dalmation* [sic], Brady and Hutton 2003) and human violence towards 'wild' animals (*Tiger Fruit*, Brady and Hutton 2004), while Brady's teenage novel *Under the Stairs* (2003) critiques a broader range of anthroparchal relations as well as providing a positive model of effective vegan activism, including direct action to rescue other animals from violence, for the reader.

Returning to *Steven the Vegan*, the way in which Bodenstein and his illustrator, Ron Robrahn, express empathic relations makes an interesting contrast with Roth's approach. While Roth eschews the cute style trope, Bodenstein and Robrahn embrace it in some respects. The animals at the farm sanctuary have cute humanized features and are often depicted as smiling (especially smiling *at* the human characters) or expressing recognizably human emotions (such as a cow with sad eyes welling with tears in the dairy factory farm (2011: 13)). While in some respects this contrasts with the construction of the wondrousness of other animals evident in Roth's work, *Steven the Vegan* shares the tactic of depicting other animals as enjoying the pleasures of life, including sociality, albeit with Steven and his classmates as much as with other members of their own species. In this respect Bodenstein's story perhaps exceeds even the optimism of Roth's post-anthroparchal utopia, in that the openness of children to rejecting anthroparchal relations leaves open the possibility of reimagining inter-species relations untainted by violence and exploitation.

In comparison with *Steven the Vegan*, Roth's work presents a self-evidently more holistic account of veganism, directly critiquing a broader range of uses of other animals (corresponding more closely to the scope of Figure 2.1) and connecting veganism to environmental concerns with deforestation, pollution and so on. On the other hand, Roth builds her case in *That's Why We Don't Eat Animals* on a claim about the benignity of human relations with 'pets' (a form of relation unmentioned by Bodenstein): 'All animals deserve the care and protection we give our pets' (2009: 5). Jarringly, although the accompanying double-page illustration depicts uncaged mammals and a bird in a cosy (human) domestic setting, it also includes five goldfish in a small bowl on a side table. The reason for highlighting these kinds of issues is not to inflict a 'vegan police' critique on the work of Roth or Bodenstein, but to highlight the difficulty of grounding a critique of anthroparchy that does not in some way draw on already-existing problematic human–other animal relations (such as 'pet'-keeping or cute style) or anti-vegan discourse (such as the reduction of veganism to an issue of dietary practice). Roth's decision to invoke human–'pet' relations as an ethical grounding for her critique makes sense in the context of connecting with children's most common close-up experience of other animals and builds on the prior cultivation of affective relations that have been

160

discussed earlier in this book. Instead of being a means of separation through (limited) incorporation as in Figure 2.1 (bringing 'pets' closer facilitates the fading into the background of the exploited masses in the south-east of Figure 2.1), in Roth's hands, 'pets' become a means of integration through exemplarity: 'We know each other by heart' (2009: 5). The choice of 'heart' is telling here; its association with empathic, or loving, relations with others invites readers to extend that form of relation to the other animals who Roth draws and writes about. The risk with this account, is that it re-spins a key strand in the web of anthroparchal relations, that 'pet'-keeping is the mutually beneficial zenith of human–animal relations and that 'pets' remain subject to human construction in practice and discourse. This raises the question as to whether domestic relations with other animals are so thoroughly compromised by anthroparchal baggage (the embedding of 'pet'-keeping within the animal-industrial complex; its integration with the slaughterhouse through the 'pet food' industry; the use of 'pet'-keeping to facilitate the duplicity of 'protect and eat' discourse and practice), that they are too risky a grounding for vegan praxis. A similar debate could be had about Bodenstein and Robrahn's use of 'cute style'; taking up the tools of cute style to ground a critique of the very situation that it legitimates in the contexts described in chapters 5–8 of this book. Nevertheless, both authors and illustrators do provide children with models for 'being vegan' as a qualitatively different experience of being human, forged through a radical reconfiguration of relations with other animals.

An alternative approach to the critique of anthroparchy within this genre comes in Carlos Patiño's *Dave Loves Chickens* (2013); 'the first in a series of books for young children examining the unique characteristics of animals and questioning why people eat them' (text from inside cover flap; at time of writing this is the only book in the series to have been published). Patiño utilises the device of an alien visitor to planet Earth, the eponymous 'monster' Dave, being mystified as to 'why people from earth eat certain animals and call it "meat"' (2013: 14–15). Dave thus invites identification between the otherness and strangeness imposed on nonhuman animals and that afforded to human children, as part of their conceptual location as not yet fully socialized or completed persons. Dave is a colourful, comical and friendly ('heart of gold'; Patiño 2013: 7) medium through which to estrange children from the taken-for-granted anthroparchal socialization process. He is drawn as a squat, bluish grey biped with three eyes and stubby green horns and a yellowed cracked tooth amidst an otherwise 'normal' set of teeth. Dave is also implicitly introduced as a vegan through his 'meatless diet' accompanied with illustrations of plant foods (and a mushroom (2013: 12)). In common with Roth, Patiño goes on to challenge anthroparchal discourses of exploited others, in his case by writing about and illustrating chickens in a positive light, for example as potentially long lived (11 years implicitly contrasted with their truncated lives within the animal industrial complex) and as enjoying their own species-specific behaviours: 'they enjoy a dust bath' (2013: 16). Like Robrahn, Patiño opts for some anthropomorphic elements in his illustrative style. For instance, chickens are depicted smiling in appreciation of the companionship of Dave (2013: 33), or 'smiling about their speed and power' (2013: 25), or wearing a t-shirt emblazoned with a chicken's 'drumstick' in a red circle with a red line drawn over it (2013: 15). Dave himself, despite his strangeness, also expresses recognizably human emotions through the text and his facial expressions, for instance wearing a police hat and stern expression when wondering why eating chicken's isn't 'banned' (2013: 29). Taken together, Patiño's stylistic and textual devices construct empathetic, rather than objectifying, knowledge as central to *Dave Loves Chickens*. To reinforce this, Patiño compares chicken's lifespans to that of white-tailed deer's (2013: 22–3); animals who children will be more likely to have a pre-existing affective disposition towards, through anthroparchal socialization (*Bambi* et al.). The articulation of chickens with animals generally located in the south-west of Figure 2.1 (except when they are repositioned eastwards in pro-hunting discourses) also invites readers to imaginatively liberate chickens by discursively repositioning them westwards too. Patiño also recalls *Steven the Vegan*'s enrolling of more celebrated nonhumans by pointing out the evolutionary connection between birds and dinosaurs and by illustrating other free-living animals who, from children's perspectives in particular, are already potentially constructed as belonging in the south-west region of Figure 2.1: an elephant, bison and orca whale. This is accompanied by the text, 'Dave loves animals as much as we do' (2013: 30).

In his formulation, 'Dave loves animals as much as we do', Patiño assumes and invokes a pre-existing empathy for other animals among child readers; entirely reasonable given the cultivation of affectivity documented in earlier chapters, but in this case that affectivity is allied to value-rational action through Dave's 'meatless diet' and direct questioning of anthroparchal norms ('why people from earth eat certain animals …'). A complicating problem for these kinds of inter-species articulations is that 'free-living' animals are commonly encountered by children in captive settings: 'zoos', aquaprisons, circuses or as 'performers' in anthroparchal films (see Molloy 2011 for an extended discussion of the latter). As we discussed in Chapter 2, ambivalently positioned animals (on the map of Figure 2.1) demonstrate the precariousness of the fates of all animals in an anthroparchal context: a deer can become prey; an elephant can become an 'entertainer'; an orca can become a spectacle. Love then, has a deeper meaning than the kind of love invoked by cute-style for Patiño; it forecloses the kind of 'love' that is reduced to an instrumental consumption of the 'cuteness' of others for human pleasure: 'chickens are great and they don't belong on our plate' (2013: 33–4). The kind of love that Dave expresses therefore also invites the reconfiguration of the human reader, along congruent lines with Roth's reconfiguration in *Vegan is Love*; although human animals are not directly represented in *Dave Loves Chickens*, Dave himself is clearly a figure that children are invited to identify with and model their ethical practice on.

The books of Roth, Bodenstein and Patiño are all aimed at younger readers (although none state an age-suitable range on the cover). To this of course must be added the embedding of the likely reading of the books within a family context, facilitating the reproduction of vegan caregivers' own ethical practice through sharing the stories themselves. Our last two examples however, differ in being either orientated primarily to older readers (which may well include adult readers), or at least not being obviously targeted at young children: Tutton's *The Amazing Adventures of Wonderpig* (2007) and the oeuvre of celebrated poet Benjamin Zephaniah's vegan-related verse.

Tutton's book (subtitled volume one, though at the time of writing no subsequent volumes have been published to our knowledge), uses a comic strip format to recount five adventures of the eponymous 'world's first and only Vegan Superhero' (2007: 1). What is striking about the tone of Tutton's work is that it invokes additional emotional responses to anthroparchal relations, especially anger, to the loving affectivity that predominates in the work of Roth, Bodenstein and Patiño. While sadness, indignation and anger at exploitation and suffering are present in the latter, they are less prominent than the theme of loving the other as fundamental to vegan praxis. Wonderpig, on the other hand, finds motivation for criminal direct action through his anger at anthroparchal practices: 'Wonderpig was livid and plotted his revenge against the [puppy farmer] offenders' (2007: 16). For instance, in his first adventure, William (Wonderpig's given name) discovers hens incarcerated on a battery farm: 'animal abuse upset him and this was serious abuse' (2007: 5). Wonderpig follows this up by finding 'the farmers family and true to his vegan values used gentle persuasion and blackmail about the farmers weekend hobbies to make them see sense' (2007: 5) and by temporarily locking the farmer in a cage as a lesson-in-kind. Wonderpig also 'rescued the birds and destroyed their prisons', who then 'finished their lives in peace and freedom as nature intended' (2007: 6). In the start of a recurring motif, Wonderpig celebrates his success with a 'bucket of vegan wine' (2007: 7). The structure established in the first story is repeated with respect of different examples of exploitation in the subsequent two stories, involving the separation of cows from calves and 'puppy farms' respectively. In each case, the humans who exploit other animals, or the relatives of those humans, are physically punished. For instance Wonderpig incarcerates the dairy farmer's children in a trailer until 'at last the farmer admitted he was wrong' and switched to growing soya beans and carrots instead (2007: 13) and puts the puppy farmer's children up for sale in a 'pet shop' until 'the dog breeder realised that it was wrong' (2007: 17). These first three strips then, offer humans a route to redemption through confronting them with a moral equivalence of imprisoning innocent children and innocent nonhuman animals. Contrastingly, the final two strips show Wonderpig firstly accessing the mass media through a globally-broadcast TV interview, in which he is able to make an environmental and health case for veganism; and secondly outlining negative health consequences of consuming cows' milk. The former results in the global overthrow of anthroparchal relations: 'overnight the planet went vegan' (2007: 23), while the latter estranges the anthroparchal 'pleasure' of drinking other species' milk: 'That's a whole zit in every glass' (2007: 27), being a reference to the pus content of commercially available cows' milk.

Described in black and white, Wonderpig's adventures, especially the first three, appear provocatively outrageous, contravening the commitment to nonviolence that is central to most anti-anthroparchal direct action, even when the latter has involved criminality, such as damage to property in the course of ALF (Animal Liberation Front) actions. Wonderpig's 'punishment' actions do not correspond with real direct actions conducted on behalf of other animals, although activists themselves do temporarily enter cages in public demonstrations, in order to inspire empathy for permanently caged nonhuman animals (for more on the history and role of nonviolence and violence in direct action for other animals, see Mann 2007 and Best and Nocella II 2004). Wonderpig's model of vegan practice is very different to that modelled by Roth, Bodenstein or Patiño, not least through his hedonistic and alcoholic celebrations of his direct action successes (William is no straight edger). However, Wonderpig has an older target audience, and a wry and knowing humour runs through the cartoons. Wonderpig's spectacular successes may offer a cathartic wish-fulfilment for the overthrow of anthroparchal relations for vegan readers, and a humorous outlet for a more enraged form of affectivity that may result from awareness of the violence of those anthroparchal relations. The playful identification of human activists with Wonderpig is arguably enhanced by its use of anthropomorphic imagery. When 'off duty', William is portrayed as naked and enjoying simple hedonic pleasures, but as Wonderpig, he dons a superhero costume: red tunic, yellow trousers, purple cape, black eye mask and purple cravat. Wonderpig also wears anthropomorphized expressions to communicate his feelings about the injustices he discovers and challenges and uses human speech. Similarly to Robrahn's illustrations in *Steven the Vegan*, Tutton also anthropomorphizes other animal characters in the cartoons, in order to communicate their objection to their exploitation, but unlike Bodenstein, the animals are also given human voices. For example, a tearful calf 'explained that although he was only 2 days old he was being taken away from his mum!' (2007: 9). Compared with Roth, Bodenstein or Patiño, Tutton therefore goes further in asserting an experiential equivalence of human–nonhuman animality as the context for intervening against anthroparchal practices. Wonderpig's adventures then, lack a 'realistic' account of personal or societal transition to a vegan future, reinforced through the evocation of the 'flying pig' metaphor, but Wonderpig may be argued to provide a sustaining resource through its articulation of a chiliastic, carnivalesque utopia, in the face of the currently overwhelming scale and power of the animal-industrial complex. However, given the 'outrage' with which a book as relatively innocuous as Roth's work can be received within the mainstream (see the discussion of *The Mail Online* article above), it is plausible that any commercial success for Tutton's book would have been met with incandescent indignation at its, for instance, 'celebration' of imprisoning or selling children, within at least some mainstream media outlets.

In contrast to the marginal cultural presence of Wonderpig, Benjamin Zephaniah is arguably one of the most celebrated of all living poets in the UK, as well as being a long-standing patron of The Vegan Society and narrator of two of the society's campaigning films: *Truth or Dairy* (1994) and *Making the Connection* (2010). A central thread of Zephaniah's poetry is woven around veganism and human relations with other animals. This is especially prominent in his collection of teenage poetry (as the book blurb describes it): *Talking Turkeys* (1995) and in *The Little Book of Vegan Poems* (2000a). In common with the examples discussed thus far, especially perhaps Bodenstein, Zephaniah empowers, celebrates and defends existing vegan children through his writing. This is achieved in a number of ways. Firstly, through providing models of vegan practice that are both light-hearted yet sincere. For example the character Vegan Steven, a young boy who appears in two humorous short poems, eschews 'animal food', hates 'foxhunting season' and wears 'some cabbage leaves with a few peas on' as his 'vegan clothes'. More soberly, 'Pride' celebrates the integrity of vegan embodiment: 'I've got no bodies inside me, All of me is me' (2000a: 14). Secondly, Zephaniah invites sympathy for vegan children in the 'warning' that opens the *The Little Book*: 'if you are offended by the strong views in these poems, just think of how vegan children are offended every day, not only by the sight and smells of burning bodies but also by being ridiculed because of their compassion' (2000a: 5). Thirdly, Zephaniah depicts vegan subjectivity as loving and loved, notably in his celebratory, 'Vegan Kisses': 'when it comes from your Mom and Dad, or someone else who really cares, your vegan kiss is truly yours, but then again it's also theirs' (2000a: 9). Zephaniah also invites readers to enjoy the pleasures of veganism, deconstructing the stereotype of veganism-as-self-denial (see Cole 2008, Cole and Morgan 2011b), in the mouth-watering verses of 'Vegan Delight' (1995: 30–31): 'What was dat question now? What do we eat?' and 'A Banana Drama' (2000a: 32–4). Veganism is a life-affirming pleasure in Zephaniah's writing, which, reminiscent of Roth's work, asserts the *human* liberatory potential of abdicating the dubious privileges of anthroparchy.

In contrast to the tongue-in-cheek retribution-redemption fantasies of Wonderpig then, Zephaniah situates loving affectivity at the centre of vegan praxis, similar to that found in the work of Roth, Bodenstein and Patiño. Like these authors and Tutton too, Zephaniah also encourages empathetic rather than instrumental knowledge of other animals, through encounters of mutual understanding, or through giving voice to other animals who thereby protest their exploitation and assert an equivalent subjecthood to human animals. These twin approaches are well-illustrated by the pair of poems 'Lost Cow' and 'Mother Cow Speaks'. In the former, the narrator recounts her/his reply to the Lost Cow's request for directions (2000a: 11). Here, the Lost Cow is not described as being the victim of any specific exploitative practice, but is subtly constructed as an agential subject, well-capable of meaningful interaction with a human animal through experiencing being lost and seeking assistance to find his way (the Lost Cow is gendered as male in the poem). In 'Mother Cow Speaks', Mother Cow herself asks the reader, 'Leave that milk for my baby, if you would be so kind' (2000a: 12). Mother Cow's plea verbally recalls the illustrated objections to exploitation of Roth, Bodenstein/Robrahn and Patiño, in which anthropomorphic illustrations are chosen to make other animals' protests against their exploitation plain to the reader. This theme of giving voice is most powerfully expressed in the tour de force 'We People Too', in which representatives of many different species of other animals address the reader and assert their people-ness on the basis of the richness and diversity of their experiences or preferences and also, in our interpretation, awareness of their positioning in Figure 2.1. For example, the pig asks, 'Please don't call me horrid names, think of me as brother', while the fly asks, 'I beg you not to squash me please, I do not want to cause you harm' (2000a: 16, 15). The poem concludes with a chorus of all the animals declaring, 'And all we want to say to you Is that We all are people too' (2000a: 19). Like Tutton, Zephaniah does also express anger against anthroparchal relations, especially through implicitly reporting on the south-east region of Figure 2.1. For example, he evokes the classic animal liberation slogan 'meat is murder' in the celebration of the nonviolence of 'veggie burgers', 'No Pain No Shame' (2000a: 36) and critiques the obfuscation of violence in 'Bloody Food': 'We don't want yu bloody food, Sold wid yu bloody lies, Most of it is simply blood, Dat is under a disguise' (2000a: 41). 'Bloody Food' also ends with a restatement of the motif of inter-species equality from 'We People Too': 'So let's look at it honestly In truth You're really eating people' (2000a: 41). In 'A Killer Lies', Zephaniah exposes the self-serving legitimation of bloodsports and its veneer of respectability: 'He's a Fox Hunter Know him by his killer eyes Something dead must be his prize He's de kind dat's *civilised*' (1995: 53, emphasised in original). The highlighting of 'civilised' by Zephaniah is significant as a critique of the masking of violence that is inherent to the anthroparchal web mapped in Figure 2.1. This motif is extended in 'Pets Control', which almost reads as a key to Figure 2.1, drawing attention to the differential (non-)sensibility of other animals consequent to human discourse and practice. The poem describes evicting nonhumans (tacitly 'vermin') from a new house, usurping them with 'pets', renaming 'wild' animals as 'strays' (itself close to being coterminous with the vermin category), while spectating 'wild' animals for entertainment on television, ironically concluding with the rhetorical, '*How civilised were we?*' (1995: 67, emphasised in original). As well as this kind of direct opposition to instrumental relations with other animals, and overt assertions of value-rational action in the form of vegan practices, or demands for human respect for other animals (arguably the principle from which vegan practices flow), Zephaniah also uses humour and incongruity to dismantle species-barriers. In 'Friends', Zephaniah assembles a motley crew of 'Monkey, snake, me, you and toad' who 'must stick together', bound by no instrumental purpose but by the value of mutuality for its own sake: 'No one understand our deep dialogue' (1995: 23).

The themes explored in *The Little Book* and *Talking Turkeys* also feature in other collections of Zephaniah's poetry, including *Funky Chickens* (1997) and *Wicked World* (2000b). By contextualizing critiques of anthroparchal relations amongst cognate themes of anti-violence, anti-exploitation and pro-empathetic understanding, Zephaniah thereby prevents the marginalization of veganism and anti-anthroparchal relations in the context of his wider work. For instance, *Funky Chickens* includes 'Danny Lives On', about an eponymous cat, apparently Zephaniah's companion, kicked to death by 'human feet', in which Zephaniah laments how 'These animal beaters Are so filled with hate' (1997: 65). Danny was previously celebrated in 'A Day in the Life of Danny the Cat' (1995: 36–9). *Wicked World* implicitly equates the importance of anti-speciesism with anti-racism or environmentalism, for instance. The collection includes 'We People Too' (featured in *The Little Book*) and the poem 'The Vegans', so that both vegans and other animals take their place alongside all human peoples as equally deserving of respect and protection, which is arguably the central theme of the collection; 'People are like you Respect people' ('One Four All', 2000b: 71). In 'The Vegans', it is vegan practice as a compassionate other-orientation that is the focus of the poem: 'He's trying to explain That the thing he hates is pain, That boy will never wear Any fox fur or horsehair, He will not follow fashion His main thing is compassion' (2000b: 51). In 'We Know', various nonhuman species are exonerated before the poem concludes with an indictment of human animals for 'killing the forest' (2000b: 55). Taken together then, Zephaniah's poetry synthesizes elements found throughout vegan literature for children: interrogating the objectification of other animals; interrogating the 'privileges' of anthroparchal relations; affirming the subjecthood of other animals; and affirming the value-rationality and affectivity of vegan practice.

Conclusion

This chapter has identified some common themes in the emerging genre of vegan children's literature. These include the evacuation of the eastern regions of Figure 2.1, through the abandonment of practices of confinement and killing and the representational architecture that sustains it. The language and imagery of vegan children's literature provides a discursive vehicle which moves other animals towards the regions *ideally* occupied by human animals ('ideally', given that many human peoples remain in practico-discursive positions imposed upon them within webs of privilege and inequality). However, vegan children's literature also sets in motion another journey, discursively transporting human animals eastwards. This occurs in two senses. Firstly, it enables readers to attain sensibility of the conditions borne by other animals in the south-east of Figure 2.1, avoiding the north-eastern diversion that the anthroparchal socialization process expends such effort in constructing, as we have recounted in chapters 5–8. Secondly, it takes readers closer to other animals themselves, perhaps meeting halfway as the latter exit the killing/cutie zones of Figure 2.1. A coalescing of species and individuals, empathetic yet respectfully ineffable, is instantiated by the disintegration of the network of instrumental relations that keeps humans and other animals so far apart.

Chapter 10
Conclusion:
Resisting the Zooicidal Imperative

Open to everything happy and sad
Seeing the good when it's all going bad. (From 'Slipping Away', Moby 2005)

We began this book with a sociological conundrum: the juxtaposition of killing and care, of death and delight, in the way we present children with affective lures alongside the corpses of other animals in 'happy meals' and other fast food—'animal' movie tie ins. The remainder of this book has been an attempt to unravel, or at least begin to unravel, that conundrum and examine the practices and discourses that make it possible. In doing so, we have pointed to the specific rationalities that govern human relations with other animals in specific contexts, but also at how those rationalities and contexts intersect and are mutually constitutive; the rationality of the cultural industry intersects with that of the fast food industry and thereby with agribusiness through the lens of children as consumers. The death and delight combo makes perfect sense for the generation of profit. But it also depends on the ceaseless extermination of other animals, the wreckage of the environment that we humans share with other animals and the price of human pain paid through hunger and chronic disease: a zooicidal imperative with suicidal and global consequences, especially given increasing consumption of 'animal products' globally and the associated export of the 'meat' and dairy-heavy SAD (Standard American Diet) (Henning 2011, Garnett 2009, McMichael et al. 2007). The anthroparchal practices and discourses explored in this book have been focused on the UK, albeit unavoidably linked with a broader Western and especially US-dominated anthroparchal culture, through Hollywood film, US 'fast food', etc. and the global spread of legitimatory representations is likely to intensify alongside any intensification in the pace and scale of exploitation of other animals. This is not to deny cultural variability in the legitimation of anthroparchal practices; these are urgent questions for social research in themselves that are beyond the scope of this book. However, the key point is to subvert the assumed inevitability of these trends through vegan praxis, which includes sociological research conducted under a Critical Animal Studies banner. As well as the food security motivation for averting a future of ever-greater global 'livestock' dependence, which often remains anthropocentric (for example see McMichael and Butler 2010), there is therefore a deeper rationality that must be counterpoised to zooicide; a rationality orientated to the ultimate values of human humility, of peaceable relations and solidarity with other animals as well as with other humans, of care for the ethical flourishing of our children; an exit from Figure 2.1. The deformation of childhood affectivity that anthroparchal relations depend on can and must be reworked in order to set our children free from dependency on the exploitation and suffering of others. New traditions can and must be embedded in the socialization experience that celebrate life, rather than death, and that restore respect, wonder and joy in our relations with other animals rather than the distancing objectification of instrumental knowledge. Recalling Moby's lyrics that open this chapter, children's affective/emotional maturity and ethical flourishing can only be enhanced through experiencing both the sadness of confronting the consequences of anthroparchal relations, as well as the happiness of their imagined and real reversal through vegan representation and practice, and we are motivated by the possibility of that reversal in spite of the apparent resilience of anthroparchal relations. How then, might this be achieved?

The emerging genre of vegan children's literature discussed in Chapter 9 began to map out a route to a post-anthroparchal future. These authors invite children to a different human ontology, one in which the incongruity of the 'happy meal' is immediately apparent and abhorrent, rather than alluring. They also honour the otherness and mystery of nonhuman animals while also asserting their capacity to experience the world in ways which are meaningful to them, beyond human experience: an invitation to empathy but an empathy that must have respectful limits and that cannot reduce other animals to infantilized ciphers for 'pre-humans':

> There is a way things look, taste, smell, feel or sound to another animal, a way of which we will have no idea as long as we insist that the only things worth knowing about are our own social constructions of the world. Although I do acknowledge that there is a sense in which we cannot know the Other [...] we must remind ourselves that other meanings exist. (Noske 1989: 160)

Vegan children's literature also wrestles with its anthroparchal context however; the cultural ubiquity of 'cute style' is difficult to evade and raises the question of how to engage a not-yet-vegan reader who is likely already to have been socialized into the normality of cutification. As Steve Baker writes, the 'ubiquity of the cute image makes it all the more important to have a go at unsettling its meanings' (2001: 226), but also that, 'complicity in the space of the popular is itself a prerequisite for any effective loosening of fixed meanings' (2001: 230). The loosening of fixed meanings that vegan children's literature facilitates is precisely the usurpation of sentimentalized instrumental relations that are sedimented into habit. They achieve this through stimulating critical questioning and also encouraging affective action: choosing veganism through love of the animal other; a love that demands the abdication of human anthroparchal privilege but that is also rewarded with the cancellation of the zooicidal-suicidal pact. Children's journey through veganism does not end with appropriated cute imagery; those appropriations are themselves invitations to learn and do more through the process of critical questioning of anthroparchal relations and in the spirit of compassion for other animals that they aim to engender. It is therefore crucial to remain mindful of the context in which vegan cultural artefacts are encountered, just as it is crucial to critique anthroparchal discourses and practices in their wider context of Figure 2.1, alongside an acknowledgement of their specificity. The analysis in Chapter 9, therefore, is only a first step in a wider enquiry into children's encounters with vegan, anti-anthroparchal discourse and practice.

This literary genre in itself is also only one small aspect of vegan children's culture and of vegan culture and practice more widely. Veganism can and must intervene across all socialization sites and furthermore, forge its own inter-textual and mutually constitutive rationalities, in order to maximize its chances of succeeding in denormalizing and ultimately ending anthroparchal relations. To an extent this process is already in train, for instance in the UK through the efforts of Vegan Society activists (the Vegan Society is an educational charity) to engage children within the education system, by delivering school talks, workshops or cookery demonstrations or disseminating vegan-themed resources for teachers, especially through the PSHE route. Likewise, the Vegan Society produces outreach materials to support vegan parenting (for example, Hood 2005). But much remains to be done in the weaving together of a thoroughgoing alternative socialization route, across the key sites we have examined in chapters 5–8 of this book and thereby across the geography of Figure 2.1. This partly requires further engagement by sociologists and Childhood Studies scholars through empirical research into how children forge relationships with other animals through practices and discourses and especially how they are able to resist anthroparchal socialization, for instance through the 'meat insight' epiphanies documented by Amato and Partridge (1989), which we discussed in Chapter 5, or through researching how children respond to anti-anthroparchal cultural artefacts such as those discussed in Chapter 9. The necessary counterpart of the exploration of anti-anthroparchal discourse and practice is therefore continued research into how anthroparchal relations are reproduced. As we stressed in the introduction to this volume, we conceived of this book partly as an invitation to further research, in recognition that human relations with other animals, and especially children's relations with other animals, ought to be significant fields of enquiry across the social sciences and humanities; or for that matter across all academic enquiry when we consider the wider context of global food production and human hunger, the challenge of climate change and the role of 'livestock' farming within that and all of the socio-practical tasks related to transitioning to plant-based societies. Even in the context of our relatively narrow focus in this book however, we have only scratched the surface. Each of the empirical chapters in Part II might easily have been developed into a book-length treatment and many important cultural fields have only been briefly touched on, such as food advertising, or children's novels, films and other cultural artefacts that feature other animals (such novels and films were the focus of an earlier paper, though that in itself was only a beginning; see Stewart and Cole 2009). Likewise, the reproduction of anthroparchal practices is ripe for sociological investigation, for instance through ethnographic work in domestic space such as family mealtimes, in public space such as fast food restaurants or 'petting zoos' or in educational space such as the classroom or the canteen. Through a fuller understanding of these discourses and representations, a sociologically-inflected critical animal studies can hope to be of service to the wider vegan movement and inform both discursive and practical interventions into children's socialization and pursue the dismantling of the anthroparchogenic environment.

Of course a key obstacle is the recalcitrance of children's caregivers, both in the home and at an institutional level; the reconstruction of children's socialization cannot proceed in isolation, not least because it runs up against the practical obstacle of, for example, how to get Ruby Roth's books into the hands of non-vegan children. In the UK context, the experience and contribution of existing vegan parents and caregivers may prove to be a vital lever in opening the education system and, by association, other parents and caregivers, to veganism, under the aegis of the existing value-rational imperatives of diversity and equality within schools. To take another example, anthroparchal digital media could also be resisted through vegan alternatives; children could play as workers/helpers on virtual animal sanctuaries that fund the rehoming of other animals through vegan-organic food growing, linked to a virtual café that served plant-based meals. The game world could be expanded to progressively open up more and more avenues of vegan outreach and activism and in-game rewards could be related to the nonhuman animals saved, the anthroparchal facilities driven out of business and replaced with veganic farms, or the numbers of in-game human characters 'converted' to veganism, through their visits to the sanctuary/farm/café. The game could also be linked to generation of revenue to support 'real world' activism in a value-rational alternative to the profit generation model of Farmville et al.

There are others far better qualified than us to imagine, design and deliver these kinds of initiatives, but, as we suggested in Chapter 2, we hope that Figure 2.1 itself can have value as a model for integrative vegan praxis, that challenges the panoply of anthroparchal relations even while acknowledging that they have their own rationalities. In fact, insisting on the specific albeit intertwined rationality of different 'positions' on Figure 2.1 arguably has value as a counterpoint to the paralyzing despair that may result from conceiving of anthroparchy as a totalizing, monolithic and therefore invulnerable system. Instead, Figure 2.1 helps keep us mindful of the precariousness of anthroparchal relations; again, as Amato and Partridge remind us, children can and do see through them, precisely through recognizing the incongruously juxtaposed constructions of affective representation and corpse-as-dinner. So, while we have argued for the responsibilities of academics to challenge the anthroparchal, zooicidal deformation of children's relations with other animals, we also draw hope and strength from children's own capacities to assert their own ethics of resistance, even in the bleakest of cultural contexts for children and other animals; 'for what is ethics, if not the practice of freedom' (Foucault 1984: 284). In that spirit, we end with an example of what one child refusing their anthroparchal socialization can achieve: Donald Watson, a co-founder of The Vegan Society (the world's first) and inventor of the word vegan in 1944, recollects his childhood witnessing of the slaughter of a pig:

> The thing that shocked me, along with the chief impact of the whole setup, was that my Uncle George, of whom I thought very highly, was part of the crew, and I suppose at that point I decided that farms, and uncles, had to be re-assessed. They weren't all they seemed to be, on the face of it, to a little, hitherto uninformed boy. And it followed that this idyllic scene was nothing more than Death Row. A Death Row where every creature's days were numbered by the point at which it was no longer of service to human beings [...] And quite early in life, I came to the conclusion that, if I was to report on Man's progress, I had to settle for the comment beloved of schoolteachers: "could do better". And from that, The Vegan Society was formed. (The Vegan Society 2002: 5)

Bibliography

AAA (*All About Animals*) 2012. April–May 2012, #62. Immediate Media Co.

AC (*Animal Cuties*) 2012. May–June 2012. Egmont.

Adams, C.J. 2004a. *The Pornography of Meat*. New York: Continuum.

Adams, C.J. 2004b. *The Sexual Politics of Meat: A Feminist-Vegetarian Critical Theory*. 20th Anniversary Edition. New York: Continuum.

Adams, C.J. 2006. The war on compassion, in *The Feminist Care Tradition in Animal Ethics: A Reader*, edited by J. Donovan and C.J. Adams. New York: Columbia University Press, 21–36.

Aesop 1998. *The Complete Fables*. London: Penguin Classics.

AF (*Animal Friends*) 2012. #129. Exeter: LCD Publishing.

Allen, R.C. 2009. *The British Industrial Revolution in Global Perspective*. Cambridge: Cambridge University Press.

Amato, P.R. and Partridge, S.A. 1989. *The New Vegetarians: Promoting Health and Protecting Life*. New York: Plenum Press.

Anderson, M.V. and Henderson, A.J.Z. 2005. Pernicious portrayals: The impact of children's attachment to animals of fiction on animals of fact. *Society and Animals*, 13(4), 297–314.

Animal Aid 2013. *Put an End to the 'Living Eggs Project'*. [Online]. Available at: http://www.animalaid.org.uk/h/f/ACTIVE/blog/ALL/1//?be_id=402 [accessed 22 February 2014].

Animal Aid 2014. *Race Horse Death Watch*. [Online]. Available at: http://www.horsedeathwatch.com/ [accessed 18 April 2014].

Archer, J. 1997. Why do people love their pets? *Evolution and Human Behaviour*, 18, 237–59.

Ariès, P. 1962. *Centuries of Childhood: A Social History of Family Life*. New York: Vintage Books.

Arluke, A. and Sanders, C.R. 1996. *Regarding Animals*. Philadelphia: Temple University Press.

Aston, L.M., Smith, J.N. and Powles, J.W. 2012. Impact of a reduced red and processed meat dietary pattern on disease risks and greenhouse gas emissions in the UK: A modelling study. [Online]. *BMJ Open*, 2(5), 1–11. Available at: http://bmjopen.bmj.com/content/2/5/e001072.full [accessed 27 May 2014].

Aune, D., Usin, G. and Veierod, M. 2009. Meat consumption and the risk of type 2 diabetes: A systematic review and meta-analysis of cohort studies. *Diabetologia*, 52, 2277–87.

AY (*Animals and You*) 2012. #145. London: D.C. Thomson & Co. Ltd.

Babe (dir. Chris Noonan, 1995).

Baker, S. 2001. *Picturing the Beast: Animals, Identity, and Representation*. Champaign, IL: University of Illinois Press.

Ball, S. 2013a. *Foucault, Power and Education*. London: Routledge.

Ball, S. 2013b. *The Education Debate*. 2nd Edition. Bristol: The Policy Press.

Baroni, L., Cenci, L., Tettamanti, M. and Berati, M. 2007. Evaluating the environmental impact of various dietary patterns combined with different food production systems. *European Journal of Clinical Nutrition*, 61, 279–86.

Bateson, P. 1976. Rules and reciprocity in behavioural development, in *Growing Points in Ethology*, edited by P.P.G. Bateson and R. Hinde. Cambridge: Cambridge University Press, 401–21.

Bauman, Z. 1988. *Freedom*. Milton Keynes: Open University Press.

Benton, T. 1993. *Natural Relations: Ecology, Animal Rights and Social Justice*. London: Verso.

Berry, G. [no date]. *First Picture Dictionary*. Loughborough: Ladybird Books Ltd.

Best, S. 2004. It's war! The escalating battle between activists and the corporate-state complex, in *Terrorists or Freedom Fighters? Reflections on the Liberation of Animals*, edited by S. Best and A.J. Nocella II. New York: Lantern Books, 300–339.

Best, S. and Nocella II, A.J. (eds) 2004. *Terrorists or Freedom Fighters? Reflections on the Liberation of Animals*. New York: Lantern Books.

Birke, L. 2003. Who – or what – are the rats (and mice) in the laboratory. *Society and Animals*, 11(3), 207–24.

BBC (British Broadcasting Corporation) 2009. Anger over school sheep slaughter. [Online]. Available at: http://news.bbc.co.uk/1/hi/england/kent/8248718.stm [accessed 22 February 2014].

BBC (British Broadcasting Corporation) 2013a. Horsemeat scandal: Withdrawn products and test results. [Online, 22 March]. Available at: http://www.bbc.co.uk/news/world-21412590 [accessed 16 December 2013].

BBC (British Broadcasting Corporation) 2013b. Newspaper review: Horsemeat scandal fallout goes on. [Online, 17 February]. Available at: http://www.bbc.co.uk/news/uk-21489560 [accessed 16 December 2013].

BBC (British Broadcasting Corporation) 2013c. Pig rearing school 'bombarded' by protest emails. [Online]. Available at: http://www.bbc.co.uk/news/uk-england-suffolk-21629888 [accessed 22 February 2014].

BBC (British Broadcasting Corporation) 2013d. PMQs: Cameron on horsemeat prosecutions and meat checks. [Online, 13 February]. Available at: http://www.bbc.co.uk/news/uk-politics-21444662 [accessed 16 December 2013].

BBC (British Broadcasting Corporation) 2013e. Primary school children rear pigs to send to butcher. [Online]. Available at: http://www.bbc.co.uk/news/uk-england-suffolk-21427695 [accessed 22 February 2014].

Bentham, J. 2000. *An Introduction to the Principles of Morals and Legislation.* Kitchener: Batoche Books.

Blackstone, W. 1765. *Commentaries on the Laws of England. Book the First.* Oxford: The Clarendon Press.

Blakemore, J.E.O. 2003. Children's beliefs about violating gender norms: Boys shouldn't look like girls, and girls shouldn't act like boys. *Sex Roles*, 8(9/10), 411–19.

Bodenstein, D. 2011. *The Tale of Eartha the Sea Turtle.* USA: Totem Tales Publishing.

Bodenstein, D. 2012. *Steven the Vegan.* USA: Totem Tales Publishing.

Box Office Mojo 2011. *Puss in Boots.* [Online]. Available at: http://boxofficemojo.com/movies/?id=pussinboots12.htm [accessed 22 December 2011].

Brady, M. 2003. *Under the Stairs.* Wolverhampton: Magpie House.

Brady, M. and Hutton, S. 2003. *The Umpteenth Dalmation.* Wolverhampton: Magpie House.

Brady, M. and Hutton, S. 2004. *Tiger Fruit.* Wolverhampton: Magpie House.

Burt, J. 2001. The illumination of the animal kingdom: The role of light and electricity in animal representation. *Society and Animals*, 9(3), 203–28.

Canning, N. 2007. Children's empowerment in play. *European Early Childhood Education Research Journal*, 15(2), 227–36.

Carroll, L. 1993 [1865/1871]. *Alice's Adventures in Wonderland & Through the Looking-Glass.* Ware: Wordsworth Classics.

Change4Life [no date]. *Healthier Lunches and Picnics.* [Online]. Available at: http://www.nhs.uk/Change4Life/Pages/healthy-lunchbox-picnic.aspx [accessed 21 December 2012].

Chicken Run (dir. Peter Lloyd and Nick Park, 2000).

Clarke, J. 2004. Histories of childhood, in *Childhood Studies an Introduction*, edited by D. Wyse. London: Blackwell, 3–12.

CLEAPSS 2013. *Student Safety Sheets.* Uxbridge: CLEAPSS.

Coats, C.D. 1989. *Old MacDonald's Factory Farm: The Myth of the Traditional Farm and the Shocking Truth about Animal Suffering in Today's Agribusiness.* New York: Continuum.

Cole, M. 2008. Asceticism and hedonism in research discourses of veg*anism. *British Food Journal*, 110(7), 706–16.

Cole, M. 2011. From 'animal machines' to 'happy meat'? Foucault's ideas of disciplinary and pastoral power applied to 'animal-centred' welfare discourse. *Animals*, 1(1), 83–101.

Cole, M. 2014. 'The greatest cause on earth': The historical formation of veganism as anethical practice, in *The Rise of Critical Animal Studies – From the Margins to the Centre*, edited by N. Taylor and R. Twine. London: Routledge, 203–24.

Cole, M. and Morgan, K. 2011a. Veganism contra speciesism: Beyond debate. *The Brock Review*, 12(1), 144–63.

Cole, M. and Morgan, K. 2011b. Vegaphobia: Derogatory discourses of veganism and the reproduction of speciesism in UK national newspapers. *British Journal of Sociology*, 61(1), 134–53.

Cole, M. and Morgan, K. 2013. Engineering freedom? A critique of biotechnological routes to 'animal liberation'. *Configurations*, 21(2), 201–29.

Cole, M. and Stewart, K. 2011a. *The Creation of a Killer Species: Cultural Rupture in Representations of 'Urban Foxes' in UK Newspapers*. Paper to the Thinking About Animals Conference, Brock University, Ontario, Canada, 31 March–1 April 2011.

Cole, M. and Stewart, K. 2011b. *The Ordering of Empathy: Socializing the Normality of 'Meat'*. Paper to Eating Meat: The Social Relationship of Humans and Animals and the Meaning of Meat Conference, Institute of Sociology, University of Hamburg, 1 July 2011.

Cole, M. and Stewart, K. 2012. Puss in boots. *Journal for Critical Animal Studies*, 10(1), 200–210.

Cole, M., Miele, M., Hines, P., et al. 2009. Animal foods and climate change: Shadowing eating practices. *International Journal of Consumer Studies*, 33(2), 162–7.

Cole, M., Stewart, K. and Williams, M. 2012. *Heteronormativity and the Co-constitution of Homophobic and Speciesist Oppression*. Paper to Sociology in an Age of Austerity, BSA annual conference, University of Leeds, 11–13 April.

Cook, D.T. 2004. *The Commodification of Childhood: The Children's Clothing Industry and the Rise of the Child Consumer*. Durham, NC: Duke University Press.

Coppin, D. 2003. Foucauldian hog futures: The birth of mega-hog farms. *The Sociological Quarterly*, 44(4), 597–616.

Corsaro, W. 2012. *The Sociology of Childhood*. 3rd Edition. London: Sage.

Cosslett, T. 2006. *Talking Animals in British Children's Fiction 1786–1914*. Farnham: Ashgate.

Craib, I. 1997. *Classical Social Theory: An Introduction to the Thought of Marx, Weber, Durkheim, and Simmel*. Oxford: Oxford University Press.

Crane, D. 2012. *Fashion and its Social Agendas: Class, Gender, and Identity in Clothing*. Chicago: University of Chicago Press.

Cudworth, E. 2008. Seeing and believing: Gender and species hierarchy in contemporary cultures of animal food, in *Eating and Believing: Interdisciplinary Perspectives on Vegetarianism and Theology*, edited by D. Grummett and R. Meurs. New York and London: T&T Clark/Continuum, 168–83.

Cudworth, E. 2011. *Social Lives with Other Animals: Tales of Sex, Death and Love*. Basingstoke: Palgrave Macmillan.

Daily Telegraph, The 2009. Pigs reared and killed at primary school. [Online]. Available at: http://www.telegraph.co.uk/education/educationnews/5314651/Pigs-re ared-and-killed-at-primary-school.html [accessed 22 February 2014].

Davis, J. 2012. *World Veganism – Past, Present, and Future.* [Online]. Available at: http://maesbury.org/history/Vegan_History.pdf [accessed 20 December 2013].

deMause, L.E. 1974. *The History of Childhood.* New York: Psychohistory Press.

DeMello, M. 2012. *Animals and Society: An Introduction to Human-Animal Studies.* New York: Columbia University Press.

DEFRA (Department for Environment Food and Rural Affairs) 2011. *UK Poultry Slaughterings.* [Online]. Available at: http://archive.defra.gov.uk/evidence/ statistics/foodfarm/food/poultry/documents/poulsl.xls [accessed 26 May 2014].

DEFRA (Department for Environment Food and Rural Affairs) 2014. *United Kingdom Poultry and Poultry Meat Statistics – March 2014.* [Online]. Available at: https://www.gov.uk/government/uploads/system/uploads/attachment_ data/file/307263/poultry-statsnotice-01may14.pdf [accessed 26 May 2014].

Department for Education 2013. *The National Curriculum in England. Framework Document.* London: Department for Education.

Department of Health 2013. DH Guidance. *Notes on the Infant Formula and Follow-on Formula Regulations 2007 (as amended).* [Online]. Available at: https://www.gov.uk/government/uploads/system/uploads/attachment_ data/file/204314/Infant_formula_guidance_2013_-_final_6_March.pdf [accessed 20 December 2013].

Dimbleby, H. and Vincent, J. 2013. *The School Food Plan.* [Online]. Available at: http://www.schoolfoodplan.com/wp-content/uploads/2013/07/School_ Food_Plan_2013.pdf [accessed 22 February 2014].

Donovan, J. and Adams, C.J. 2007. *The Feminist Care Tradition in Animal Ethics: A Reader.* New York: Columbia University Press.

Dunayer, J. 2002. *Animal Equality: Language and Liberation.* New York: Lantern Books.

Eisnitz, G.A. 2007. *Slaughterhouse: The Shocking Story of Greed, Neglect, and Inhumane Treatment Inside the U.S. Meat Industry.* Amherst, NY: Prometheus Books.

Elias, N. 1978. *The History of Manners: The Civilizing Process, Vol. 1.* New York: Pantheon.

Erickson, R. 1985. Play contributes to the full emotional development of the child. *Education,* 105(3): 261–3.

European Commission [no date a]. *Doing Your Shopping.* [Online]. Available at: http://farmland-thegame.eu/tech_sheet_08_shopping_en.html [accessed 22 February 2013].

European Commission [no date b]. *Farmland the Game.* [Online]. Available at: http://www.farmland-thegame.eu/ [accessed 22 February 2013].

European Commission [no date c]. *Pupils' Handbook.* [Online]. Available at: http://farmland-thegame.eu/downloads/pdf/Farmland_Toolkit_Teacher. pdf [accessed 22 February 2013].

European Commission [no date d]. *Teachers' Handbook.* [Online]. Available at: http://farmland-thegame.eu/downloads/pdf/Farmland_Toolkit_Teacher. pdf [accessed 22 February 2013].

European Commission [no date e]. *The Life of Calves.* [Online]. Available at: http://farmland-thegame.eu/tech_sheet_05_calves_en.html [accessed 22 February 2013].

European Commission [no date f]. *The Life of Dairy Cows.* [Online]. Available at: http://farmland-thegame.eu/tech_sheet_06_dairy_cows_en.html [accessed 22 February 2013].

European Commission [no date g]. *The Life of Laying Hens.* [Online]. Available at: http://farmland-thegame.eu/tech_sheet_03_hens_en.html [accessed 22 February 2013].

European Commission [no date h]. *The Life of Pigs.* [Online]. Available at: http:// farmland-thegame.eu/tech_sheet_02_pigs_en.html [accessed 22 February 2013].

European Commission [no date i]. *The Transport of Animals.* [Online]. Available at: http://farmland-thegame.eu/tech_sheet_07_transport_en.html [accessed 22 February 2013].

F Word, The 2005–2010. Channel 4. 27 October 2005–7 January 2010.

Fairlie, S. 2010. *Meat: A Benign Extravagance.* East Meon: Permanent Publications.

Faubion, J. (ed.) 2002. *Power.* London: Penguin Books.

Fiddes, N. 1991. *Meat: A Natural Symbol.* London: Routledge.

Fletcher, A., Jamal, F., Fitzgerald-Yau, N., and Bonell, C. 2013. 'We've got some underground business selling junk food': Qualitative evidence of the unintended effects of English school food policies. *Sociology* DOI: 10.1177/0038038513 500102.

Food for Life Partnership 2013. *Homepage.* [Online]. Available at: http://www. foodforlife.org.uk/ [accessed 22 February 2014].

Foucault, M. 1973. Truth and juridical forms, in *Power*, edited by J. Faubion. London: Penguin Books, 1–89.

Foucault, M. 1980. Questions of method, in *Power*, edited by J. Faubion. London: Penguin Books, 223–38.

Foucault, M. 1982a. Space, knowledge and power, in *Power*, edited by J. Faubion. London: Penguin Books, 349–64.

Foucault, M. 1982b. The subject and power, in *Power*, edited by J. Faubion. London: Penguin Books, 349–64.

Foucault, M. 1984. The ethics of the concern of the self as a practice of freedom, in *Ethics*, edited by P. Rabinow. London: Penguin Books, 281–301.

Foucault, M. 1991. *Discipline and Punish: The Birth of the Prison.* London: Penguin Books.

Foucault, M. 1998. *The Will to Knowledge: The History of Sexuality Volume 1.* Penguin: London.

Foucault, M. 2000. Penal theories and institutions, in *Ethics*, edited by P. Rabinow. London: Penguin Books, 17–21.

Fox, M.A. 2000. Vegetarianism and planetary health. *Ethics and the Environment*, 5(2), 163–74.

Franklin, A. 1999. *Animals and Modern Cultures.* London: Sage.

Garnett, T. 2009. Livestock-related greenhouse gas emissions: Impacts and options for policy makers. *Environmental Science & Policy*, 12(4), 491–503.

Giddens, A. and Sutton, P.W. 2013. *Sociology.* 7th Edition. Cambridge: Polity Press.

Gordon, C. 2002. Introduction, in *Power*, edited by J. Faubion. London: Penguin Books, xi–xli.

Greger, M. 2006. *Bird Flu: A Virus of Our Own Hatching.* New York: Lantern Books.

Griffin, E. 2010. *A Short History of the British Industrial Revolution.* Basingstoke: Palgrave Macmillan.

Guardian, The 2009. Marcus the sheep slaughtered after being raised by schoolchildren. [Online]. Available at: http://www.theguardian.com/uk/2009/sep/14/marcus-the-sheep-slaughtered [accessed 22 February 2014].

Guerrini, A. 1989. The ethics of animal experimentation in seventeenth-century England. *Journal of the History of Ideas*, 50(3), 391–407.

Hall, J. 2008. *Organic Alice and the Wiggly Jiggly Worms.* St. Helen's: Sow & Grow Organics.

Hamleys [no date]. *Life at Hamleys.* [Online]. Available at: http://www.hamleys.com/explore-life.irs [accessed 1 May 2014].

Hansard HL Deb. col. XIV col. 555–6, 15 May 1809.

Haraway, D. 2007. *When Species Meet.* Minnesota: University of Minnesota Press.

Harris, M. 2002. Vivisection, the culture of science, and intellectual uncertainty in The Island of Doctor Moreau. *Gothic Studies*, 4(2), 99–115.

Harrison, B. 1973. Animals and the state in nineteenth-century England. *English Historical Review*, LXXXVIII(CCCXLIX), 786–820.

Henning, B.G. 2011. Standing in livestock's 'long shadow': The ethics of eating meat on a small planet. *Ethics and the Environment*, 16(2), 63–93.

Hirschman, E.C. and Sanders, C.R. 1997. Motion pictures as metaphoric consumption: How animal narratives teach us to be human. *Semiotica*, 115(1/2), 53–79.

Hogarth, W. 1742. *The Graham Children.* Oil on canvas, 160.5 × 181 cm, The National Gallery, London.

Hood, S. 2005. *Feeding Your Vegan Infant with Confidence: A Practical Guide from Pre-conception Through to Pre-school.* St. Leonards-on-Sea: The Vegan Society.

Horrigan, L., Lawrence, R.S. and Walker, P. 2002. How sustainable agriculture can address the environmental and human health harms of sustainable agriculture. *Environmental Health Perspectives,* 110, 445–56.

Howard Moore, J. 1895. *Why I Am a Vegetarian: An Address Delivered Before the Chicago Vegetarian Society.* Chicago: Purdy Publishing Co.

Hribal, J. 2010. *Fear of the Animal Planet. The Hidden History of Animal Resistance.* Petrolia/Oakland: Counter Pounch/AK Press.

Humphries, J. 2010. *Childhood and Child Labour in the British Industrial Revolution.* Cambridge: Cambridge University Press.

Independent, The 2009. Marcus the sheep falls victim to ruthless primary school pupils. [Online]. Available at: http://www.independent.co.uk/news/uk/ho me-news/marcus-the-sheep-falls-victim-to-ruthless-primary-school-pupils-1786138.html [accessed 22 February 2014].

Jack, L. 2007. BBC launches animal magazine for kids. *Marketing Week.* [Online]. Available at: http://www.marketingweek.co.uk/bbc-launches-animal-maga zine-for-kids/2057188.article [accessed 26 January 2013].

James, A. and James, A. 2012. *Key Concepts in Childhood Studies.* London: Sage.

Jamie's Great Italian Escape 2005. Channel 4. 19 October–23 November.

Jenks, C. 2005. *Childhood.* 2nd Edition. Abingdon: Routledge.

Jerolmack, C. 2008. How pigeons became rats: The cultural-spatial logic of problem animals. *Social Problems,* 55(1), 72–94.

Johnson, L. 2012. *Power, Knowledge, Animals.* London: Palgrave.

Jungle Book, The (dir. Wolfgang Reitherman, 1967).

Kalof, L. and Fitzgerald, A. (eds) 2007. *The Animals Reader. The Essential Classic and Contemporary Writings.* Oxford: Berg.

Kean, H. 1998. *Animal Rights. Political and Social Change in Britain Since 1800.* London: Reaktion.

Kehily, M.-J. 2009. Understanding childhood, in *An Introduction to Childhood Studies.* 2nd Edition, edited by M-J. Kehily. Maidenhead: Open University Press, McGraw Hill Education, 1–16.

Kheel, M. 2008. *Nature Ethics: An Ecofeminist Perspective.* Lanham, MA: Rowman & Littlefield.

Kheel, K. 2009. Communicating care: An ecofeminist perspective. *Media Development* (February 2009): 45–50.

Kipling, R. 1894. *The Jungle Book.* [Online]. Available at: http://www.gutenberg. org/files/35997/35997-h/35997-h.htm [accessed 6 February 2013].

Kirby, P. 2003. *Child Labour in Britain 1750–1870.* Basingstoke: Palgrave Macmillan.

Kowalczyk, A. 2014. Mapping non-human resistance in the age of biocapital, in *The Rise of Critical Animal Studies: From the Margins to the Centre,* edited by N. Taylor and R. Twine. London: Routledge, 183–200.

Lansbury, C. 2007. The Brown Dog Riots of 1907, in *The Animals Reader: The Essential Classics and Contemporary Writings*, edited by L. Kalof and A. Fitzgerald. Oxford: Berg, 307–22.

Leneman, L. 1999. No animal food. The road to veganism in Britain: 1909–1944. *Society and Animals*, 7(3), 219–28.

Lenzer, G. 2001. Children's studies: Beginnings and purposes. *The Lion and the Unicorn*, 25(2), 181–6.

Lion King, The (dir. Roger Allers and Rob Minkoff, 1994).

Little Dish no date. *Our Food.* [Online]. Available at: http://www.littledish.co.uk/our-food/ [accessed 30 April 2014].

Living Eggs 2013a. *About Us.* [Online]. Available at: http://www.livingeggs.co.uk/aboutus.htm [accessed 6 February 2013].

Living Eggs 2013b. *Teachers' Resources.* [Online]. Available at: http://www.livingeggs.co.uk/TeachersResources.asp [accessed 26 January 2013].

Living Eggs 2013c. *Using Animals in Schools. Ethical Considerations for the Use of Animals in Schools.* [Online]. Available at: http://www.livingeggs.co.uk/hatch-a-chick/wp-content/uploads/2013/02/Animal-Ethics.pdf [accessed 26 January 2013].

Living Eggs 2014a. *Rehoming Chicks.* [Online]. Available at: http://www.livingeggs.co.uk/hatch-a-chick/wp-content/uploads/2013/02/Re-homing-chicks1.pdf [accessed 22 February 2014].

Living Eggs 2014b. *Thematic Planning with Living Eggs.* [Online]. Available at: http://www.livingeggs.co.uk/hatch-a-chick/wp-content/uploads/2013/09/Living-Eggs-English-KS1-KS2-A2-Poster-3-1.pdf [accessed 22 February 2014].

Living Eggs 2014c. *National Curriculum – Living Eggs.* [Online]. Available at: http://www.livingeggs.co.uk/hatch-a-chick/wp-content/uploads/2013/02/Living-Eggs-KS3-Planner.-England.pdf [accessed 22 February 2014].

Ludvigsen, A. and Sharma, N. 2004. *Burger Boy and Sporty Girl: Children and Young People's Attitudes Towards Food in School.* Ilford: Barnardos

Luke, B. 2007. Justice, caring and animal liberation, in *Feminist Care Tradition in Animal Ethics*, edited by J. Donovan and C.J. Adams. New York: Columbia University Press, 125–52.

Madagascar (dir. Eric Darnell and Tom McGrath, 2005).

Mail Online, The 2012. New children's book promoting veganism sparks outrage for graphic images and unhealthy diet message – but how bad is a veggie food plan for kids? [Online]. Available at: http://www.dailymail.co.uk/femail/article-2131090/Ruby-Roths-new-childrens-book-Vegan-Love-sparks-outrage-graphic-images-unhealthy-diet-message.html [accessed 18 April 2014].

Making the Connection (dir. Ella Todd, 2010).

Mann, K. 2007. *From Dusk 'til Dawn: An Insider's View of the Growth of the Animal Liberation Movement.* London: Puppy Pincher Press.

Marcus, E. 2001. *Vegan: The New Ethics of Eating*. Revised Edition. Ithaca, NY: McBooks Press.

Marcus, E. 2005. *Meat Market: Animals, Ethics & Money*. Boston, MA: Brio Press.

Marx, K. 1887. *Capital: Volume 1*. Moscow: Progress Publishers.

Marx, K. and Engels, F. 1985. *The Communist Manifesto*. London: Penguin Books.

Mason, J. 2005. *An Unnatural Order*. New York: Lantern Books.

Mason, K. 2012. *Bound to the Back of a Tiger: Critical Explorations at the Animal/ Human Frontier*. Unpublished PhD Thesis, Queen's University Belfast.

Masson, J.M. 2009. *The Face on Your Plate: The Truth about Food*. New York: W.W. Norton.

McCance, D. 2013. *Critical Animal Studies: An Introduction*. Albany, NY: State of New York University Press.

McKeown, T. 1977. *The Modern Rise of Population*. London: Academic Press.

McMichael, A.J. and Butler, A.J. 2010. Environmentally sustainable and equitable meat consumption in a climate change world, in *The Meat Crisis: Developing More Sustainable Production and Consumption*, edited by J. D'Silva and J. Webster. London: Earthscan, 173–89.

McMichael, A.J., Powles, J.W., Butler, C.D. and Uauy, R. 2007. Food, livestock production, energy, climate change, and health. *The Lancet*, 370(9594), 1253–63.

Melson, G. 2005. *Why the Wild Things Are*. Cambridge, MA: Harvard University Press.

Midgley, C. 1992. *Women Against Slavery: The British Campaigns 1780–1870*. London: Routledge.

Midgley, C. 2007. *Feminism and Empire: Women Activists in Imperial Britain 1790– 1865*. Abingdon: Routledge.

Miller, J. 2010. *Teddy Bears*. London: Miller's.

Moby 2005. Slipping away. *Hotel*. [CD]. London: Mute.

Molloy, C. 2011. *Popular Media and Animals*. London: Palgrave Macmillan.

Morgan, K. and Cole, M. 2011. The discursive representation of nonhuman animals in a culture of denial, in *Humans and Other Animals: Critical Perspectives*, edited by R. Carter and N. Charles. London: Palgrave, 112–32.

Murray, J.K., Browne, W.J., Roberts, M.A., Whitmarsh, A. and Gruffydd-Jones, T.J. 2010. Number and ownership profiles of cats and dogs in the U.K. *Veterinary Record*, 166, 163–8.

Natural England 2013. *About Us*. [Online]. Available at: http://www. naturalengland.org.uk/about_us/default.aspx [accessed 13 December 2013].

Nelson, M., Nicholas, J., Riley, K. and Wood, L. 2012. *Seventh Annual Survey of Take-Up and School Lunches In England*. London: School Food Trust.

NHS Choices 2013. *Your Baby's First Solid Foods*. [Online]. Available at: http:// www.nhs.uk/Conditions/pregnancy-and-baby/Pages/solid-foods-weaning. aspx [accessed 22 February 2014].

Nibert, D. 2002. *Animal Rights/Human Rights: Entanglements of Oppression and Liberation*. Lanham: Rowman and Littlefield.

Nibert, D. 2003. Humans and other animals: Sociology's moral and intellectual challenge. *International Journal of Sociology and Social Policy*, 23(3), 4–25.

Nibert, D. 2013. *Animal Oppression and Human Violence: Domesecration, Capitalism and Global Conflict*. New York: Columbia University Press.

Nintendo 2011a. *About Nintendogs + cats*. [Online]. Available at: http://nintendogspluscats.nintendo.com/about/ [accessed 14 December 2013].

Nintendo 2011b. *Iwata Asks: Nintendo 3DS: Bragging About Your Pet to the World*. [Online]. Available at: http://iwataasks.nintendo.com/interviews/#/3ds/how-nintendo-3ds-made/3/3 [accessed 15 December 2013].

Nintendo 2011c. *Pose with Your Pet!* [Online]. Available at: http://nintendogspluscats.nintendo.com/pose/ [accessed 15 December 2013].

Nintendo 2011d. *Testimonials*. [Online]. Available at: http://nintendogspluscats.nintendo.com/testimonials/index.html [accessed 14 December 2013].

Noske, B. 1989. *Humans and Other Animals*. London: Pluto Press.

Novek, J. 2005. Pigs and people: Sociological perspectives on the discipline of nonhuman animals in intensive confinement. *Society and Animals*, 13(3): 221–44.

Oppose Living Eggs [no date]. *Oppose the Living Eggs Project*. [Online]. Available at: http://opposelivingeggs.wordpress.com/ [accessed 22 February 2014].

Osborne, M.A. 1996. Zoos in the family: The Geoffrey Saint-Hillaire clan and the three zoos of Paris, in *New Animals. From Menagerie to Zoological Park in the Nineteenth Century*, edited by R.J. Hoage and W.A. Deiss. Baltimore: Johns Hopkins University Press, 33–42.

Pallotta, N.R. 2008. Origin of adult animal rights lifestyle in childhood responsiveness to animal suffering. *Society and Animals*, 16(2), 149–70.

Pan, A. et al. 2012. Red meat consumption and mortality. *Arch Intern Med*, 172(7), 555–63.

Paramount Pictures 2011. *Puss in Boots Official UK Website*. [Online]. Available at: http://www.pussinbootsmovie.co.uk/?utm_source=google&utm_medium=ppc&utm_term=puss+in+boots+film&utm_campaign=Puss+In+Boots+-+Brand+[accessed 17 December 2011].

Parry, J. 2010. Gender and slaughter in popular gastronomy. *Feminism & Psychology*, 20(3), 381–96.

Pascoe, D. 1997. *Charles Dickens: Selected Journalism 1850–1870*. London: Penguin Books.

Patterson, C. 2002. *Eternal Treblinka: Our Treatment of Animals and the Holocaust*. New York: Lantern Books.

Peggs, K. 2012. *Animals and Sociology*. Basingstoke: Palgrave Macmillan.

Pellegrini, A.D. and Smith, P.K. 1998. The development of play during childhood: Forms and possible functions. *Child and Adolescent Mental Health*, 3(2), 51–5.

PetSmart [no date]. *Homepage*. [Online]. Available at: www.petsmart.com [accessed 1 May 2014].

PFMA (Pet Food Manufacturer's Association) 2014. *Pet Food Manufacturers' Association Annual Survey*. [Online]. Available at: http://www.pfma.org.uk/pet-population-2014/ [accessed 1 May 2014]

Piaget, J. 1962. *Play, Dreams, and Imitation*. New York: Norton.

Pollock, L.A. 1983. *Forgotten Children: Parent-child Relations from 1500 to 1900*. Cambridge: Cambridge University Press.

Pomerleau, A., Bolduc, D., Malcuit, G. and Cossette, L. 1990. Pink or blue: Environmental gender stereotypes in the first two years of life. *Sex Roles*, 22(5–6), 359–67.

Postman, N. 1994. *The Disappearance of Childhood*. New York: Vintage Books.

Potter, B. 1902. *The Tale of Peter Rabbit*. London: Frederick Warne and Co.

Potter, B. 1904. *The Tale of Two Bad Mice*. London: Frederick Warne and Co.

Potter, B. 1908. *The Tale of Jemima Puddle Duck*. London: Frederick Warne and Co.

PR *Newswire* 2000. *Burger King corporation invites customers to take part in the most daring escape ever hatched with 'Chicken Run' from DreamWorks*. [Online]. Available at: http://www.prnewswire.com/news-releases/burger-king-corporation-invites-customers-to-take-part-in-the-most-daring-escape-ever-hatched-with-chicken-run-from-dreamworks-73569452.html [accessed 12 September 2008].

Primatt, H. 1776. *The Duty of Mercy and the Sin of Cruelty to Brute Animals*. London: T. Cadell.

Puss in Boots (dir. Chris Miller, 2011).

Rabinow, P. (ed.) 2000. *Ethics*. London: Penguin Books.

Rentokil 2013a. *Pest Control and other Rentokil Services*. [Online]. Available at: http://www.rentokil.co.uk/index.html [accessed 29 March 2013].

Rentokil 2013b. *Rat Control*. [Online]. Available at: http://www.rentokil.co.uk/commercial-pest-control/pest-problems/rat-control/index.html [accessed 29 March 2013].

Ridgway, N.M., Kukar-Kinney, M., Monroe, K.B. and Chamberlin, E. 2008. Does excessive buying for self relate to spending on pets? *Journal of Business Research*, 61, 392–6.

Ritson, J. 1802. *Essay on Abstinence from Animal Food as a Moral Duty*. London: Richard Phillips.

Ritvo, H. The order of nature. Constructing the collections of Victorian zoos, in *New Animals. From Menagerie to Zoological Park in the Nineteenth Century*, edited by R.J. Hoage and W.A. Deiss. Baltimore: Johns Hopkins University Press, 43–50.

Roth, R. 2009. *That's Why We Don't Eat Animals: A Book About Vegans, Vegetarians and All Living Things*. Berkeley: North Atlantic Books.

Roth, R. 2012. *Vegan is Love: Having Heart and Taking Action*. Berkeley: North Atlantic Books.

Roth, R. 2013. *V is for Vegan: The ABCs of Being Kind*. Berkeley: North Atlantic Books.

Royal Society of Chemsitry 2005 *'Surely that's banned?' A Report for the Royal Society of Chemistry on Chemicals and Procedures Thought to be Banned from Use in School*. London: Royal Society of Chemistry.

RSPCA no date. *Education and Animals: Guidance for Educational Establishments*. [Online]. Available at: http://www.rspca.org.uk/ImageLocator/LocateAsset? asset=document&assetId=1232721459275&mode=prd [accessed 22 February 2014].

Sandberg, A. and Heden, R. 2011. Play's importance in schools. *Education 3–13: International Journal of Primary, Elementary and Early Years Education*, 39(3), 317–29.

Scarry, R. 2010. *What Do People Do All Day?* London: HarperCollins Children's Books.

Schlosser, E. 2002. *Fast Food Nation*. London: Penguin Books.

Schluchter, W. 1985. *The Rise of Western Rationalism: Max Weber's Developmental History*. Berkeley: University of California Press.

Sewell, A. 1877. *Black Beauty*. [Online]. Available at: http://www.gutenberg.org/ files/271/271-h/271-h.htm [accessed 6 February 2013].

Serpell, J. 1999. *In the Company of Animals*. Cambridge: Cambridge University Press.

Serpell, J. 2002. Anthropomorphism and anthropomorphic selection – beyond the 'cute response'. *Society and Animals*, 10(4), 437–54.

Simmel, G. 1984. *Georg Simmel: On Women, Sexuality and Love*. Newhaven: Yale University Press.

Singer, P. 1975. *Animal Liberation*. New York: Avon Books.

Smith, C.S. 1999. *The Market Place and The Market's Place in London c.1660–1840*. Unpublished PhD Thesis, University College London.

Smith, M. 2002 The 'ethical' space of the abattoir: On the (in)human(e) slaughter of other animals. *Human Ecology Review*, 9(2): 49–58.

Spiegel, M. 1996. *The Dreaded Comparison: Human and Animal Slavery*. New York: Mirror Books.

Steinfeld, H., Gerber, P., Wassenaar, T., et al. 2006. *Livestock's Long Shadow: Environmental Issues and Options*. Food and Agriculture Organization of the United Nations: Rome.

Stewart, K. and Cole, M. 2009. The conceptual separation of food and animals in childhood. *Food, Culture and Society*, 12(4), 457–76.

Stewart, K. and Cole, M. 2013. *Plant Foods and Public Health*. Poster to BSA Medical Sociology Group 45th Annual Conference, University of York, 11–13 September.

Suicide Food 2011. *Suicide Food. Animals That Desire to be Eaten. Sickening*. [Online]. Available at: http://suicidefood.blogspot.co.uk/ [accessed 13 December 2013].

Szreter, S. 2001. The importance of social intervention in Britain's mortality decline c.1850–1914: A re-interpretation of the role of public health, in *Health and Disease: A Reader*. 3rd Edition, edited by B. Davey et al. Maidenhead: OUP McGraw Hill Education, 219–26.

Tantamango-Bartley, Y., Jaceldo-Siegl, K., Fan, J. and Fraser, G. 2012. Vegetarian diets and the incidence of cancer in a low risk population. *Cancer Epidemiol Biomarkers*, 22(2), 286–94.

Taylor, N. and Twine, R. (eds) 2014. *The Rise of Critical Animal Studies: From the Margins to the Centre*. London: Routledge.

Tester, K. 1991. *Animals and Society: The Humanity of Animal Rights*. London: Routledge.

The Happy Chick Company 2009. *Homepage*. [Online]. Available at: http://www.thehappychickcompany.co.uk [accessed 22 February 2014].

Thompson, M. 1866. *Sheep Walk, Cronkley Crags, Teesdale, County Durham*. Oil on canvas, 86 × 145 cm, The Bowes Museum, Barnard Castle.

Toke, D. 2010. Foxhunting and the Conservatives. *The Political Quarterly*, 81(2), 205–12.

Tonstad, S., Stewart, K., Oda, K., et al. 2013. Vegetarian diets and incidence of diabetes in the Adventist Health Study – 2. *Nutr Metab Cardiovasc Dis*, 23(4), 292–9.

Torres, B. 2007. *Making a Killing: The Political Economy of Animal Rights*. Edinburgh: AK Press.

Truth or Dairy (dir. Franny Armstrong and Rachel Armstrong, 1994).

Tutton, P. 2007. *The Amazing Adventures of Wonderpig: Volume One*. Hull: Wonderpig Publishing.

Twigg, J. 1979. Food for thought: Purity and vegetarianism. *Religion*, 9(1), 13–35.

Twigg, J. 1983. Vegetarianism and the meanings of meat, in *The Sociology of Food and Eating: Essays on the Sociological Significance of Food*, edited by A. Murcott. Aldershot: Gower, 18–30.

Twine, R. 2010. *Animals as Biotechnology: Ethics, Sustainability and Critical Animal Studies*. London: Earthscan.

Twine, R. 2012. Revealing the 'animal-industrial complex' – A concept and method for critical animal studies? *Journal for Critical Animal Studies*, 10(1), 12–39.

Vegan Society, The [no date]. *Compassion for Animals*. [Online]. Available at: http://www.vegansociety.com/sites/default/files/CompassionForAnimals.pdf [accessed 27 May 2014].

Vegan Society, The 2002. *Interview with Donald Watson on Sunday 15 December 2002*. [Online]. Available at: http://www.vegansociety.com/sites/default/files/DW_Interview_2002_Unabridged_Transcript.pdf [accessed 28 May 2014].

Vialles, N. 1994. *Animal to Edible*. Cambridge: Cambridge University Press.

Walters, K.S. and Portmess, L. 1999. *Ethical Vegetarianism: From Pythagoras to Peter Singer*. Albany, NY: State University of New York Press.

Walters, K.S. and Portmess, L. 2001. *Religious Vegetarianism: From Hesiod to the Dalai Lama*. Albany, NY: State University of New York Press.

Ward, A. 2012. 'Recession's silent victims': More than 100 pets are being abandoned every day in Britain as families can no longer afford to feed them. *The Mail Online*. [Online, 1 November]. Available at: http://www.dailymail.co.uk/news/article-2226089/RSPCA-Over-100-pets-abandoned-day-Britain-families-longer-afford-feed-them.html [accessed 16 December 2013].

Weber, M. 1992 [1930]. *The Protestant Ethic and the Spirit of Capitalism*. London: Routledge.

Weber, M. 2004. Basic sociological concepts, in *The Essential Weber: A Reader*, edited by S. Whimster. London: Routledge, 311–58.

Wesley, J. 1993. *The Works: Journals and Diaries v.22 (Journals and Diaries, 1765–1775)*. Edited by W.R. Ward and R.P. Heitzenrater. Nashville: Abingdon Press.

White, T. 2000. Diet and the distribution of environmental impact. *Ecological Economics*, 34(243), 145–53.

Wollstonecraft, M. 1906. *Original Stories*, with an introduction by E.V. Lucas. London: Henry Frowde.

Wright, J. 1768. *An Experiment on a Bird in the Air Pump*. Oil on canvas, 183 × 244 cm, The National Gallery, London.

WWF (World Wildlife Fund) [no date]. *Leopard Adoption*. Godalming: WWF.

Yates, R. 2004. *The Social Construction of Human Beings and Other Animals in Human-Nonhuman Relations*. [Online]. Available at: http://roger.rbgi.net/ [accessed 22 February 2014].

Zephaniah, B. 1995. *Talking Turkeys*. London: Puffin Books.

Zephaniah, B. 1997. *Funky Chickens*. London: Puffin Books.

Zephaniah, B. 2000a. *The Little Book of Vegan Poems*. Edinburgh: AK Press.

Zephaniah, B. 2000b. *Wicked World*. London: Puffin Books.

Index